Myth, Realism, and the West African Writer

Myth, Realism, and the West African Writer

Richard K. Priebe

AFRICA WORLD PRESS
TRENTON, New Jersey

African and Caribbean Literatures Section
Division des litteratures africaines et caribeennes

Research Institute for Comparative Literature
Institut de recherches en littérature comparée
University of Alberta
Edmonton, Alberta, Canada T6G 2E6

Africa World Press, Inc.
P.O. Box 1892
Trenton, N.J. 08607

First Printing 1988

Typeset by Gabriella Baltes

Cover design by Peter Drummond

Library of Congress Catalog Card Number: 88-71174

ISBN: 0-86543-097-7   Cloth
        0-86543-098-5   Paper

Printed in Canada

Comparative Studies in African/Caribbean Literature Series

Series Editor: Stephen H. Arnold
Associate Editor: George Lang

African and Caribbean Literatures Section
Research Institute for Comparative Literature
The University of Alberta
Edmonton, Alberta
CANADA T6G 2E6

Contents

For Barbara and Adam

Foreword

"If you see an elephant, you don't say 'I saw something flash by;' you'd better acknowledge that what you saw was the mightiest of beasts." Critics have certainly acknowledged modern African literature for the formidable animal it is. Indeed, they have erected such a towering apparatus of literary history, commentary and analysis around it that we are likely to forget that less than thirty years ago it did seem, precisely, to flash onto the scene, arriving suddenly with a turbulent dazzle. The great weight of institutionalisation since then cannot really obscure the continuing profusion, diversity and creative energy of this literature; but it can cause us to take it too much for granted.

For the circumstances in which African writers were, and still are, working were extraordinarily inauspicious. A tiny and precarious intelligentsia, they were removed by their education from the culture and experience of the majority of the population, and assigned to a ruling elite which was both unstable and rapacious. They were politically disaffected from this elite, often at great personal risk, and alienated from the metropolitan powers that kept it in place. As pre-Independence nationalism gave way silently and almost instantly to neo-colonial complicity and corruption, they articulated in their own idiom an anger and disgust which was shared by the whole population. But those for whom they declared themselves to be writing could hardly read them. They were read — eagerly and enthusiastically read — by a foreign audience who had never experienced the conditions of which they wrote. This audience was primed by the controlling interests of the European and American publishing industry, and its frame of reference was set by the dominant Western academic establishment. At the same time, the ordinary people in Africa were vigorously engaged in the creation of their own culture, a popular urban-oriented culture more or less invisible to the outsider's eye but of great importance to those who inhabited it. This culture existed in an ambiguous and variable relationship to the work of elite writers, who both envied and deplored it. All of these writers, then, had to root their work in the thin soil of a shadowy, insecure and displaced relationship with their public. Only by courtesy of hindsight do we accept it as natural that this soil should have produced such an abundance of blooms.

But in literary criticism, these same conditions produced the opposite result. By a curious inversion, a literature exploding with possibilities seemed to attract, initially at least, a commentary of deadening dulness. The domination of Western publishing and academic establishments produced an effect of distortion. The European and American critics who "discovered" African writing approached it, understandably enough, as a privileged entry into an unknown world. To most of them, literature written in English or French was the only aspect of present-day African cultures that was visible or accessible to them. They were therefore interested in the Africanity of African literature, in just what it was that made it different from their own literatures. To get at this question, they inevitably proceeded from the known to the unknown. That is, they started from the fact that modern written Anglophone and Francophone African literature uses language and forms derived from Europe. Into this, they then postulated, must have been infused something else: something indigenous, traditional and authentically African. Studies of African writing therefore had to propose a cultural "other," something often only vaguely apprehended, and represented by such notions as "traditional folklore," "oral poetry" or "ritual/festival drama." These "traditions" were thought to have exercised some kind of subterranean influence on the conventions of Western literature, pushing through from underneath to break up, transform and reshape the smooth surface of recognised form. From the first, then, African literature was presented primarily in terms of its hybrid character, and much effort was devoted to locating the indigenous, traditional elements. All too often this procedure led to the invention of spurious evolutionary sequences. Soyinka's drama was pictured as having somehow "emerged" from an earlier phase of traditional masquerade theatre; the modern novel somehow "had its roots" in the folktale. Titles like "from oral art to written poetry" were common. This is not to say that the questions they asked were without interest; but conceived as they so often were in terms of "culture clash" they could not avoid a formalism which was further exacerbated by ignorance of the "traditional" half of the equation.

Those African critics who avoided working wholly within the terms set by the foreign critical establishment brought a more activist perspective to bear on what were fundamentally the same questions. What is the African writer's role in society? What should his or her relationship to be the pre-colonial past, to "tradition"? What is he or she to do with the materials and resources of the indigenous culture? Can something be rescued from under the intolerable mass of cultural distortions imposed by colonisation, and reasserted or recreated? The most famous formulation of these issues was the theory of Negritude; the debate arising from which, surprisingly enough, is still being reheated and served up in a variety of theoretical dishes.

These are important questions, but they did not, on the whole, lead to a rewarding critical practice. Proposing an authentic "traditional" indigenous culture or aesthetic as the sole opponent to "Western" values had the effect of immobilising history into a permanent duality. Like the Euro-American criticism, the Africanist criticism accepted as empirical reality what is an ideological construct, the notion of "tradition" itself. They both usually failed to specify the content, form or aesthetic principles of the "traditional" culture they postulated. They both also had the effect of by-passing almost without comment what is actually going on in West African towns today — that explosion of popular creativity in fiction, drama, music and visual art which is often self-consciously *not* "traditional" but which nonetheless is an authentic expression of the ordinary people's fears and aspirations. And the Africanist criticism implicitly accepted the specious evolutionary schema of Euro-American criticism — even though with intent to reverse it and go *back* to recuperate a lost past — which fails to take into account the fact that all the cultural forms under discussion are actually going on simultaneously, and exist in complex and problematic relations to each other — relations which are being continually reworked in response to people's actual struggles in changing historical circumstances.

The preoccupations and assumptions that inform this early criticism have not been entirely superseded. But other kinds of criticism have appeared. There is now a growing number of critics, working from a variety of standpoints, who do not see "culture clash" as a fundamental explanatory paradigm. Instead, they take works of African literature to be — like any other literature — complex and polysemous constructs, forged out of the materials of specific historical, political and cultural experience. The first question is not how to disentangle foreign and indigenous elements, but how the texts *work* in their own terms: that is, what they say and by what means they say it.

To this growing body of criticism, Richard Priebe's book must be considered a major contribution. Priebe's exploration of a number of West African texts recognises them as the products of definite contemporary realities: addressing themselves to the state of a specifically West African nation and with much to say that is implicitly or explicitly political. Nonetheless, he is able to show that they also transcend the immediate local experience in which they are rooted, and speak, over space and time, in a symbolic language that is much more widely understood. They are accessible to a foreign audience not because they borrow foreign forms and conventions but because they share, with other literatures from all over the world, fundamental imaginative structures. His suggestion is that the link between a text and its social context can be seen in terms of *rhetoric*. A rhetoric is a way of saying things, a form of persuasion, involving purpose and ends as well as means; but it is more than a matter of form, organisation and style. The two rhetorical modes which Priebe discerns in West African literature have very deep roots, reaching into universal literary resources.

These two rhetorics are the ethical and the mythical. The ethical is a realist rhetoric; it deals with outer reality, establishes an illusion of quotidian historical continuity, works through simile, and is didactic. Because of its surface similarity to "real life," the ethical mode is accessible and popular; it is no accident that its greatest West African exponent, Chinua Achebe, is also the most widely-read of all African authors. In this mode, the hero/heroine is central to the society in which he or she is depicted; if s/he goes mad, this is a tragedy, for society, by whose standards s/he is judged, is sane. The text's viewpoint coincides with that of the society it depicts. The mythical on the other hand is a metaphorical and paradoxical mode, presenting an inner reality in an ahistorical, cyclical or disjunctive manner. The hero is marginal to the society in which s/he is depicted, a liminal figure who thereby becomes a source of social regeneration, for it is society and not the hero who is mad. Mythical rhetoric employs expressionistic, often apocalyptic imagery and projects a vision of the world that ranges from the fantastic to the prophetic. It is a more "difficult" rhetoric than the ethical, but it is also the dominant one in West African elite literature today. Armah, Soyinka, Awoonor, and Tutuola are all "mythical" writers, and Priebe gives this mode most of his space.

In his exploration of mythic rhetoric, Priebe combines the ideas of Van Gennep, Turner, Mary Douglas and Joseph Campbell, to propose a basic paradigm of the mythic hero: he is someone who undergoes separation or alienation from his society, initiation into another realm of experience, followed by return to his own world with the fruits of his journey. As a liminal figure, he is both an outcast and a potential healer of the society's malaise. This symbolic narrative structure, found all over the world, is here used to illuminate different African texts in very particular ways. In close readings of four "mythic" writers, Priebe draws out a different aspect of the rhetoric in each case. By developing it from different angles, his paradigm becomes a source of varied insights rather than a classificatory straitjacket or an obsessional rediscovery of the same thing in every text. It enables him fruitfully to reinterpret well-known works, as when he reads "the man" in Armah's *The Beautyful Ones are Not Yet Born* as a liminal figure in a society which is itself liminal. It also enables him to write illuminatingly about notoriously difficult texts, such as Soyinka's *Idanre* and Armah's later work. And it puts him in a position to relocate Amos Tutuola — consigned by previous scholarship to a quaint cul-de-sac — in the literary mainstream, in company which illuminates aspects of his work that were previously ignored.

Mythic and ethical rhetoric are to be understood as complementary rather than exclusive and opposed modes. In Priebe's interpretation, their complementarity echoes what he sees as a fundamental notion in African thought in general, that of the interdependence and inseparability of contraries. The ethical mode works like a proverb; the mythical, like a riddle. His development of this idea, drawing on the work of Kenneth Burke, results in brilliantly suggestive readings of Achebe and Tutuola. Achebe's realism is an active realism, a living didacticism which charts the possibilities of action; Tutuola's *The Palm-Wine Drinkard*, read as a series of interlocking riddles, becomes — for me at least — for the first time, dazzlingly clear.

One may well feel wary of sweeping dichotomies, especially when the picture is filled out by generalised references to something called "African thought." But Priebe uses his dual model not to classify but to interpret. A great advantage of his distinction between the two rhetorics is that it enables him to bring into view the whole of contemporary literary creation. Not only elite literature, but oral ("traditional") and popular literature can be understood in this framework. Rejecting any attempt to periodise ethical and mythical modes into a quasi-evolutionary model — along the lines, for instance, of the European shift from 19th-century realism to 20th-century modernism — Priebe suggests a way of seeing the whole spectrum of contemporary literatures as simultaneous and complementary symbolic statements about a common social reality. Especially interesting is the observation that while "traditional" oral literature uses both modes, popular urban-based literature exists only in the ethical mode. The penultimate chapter, in some ways the most original, is an analysis of Ghanaian popular fiction. It is admirable for its detailed and perceptive attention to a much-neglected popular literature, which he locates clearly in its concrete context of production and consumption (an approach which could well be extended to the elite literature he considers in the rest of the book). He is thus able to read the rhetoric in terms of what it does, and his reading of "sub-texts" in these apparently simple texts repays close attention. But also, his approach offers a way of seeing popular fiction *in relation* to the elite texts. His analysis shows how close is the complementarity between modern popular fiction and modern elite fiction. The popular writers, in their ethical idiom of personal sexual morality, were addressing the same social malaise as were the elite novelists in their predominantly mythic symbolic idiom. To look at only one half at a time is a grave impoverishment of our understanding of both.

This is not a book to provide a definitive reading of West African literature: it is a book to stimulate the imagination, and re-open the eyes to the mightiest of animals as it continues to flash by in all directions. It should be judged by the extent to which it communicates the author's own lively and intelligent enthusiasm for a literature which is, as he says, "simply much too good to resist writing about."

Karin Barber
Centre of West African Studies
University of Birmingham
England

Acknowledgements

It is a very great pleasure to acknowledge present colleagues and past teachers, as well as the many friends who helped, encouraged, and inspired me in this undertaking. Roger Abrahams, Sunday Anozie, and Joseph Jones gave a considerable amount of useful advice in the early stages of this book. Bernth Lindfors, the most selfless mentor a student could ever have, has given me invaluable criticism through the manuscript's many transformations. What I have written on Kofi Awoonor, I hope reflects clearly my admiration for his work, but I also owe him a great debt as a friendly critic. His numerous letters and extensive criticism, and especially some conversations we had while on hunting and fishing expeditions, kept me on track through dark periods. Ann Woodlief and Boyd Berry gave generously of their time to straighten out parts of my argument. The crookedness that remains is mine; what straight cogency there is owes much to them. Stephen Arnold, as critic, editor, and friend, prodded, pushed, and aided me in more clever and gentle ways than any writer could hope for. Finally, I would like to thank Karen Cox for her patient help in proofreading and Gene Dunaway and Diane Marshall for their untiring professional help in word processing. Clearly, without these three, this book would not be.

I am very grateful to *Research in African Literatures, Yale French Studies*, and *Ariel* for permission to include parts, which in different form, appeared first as articles in those journals. Likewise, I am grateful to Bernth Lindfors and Three Continents Press, as well as Ulla Schild and B. Heymann Verlag, for early versions of chapters that appeared, respectively, in *Critical Perspectives on Amos Tutuola* and *Neo-African Literature and Culture: Essays in Memory of Janheinz Jahn*.

Finally, I owe much to Virginia Commonwealth University where generous support in a grant-in-aid enabled me to do the research on a portion of this book, and to the Fulbright Program whose generous support for a year in Ghana enabled me to complete the manuscript.

Introduction

Much of this book deals with the work of five prominent West African writers who write in English: Chinua Achebe, Amos Tutuola and Wole Soyinka from Nigeria; Kofi Awoonor and Ayi Kwei Armah from Ghana. I have selected some of their most widely read works and analyzed them to illustrate a critical theory. I make no attempt to give a broad survey of African literature, and I avoid giving even a broad survey of the individual author. I am more concerned with being thorough in my treatment of the works I do cover. The explications can be read individually, but my larger aim with each one is to advance or amplify aspects of the theory. In fact, I hope it is the theory that unifies this study, making the explications meaningful and showing a way of making connections among a wider range of works than I have specifically examined. To clarify the theory and the works, and thus balance breadth and depth, I have, in other words, chosen an intensive rather than an extensive approach, inductively arguing theory from a selected body of literature. My reasons for doing this kind of book have to do with my desire to reach a broad range of students and scholars and also with some very practical considerations concerning the present state of scholarship in African literature.

Written literature has developed very rapidly in West Africa. The amount of creative writing coming out of the entire sub-Saharan continent has increased in geometric progression over the past thirty years. Were it possible for astronomers to witness the rapid expansion of a new galaxy, we might have a situation analogous to what the critics now face. It has been cause for much excitement and enthusiasm, with the result that a body of criticism has developed almost as quickly as the creative writing. As critics, though, we have been caught in a trap. The literature is simply much too good to resist writing about, and yet we have not really waited to develop all the tools we need to effectively deal with it. As a colleague of mine commented, a West African novel very often does not even have a chance to cool down from its run off of a printing press before a critic is at work on an article. The enthusiasm is catching, though we are often left working not merely without the right tools, but also without very much historical perspective. We might grope toward linking our perceptions and talk about "trends" in African literature or "new perspectives" in criticism, but we generally have trouble seeing the forest through the trees.

It has become commonplace for scholars to assert that one must know something about African society before one can write critically about the literature, and that the criticism must really clarify the literature in terms of the society from which it has come. There are, then, numerous studies that explain social and political thought, examine the way folklore is used, or compare European and African literary form. In several cases these studies provide excellent insight into particular works, but, generally speaking, there are few perceptions that can then be taken to works not covered in the studies. In other words, little in the way of critical theory has emerged, for we have not been given very much information about the aesthetics of African literature.

If we must examine African literature in relation to particular African societies (and I accept this commonplace), we will presumably want to understand the nature of the relationship between the literature and the culture. Regardless of the genre he chooses to write in, the West African writer, as any writer, necessarily defines a relationship with his culture through the rhetoric he employs. The elements of his art, such as characterization, theme and formal patterning, will all reflect a consciousness of the social reality he is drawing from. There is a sense in which all literature, perhaps all art, is based on comparison. The writer who chooses to set up a very direct, explicit relationship between his work and his society chooses the rhetoric of realism and is guided by what I term an ethical consciousness. The writer, on the other hand, who chooses to set up an indirect, implicit relationship between his work and his society chooses the rhetoric of myth and is guided by what I call a mythic consciousness. In this study, then, I describe the aesthetics of West African literature in terms of the rhetoric the author employs, specifically in terms of relationships he sets up between his work and his society, and between his work and his readers.

At a conference a few years ago, an African scholar was upset with the way I was using the term "myth" in a paper I presented. He felt I was looking at African myths with an attitude that I would not assume in studying the myths of my own society. In effect, he was saying "What you call myths are my sacred beliefs." The misunderstanding was based in part on semantic confusion which was easily resolved. To be sure, I was talking about African myths from the vantage point of a scholar and not a participant in the culture, but the African scholar soon understood that I was not using the term in the pejorative manner in which it can be employed (i.e., "myth" as lie or untruth). There was, and still is a more fundamental problem which is not so easily resolved. As scholars we can easily point to the general sense in which we employ the term, but I think only rarely do our various concepts of myth coincide in any detail. It would be a lengthy exercise were I to review here the definitions of myth offered by anthropologists, linguists, philosophers, and literary critics, and I am not sure it would clarify what I have to say about African literature. My point is, however, that even a very cursory look at the scholarship from Claude Lévi-Strauss to Northrop Frye on the subject of myth will show that definition is a major problem.

If there are problems involved with the use of the terms "myth" and "mythic," they are small compared to the problems we confront with the word "realism." Our references are highly personal, highly subjective. Whether we say something is "realistic" in the course of a commonplace conversation or in a more academic discussion of art, there is, I am convinced, little difference. I know of no other term in literary criticism which is used so freely, and so vaguely, as the term "realism." We need only consider how essential this term is to any discussion of the novel as a literary form to understand its central importance. We need only look at any two articles on the novel by different critics to see how much we assume when we employ the term. We are left with the commonplace that the African scholar pointed out in relation to myth, namely that what is realism to one person may not be to another.

I do not wish to add to any controversy regarding the use of terminology. It should, in fact, be clear to most scholars that the terms "myth" and "realism" cover a range of meanings, dependent not only on the ways different scholars employ them, but also on the ways they are employed by members of different cultures. I approach this subject of meaning with some trepidation, but also with the hope that as a literary critic I am presenting an operational model to aid in the understanding of a particular body of literature. The distinction I draw between two types of consciousness in West African literature is, in part, based on formal criteria, structures and patterns that are particular to the products of each type of consciousness, the ethical and the mythic. It is not, however, just a formal distinction, a distinction, say, between verisimilitude and fantasy, concerned only with the way the artist has organized experience in the work. The distinction is also based on the type of philosophical or value system the work encompasses, though I am not really concerned with the intentions of the artist. However, an examination of the rhetoric of a work in terms of the guiding consciousness does include consideration of ends as well as means, that is, consideration of where the artist is leading us and why he is taking us there. The "why" has less to do with what the artist may or may not have felt, than it has to do with our understanding of the work in the context of the society in which it was created. The distinction, then, additionally has to do with the social and economic realities that have influenced the structure of the work and have aided or even impeded its production.

In short, my thesis here is that a piece of modern West African writing of English expression and its socio-economic realities can be characterized by its position along a spectrum from literature of ethical consciousness to literature of mythic consciousness.

Though I have developed it around a binary distinction, I hope that the theoretical orientation of my book is not taken as reductive. In relation to specific works, the terms "mythic" and "ethical" apply to gradients along a continuum and not to a clear-cut polar contrast. A given work may have elements that are "mythic" and elements that are "ethical," and clearly no writer is bound to write all his works so that they reflect one consciousness. I am simply presenting a model; its value is heuristic. While I will examine works on both sides of the continuum, I have found the theory to be of particular value in understanding the literature on the "mythic" side.

The model I am proposing is, I believe, one that is useful in examining other modern African literatures: East and South African as well as West African; Francophone and Lusophone as well as Anglophone; vernacular as well as those written in European languages. My immediate aim, however, is a more modest one than to prove the general application of the theory. I am not, at any rate, sure that any critical theory can be proven. At best a scholar can cogently show that a theory is useful. My interest, then, is not just in advancing a critical theory, but also as I indicated earlier, in offering close interpretations of works of a group of authors who, for the most part, are generally accepted as being among the most important writers in Africa today. The chapter on Ghanaian popular writing is intended as an exception to prove (in the original sense of "to test") the rule. The material I look at in this chapter is not readily available to students or scholars outside of Africa, but is very representative of what the masses in Africa read and is important in allowing us to look at elements in the relationship between literature and society that we cannot so readily re-construct in the case of "elite" literature. (Works by writers such as Soyinka and Achebe are still, for the most part, published outside of Africa and read mainly by an educated elite in Europe and Africa.) Many of the same arguments I am sure could have been made with the better-known Onitsha literature of Nigeria, but in using this material I can draw on my own first-hand field work in Ghana.

I would now like to turn to a brief sketch of the critical theory as I develop it in relation to the authors I cover.

Seeing the similarities of four Anglophone West African writers, Ayi Kwei Armah, Kofi Awoonor, Wole Soyinka, and Amos Tutuola, encompassed by the idea of a mythic consciousness, I define the term in contradistinction to an ethical consciousness found in the work of Chinua Achebe. The style of the latter tends to be realistic with little being left unexplained by the action or the description, historical in its specificity of time and place, didactic in its rendering of the human condition, and continuous in its rhythm as we are led from a clear beginning through a definite end. In contrast, the mythic style is expressionistic with much that is seemingly obscure or incomplete, ahistorical in that we find a move towards time *ab origine*, problematic with regard to the human condition, and cyclical in its rhythm, symbolic or real death being followed by resurrection. At one time I considered using the phrase "mythopoeic sensibility," but I am not simply discussing a mythmaking process in literature. I prefer the phrase "mythic consciousness," for I examine the motifs, symbols, and images employed by these four mythic writers within the context of the tradition of myths and rituals found in their societies and find the writers engaged in a process of consciously reinterpreting traditional myths, not of creating new ones. In discussing the development of a mythic consciousness in these writers, my implicit assumption has been that there is a discernible continuity between traditional verbal and nonverbal art and their written literature.

The central characters in the works (and *personae* of the poetry) shaped by a mythic consciousness tend to be marginal men, liminal figures who appear to be partly in this world and partly in another. Like Murano in Soyinka's *The Road*, they have one foot in this world and the other "on the slumbering chrysalis of the word." Their liminal condition, their contact with the embryonic word, gives them potential power to shape and direct society. The central characters in the works informed by an ethical consciousness are entirely in and of this world. What power they have is functional, not potential, and thus in the case of Okonkwo, in Achebe's *Things Fall Apart*, it is the loss of real power that to a great extent defines his tragedy. In *Arrow of God*, perhaps a more complex work, the tragedy of the priest, Ezeulu, is directly related to his confusion of the two types of power. In this novel more than in anything else he has written, Achebe reflects elements both of a mythic and an ethical consciousness.

Binary contrasts can all too easily proliferate in the abstract and seemingly take on a life of their own. I hope I have effectively grounded mine in specific works, but in such a manner that the general patterns may be seen in relation to works I have not discussed. Having briefly developed my theoretical statement in the opening chapter, I expand it through an examination of Armah's novels. These novels appear to have little to do with traditional African myths and rituals, the early ones being easily seen in terms of European existentialism and Frantz Fanon's philosophy regarding the colonized individual. In his most recent novels, *Two Thousand Seasons* and *The Healers*, Armah might be seen as writing from an ethical consciousness. The novels seem to be very historical and stylistically simple. However, the alienation of all Armah's heroes can be most fully explained as the anguish which is a concomitant of their priest-like relation to society. They are, in one sense, mythic heroes, albeit specifically African mythic heroes, whose experiences conform to the monomythic pattern of separation, initiation, and return, where the magical boon that they bring their societies is implied in their experiences of liminality and their questioning of the social order. They step far enough away from their societies so that they can see some of the accepted order there as disorder and can learn new ways of ordering. Yet they remain close enough to their societies to keep their new perspectives grounded in the essential values of their people. The demonic landscapes of Armah's novels, including the scatological imagery and death, insanity or emasculation of the heroes, are symbolic inversions, negations that imply utopian or mythic visions.

The two chapters that follow, one on Achebe's *Things Fall Apart* and another on Tutuola's *The Palm-Wine Drinkard*, I have set up as contrasting studies of the two types of consciousness. The two works are about as far apart on my continuum as any two that could be found in West Africa. They are, moreover, the two works with which even the least experienced student of African literature is most likely to have some familiarity. Achebe gives us an ethical orientation toward a fully functional society. In the penultimate chapter I examine a similar orientation in the works of Ghanaian popular writers. Their fiction, like the novels of Achebe (and I might have also included the works of T.M. Aluko, Elechi Amadi, and several other "elite" writers), directs us toward a range of specific responses to specific problems in much the same way that a proverb directs us to see a particular social situation in terms of a clearly defined ethical position. Tutuola, however, leads us into the world of myth where we see limitless potential. In his quest for his dead palm-wine tapster, Tutuola's Drinkard moves through a realm where cultural and natural laws can be, and often are, easily violated. This violation is akin to a riddler's violation of ordinary language, and a look at the extraordinary aids us in reconsidering the ordinary. Just as a riddler, Tutuola raises questions that direct us toward new ways of perceiving reality.

In Awoonor's novel, *This Earth, My Brother*, as well as in *The Palm-Wine Drinkard* and Armah's novels, theme emerges more as question than statement: how can a dying society be saved? The hero of *This Earth* bears the anguish of his people in a priest-like manner, and he quests after salvation, not just for himself, but for the whole group. The carrying of this anguish leads the hero to his death, but not just in the manner of a simple tale of self sacrifice. In *This Earth*, symbolic inversion and the hero's liminality exist in the more explicitly traditional context of an Ewe dirge. In fact, I attempt to show that the novel thematically as well as stylistically is a dirge, and that the reader is drawn into a mimetic recreation of a funeral celebration.

The West African writer, and I believe this applies to the African writer in general, has an intense concern for the well-being of culture and society. This is no less true for the writer working from a mythic consciousness than it is for the writer working from an ethical consciousness. Two elements that specifically distinguish the two groups, and account for the special difficulty we usually have in approaching the former, are thematic development and the role of the central figure or figures. Achebe's themes emerge as sharply and directly as the proverbs he employs to aid in developing them, and his central characters are generally in and of their societies. In the works of Tutuola, Armah, Awoonor and Soyinka, we find the liminal or marginal heroes I have been discussing, men who are paradoxically both inside and outside their societies. Where Achebe gives us a novel that has the directness of an extended proverb, these writers give us works that have the indirection of a riddle. Hence, their themes emerge as the questions in the riddles they pose.

Scholars as well as students find Awoonor's *This Earth* and Soyinka's *The Interpreters* difficult, even taxing works to read. The characters in these two novels are clearly critical of their societies, but they do not seem to do very much. Except in negative terms (e.g., scatological imagery and death such as we find in Armah's work), there is no clear resolution of the questions the protagonists confront. What the characters do, in fact, is far less important than what they are, their mode of being. Their existence is defined in relation to traditional values, values that are no longer the wellspring of the society at large. In *This Earth* we come to an understanding of these values and their importance through Awoonor's use of the Ewe dirge. The marginality and the values of the several protagonists in *The Interpreters* are connected with their individual affinities with Yoruba deities. Soyinka's characters move in relation to an implied backdrop of Yoruba cosmology. They serve as bridges, hence "interpreters," between the spiritual and physical worlds. Once again we see that inherent in this betwixt and between positioning is the power to revitalize society. The conflicts within each of the characters, and among them, are struggles to realize this potential. As in Yoruba cosmology, balance and harmony are asserted by Soyinka as the ideal, even though he and his culture recognize the necessity for the tension and revitalizing energies of conflict.

The poetry of Awoonor and Soyinka, as well as Soyinka's play, *The Trials of Brother Jero*, support my contention that these two writers are deeply immersed in traditional African myths and rituals even when they appear to be employing European forms. Their collections of poetry, *Night of My Blood* and *Idanre*, are structured around the monomythic pattern, the major *personae* being cast in the roles of poet-priests. Moreover, the traditional Ewe dirge form again clarifies much of Awoonor's work, while traditional Yoruba mythology sheds light on Soyinka's poetry and his play. I look very closely at the liminal figure's comic power of inverting societal order and his potential revitalizing energies in this shortest of Soyinka's comedies.

The chapter on Ghanaian popular writing is in many ways the least theoretical and most concrete assertion in this book. Throughout the book I attempt to approach West African literature from a cultural perspective, though here my orientation is more social and historical than literary. The aim of any literary criticism should ultimately be humanistic, but the Western literary critic is limited if he does not seek to employ the tools of the social scientist. I felt that my understanding of African literature had to be grounded in actual field work in Africa. I could read some Ghananian popular writers in the United States (many of their works have never been systematically collected for libraries here or even in Africa), but I could only gain a sense of their significance by studying the production and impact of the literature in context. Out of context any popular literature is at best quaint and amusing, and at worst simply boring. Either response is understandable, but both responses are limiting in terms of the perceptions such a literature affords.

In the concluding chapter I return to the broader theoretical issues and consider the significance of the theme of death to the African writers who employ the rhetoric of myth, the reasons for my giving more attention to these writers than writers like Achebe, and the implications of my general theory to the study of African literature, oral and written.

Mankind and the gods can participate in maintaining a social life only under the assurance that the cosmos is eternal in its structure and that change is growth — whether it be the ageing of the individual, the development of towns, or new variations in culture, change must not be thought random or obliterating. Death as absolute extinction is denied because it conflicts with the presuppositions not only of the worth of individual effort, but also of the whole culture.

Peter Morton-Williams, "Yoruba Responses to the Fear of Death."

Myth and the Contemporary West African Writer

In "New Directions in African Writings," a paper presented in 1971 at the Annual Meeting of the African Studies Association,[1] Emile Snyder took a large step in defining what are now obviously two mainstreams of African literature. The paper affords considerable insight into the relationship of Armah, Awoonor and Soyinka's work, yet he implicitly takes a position I would question. Snyder begins by asserting that we can now see two "generations" of African writers, separated more by their aesthetics than their age. On the one hand, we have the first generation of African writers epitomized by Achebe, and on the other, the second generation epitomized by Soyinka. In making his distinction he draws comparisons with European writers, showing parallels between Achebe's work and the Victorian realistic novel and between Soyinka's work and the modern experimental novel. Certainly the writers of both "generations" have been very much influenced by European writers, and such comparisons are often useful, but we should never let this lead us away from the fact that a writer is usually writing from the perspective of his own cultural milieu. In effect, the implication of the generational idea is that Africa has been following the literary movements of Europe, and it is doubtful that this could be fully substantiated. I would agree with Snyder that the writers of the new novels use a universal language, but it is on a level that can only be comprehended through an understanding of their particular cultures.

A key statement in Snyder's argument is that "With *The Interpreters* the African novel transcends history and enters into the realm of metaphysics."[2] A question immediately arises concerning what we could say about Camara Laye's *The Radiance of the King*, Thomas Mofolo's *Chaka*, and numerous works by D.O. Fagunwa, earlier African novels that had already entered "the realm of metaphysics." I plan to limit my investigation to West African literature in English, but I still would be hard put to agree with the statement, since the metaphysics of *The Interpreters* can also be found in Soyinka's earlier work, and perhaps more importantly, in the work of Amos Tutuola.

Several years ago in *Seven African Writers*, Gerald Moore wrote one of the finest essays on Amos Tutuola. Yet the most hazardous task any critic can undertake is to predict what the influences on future literature will or will not be. In a rather infelicitous statement at the end of his essay, Moore asserted that "Tutuola's books are far more like a fascinating cul-de-sac than the beginning of anything directly useful to other writers. The cul-de-sac is full of wonders, but is nonetheless a dead end."[3] Moore was countering an earlier statement by Geoffrey Parrinder that Tutuola's work was the beginning of a new direction in African literature. At the time Moore's prediction would have seemed the more sensible and Parrinder's the more foolish. Aside from the fact that Tutuola's books had been very unfavorably received by African critics, much of the literature that had been published in the decade between the publication of Tutuola's *The Palm-Wine Drinkard* and Moore's book was social protest. Though the emphasis shifted from colonial criticism to self-criticism, the mainstream of West African literature continued to be concerned directly with social issues treated in a realistic manner.

Bernth Lindfors has argued that Tutuola has had an influence on African writing, albeit an indirect one. In getting world recognition Tutuola opened the doors of Western publishing houses to West African writers and showed that they could write on their own terms. Still, with most critics, Lindfors insists that Tutuola's works are *sui generis*, "unique because his background, imagination, and linguistic equipment are unique."[4] Certainly it would be difficult to prove that Tutuola's language has had a direct influence on other writers, but another writer from his home town of Abeokuta, Wole Soyinka, has shown an imagination very similar to Tutuola's. Moreover, a fundamentally similar sensibility is evident in two Ghanaian writers, Kofi Awoonor and Ayi Kwei Armah. The common denominator is a mythic consciousness that orders the underlying structure of their work. Other writers, notably Chinua Achebe and Elechi Amadi, have employed myths, but an ethical consciousness, their pervading didactic purpose, has led them to structure their work in a different way.

Some definitions are now in order if we are to come to a clear understanding of the nature of the differences. As I mentioned in my preface, any survey of the myth scholarship done by linguists, anthropologists, folklorists, and literary critics reveals that a consensus of what the term "myth" means has never been achieved within any of these fields, let alone among them. A rehashing of the arguments that have taken place would lead far away from my topic, so I will simply give a working definition of myth: a narrative that explains, explores or attempts to resolve the primary ontological, psychological and physical contradictions that man has recurrently faced. The essential characteristic of any myth is that in one or more ways we are led outside of a time referent. The writer who holds a mythic awareness of literature retreats from the openly didactic and insists on viewing life with regard to open and perpetual contradiction.

Northrop Frye has shown that myth is one end of literary design and realism the other, the two respectively being arts of implicit metaphor and simile.[5] Myth represents an ahistorical inner reality, though that reality is necessarily revealed in objective symbols that we can recognize and a cyclical rhythm that we can feel. On the other hand, realism shows us an outer reality that is like the historical one we daily experience and is thus controlled by a corresponding continuity. To borrow Frye's terms, but employ them in a different sense than he uses them, I would say that the writer whose imagination is governed by an ethical consciousness feels the rhythm of continuity, while the writer whose imagination is governed by a mythic consciousness feels the rhythm of recurrence.

Shortly after the publication of Moore's book, Soyinka had begun to make a similar distinction in an essay for *The American Scholar*. He saw Achebe and Tutuola as epitomizing two diametrically opposite styles, yet completely rejected the all too facile observation that the one style is sophisticated and the other primitive. Though he takes nothing away from Achebe, Soyinka understandably has more praise for Tutuola whose poetic sensibility is closer to his own and in whose writing is to be found:

... a largeness that comes from an acceptance of life in all its manifestations; where other writers conceive of man's initiation only in terms of photographic rites, Tutuola goes through it as a major fact of a concurrent life cycle, as a progression from physical insufficiency, through the Quest into the very psyche of Nature. The *Palm-Wine Drinkard*, as with Fagunwa's *Ogboju Ode* and universal myth, is the epic of man's eternal restlessness, symbolized as always in a Search ....

For Tutuola involves us in a coordination of the spiritual and the physical, and this is the truth of his people's concept of life. The accessories of day-to-day existence only become drawn into this cosmic embrace; they do not invalidate it .... [6]

In contrast he writes the following of Achebe:

In a sense — not a pejorative one— he is a chronicler, content to follow creases and stress lines, not to impose his own rearrangement on them. That this can be a creative process is demonstrated by the inexorable fate that overtakes his hero, Okonkwo, in *Things Fall Apart*. The demand we make of an expressed way of life is, first and foremost, reality....

There is no good and evil, however, only concepts of continuity — what works for society and what does not. And this knowledge, this magic is achieved from within society itself. The author, understanding this, has excluded all private imposition.... [7]

When Soyinka speaks of the writers who "conceive of man's initiation only in terms of photographic rites" he is certainly not speaking of Achebe, but rather only those writers who could not transform their anthropological and sociological material into art. Nevertheless, though he admires Achebe, he is deeply excited by the mythic consciousness of Tutuola. This excitement is nowhere more clearly indicated than in a review he wrote of E.K. Ogunmola's folk opera adaptation of *The Palm-Wine Drinkard.* Soyinka had nothing but praise for the opera, except for the ending of the production where he was quite severe in his criticism of a slight alteration of the original story. Ogunmola has his hero wake to find that he had been dreaming that his tapster, whom he had thought dead was in fact still alive. Soyinka complained that this ending robbed the drama of the mythic vitality of Tutuola's story: "There was no need to fear that *The Palm-Wine Drinkard* would not exact implicit acceptance on the terms of Tutuola's cosmological reality. For it did. Until the dream gimmick, it did. The production explored theatre and plumbed it to its imaginative depths; it should have retracted nothing."[8] That the criticism relates logically to his own creative impulse can be seen from the fact that of the four plays he published in 1963, the same year as this review, only one, *The Lion and the Jewel,* does not demand our acceptance of a "cosmological reality."

The objection might be raised that this does not apply to Armah, that he is no less a didactic writer than Achebe, for we are continually confronted with his sense of moral outrage at the political corruption he sees in Africa. But unlike Achebe, he is much less a moralist teaching his audience about the African experience than an interpreter seeking to find meaning in that experience. Thus it is not surprising that a key concern of Armah and Awoonor, as well as Soyinka, has been to explore the role of the artist as interpreter. Each of the three has sought to function "as the record of the mores and experience of his society and as the voice of vision in his own time."[9] Hence, I have referred to their distinctive awareness as a mythic consciousness in preference to the phrase "mythopoeic sensibility" in order to avoid the implication that they are myth-makers. The element of creativity is there, just as it had to be present among the priests of traditional societies, but ascendance is given to the aspect of conscious communal interpretation over private creativity.

The most obvious starting points for these writers in their explorations into the contradictions inherent in their cosmological reality are their own traditional myths. Yet where this appears to be clear in the pantheon of gods in Soyinka's *A Dance of the Forests* or *The Interpreters* or the Mammy Water figure in Awoonor's *This Earth, My Brother,* it is something that needs closer examination in the case of the trickster figure in Soyinka's *The Trials of Brother Jero* or in the ghost and cargo cult metaphors employed by

cosmological reality

Armah in *Fragments*. But appearances are deceiving, and little work has been done to study the ways in which even the obvious borrowings from traditional myth are transformed by the artists. Writers like Achebe have regularly used traditional myths, but they have done so primarily within a historical perspective. Armah, Awoonor, Soyinka and Tutuola, however, have used myth in that mythic sense of movement towards time *ab origine*, towards, as it were, a utopian vision.[10] Myth, then, is not just an element of their work, it is *the* defining element. In talking about his novel Awoonor has said: "I think if we go back to the festival of the senses, our destruction of things and people will cease. In a way, that long journey that Amamu takes through Nima is a journey at a very realistic level, not only at the mythical level. It is also a journey into himself, into the society — into the very entrails of his society in order to turn from it.... It may be lonely and anguished, but it is achieved and fulfilled."[11] Amamu's journey is the antithesis of what Snyder meant when he spoke of the way in which these writers internalized the collective consciousness of history into the consciousness of their characters,[12] for such a journey is really ahistorical. The problems, the contradictions that Amamu must face, are fundamental questions regarding the nature of his existence and are thus ontologically, not historically, specific.

In his criticism, as well as his creative writing, Soyinka has continually made the point that the gods may change their outer appearance, but they are still very much with us. He tells us that *"Sango* (Dispenser of Lightning) now chairmans the Electricity Corporation, *Ogun* (God of Iron) is the primal motor-mechanic."[13] Along with Tutuola he may be having fun, but it in no way undercuts his ultimate seriousness. In *Idanre*, for example, the gods and their battles are shown to be as real and as present as the course of the seasons and the journey of the poet through the night.

The dominant images of the writers who employ the rhetoric of myth fall into two main categories, demonic and apocalyptic. Through *agon*, that is, conflict and suffering, the characters are reborn into a higher state of consciousness about the human condition. In effect, the conflict is between these states of consciousness as indicated by two opposing clusters of images. Once again I can take my frame of reference from Awoonor who had the following to say about his images in *This Earth, My Brother*: "People have clearly pointed out the two images of the dunghill and the field of butterflies, which you may say have taken over my earlier duality. I saw the traditional society almost stupidly as a golden age, a beautiful and sinless kind of world. I no longer have that perception. I'm aware that suffering comes out of that condition. Thus I created these two images, let them fight against one another and then had the image of this woman who will eliminate the conflict and the sorrows, and almost in an atavistic sense, take us back to the primal good nature of all ourselves."[14] In short, the action centers around the mythic move and the image clusters are the vehicles for effecting that move.

The landscape through which the protagonists move is a scatological nightmare relieved only occasionally by a flower or a moment of respite found in the act of making love. These characters are, in a sense, shaman priests painfully aware of the ontological gap between the demonic world in which they live and the apocalyptic world they envision. It is just this gap that Soyinka has referred to as the "anguish of severance,"[15] a primal awareness of the separation of man and the gods (and, I might add, man from man). As these "priests" make the journey into "the entrails of society," the anguish is followed by a sense of despair, for every move that would lead them out also leads to a checkmate. The very titles of Armah's books are indicative of the frustration and despair of being trapped: The *Beautyful Ones Are Not Yet Born, Fragments,* and the ironic *Why Are We So Blest?*. Perhaps the demonic imagery is more overwhelming in Armah than in the other writers, but one does not have to get very far into either Awoonor or Soyinka's novels to find it.

The demonic imagery and the concomitant anguish in the psyches of the protagonists has been a real stumbling block for critics. It is easy to be struck by the deep sense of despair and blinded from seeing beyond it. Despite the dazzling brilliance of Armah's language, it is possible to feel about *The Beautyful Ones Are Not Yet Born* the same thing that E.M. Forster felt about Joyce's *Ulysses*: "... it is a dogged attempt to cover the universe with mud, an inverted Victorianism, an attempt to make crossness and dirt succeed where sweetness and light failed, a simplification of the human character in the interests of Hell."[16] Perhaps this is too harsh a statement; first of all, Armah is African not British, and secondly, we can understand existentialism where Forster could not. And yet as critics we are in the embarrassing position of those nineteenth-century ethnographers who saw that the distinguishing characteristic between advanced and primitive religions was in the ability to separate the sacred and the profane. Contamination, so the argument runs, is simply a negation of the purity of the sacred.

But it is not all that simple. Mary Douglas's book, *Purity and Danger: An Analysis of Concepts of Pollution and Taboo,*[17] is suggestive of a much more revealing way we can approach Armah's work. She demonstrates that dirt is that which is out of place in an organized system; thus, the very existence of dirt implies a prior concept of order. The very demonic, the scatological and the insane are categories which are outside and powerful, hence potentially dangerous to the established structure of society. Tutuola's Unreturnable-Heaven's Town is the very antithesis of what we would expect a well-ordered society to be; the people are cruel, filthy and entirely mad. What happens in Tutuola, as well as Armah, is a kind of symbolic inversion whereby the ineffable — Heaven, Utopia, the perfect society, call it what you will — gets named in terms of its opposite.

Contemplation of either the demonic or the apocalyptic is not something the mundane world can long endure. Those who persist in such contemplation are seen either as madmen or priests who can only exist on the margins of society. They are in touch with powers that are paradoxically a threat to society, while being essential to the continuing vitality of the social structure. They are a threat in that they are beyond human control, essential in that they are necessary to prevent social structures from becoming too rigid and thus dying. The marginal man, by virtue of his liminality, exists as a mediating agent filtering new energy into society and cushioning society from the dangers of that energy. The central characters, in the works of the writers I am considering, all exist as liminal figures.

Usually in these works, however, the marginal figure is more of a priest, an individual who, as a mediating agent between man and the gods, must bear more anguish than the ordinary man could live with. And while the authorial presence guides us into seeing the protagonists as priests, their societies see them as insane. When they reach the very nadir of their journeys, they must devise a strategy to live with an impossible situation. As the British psychiatrist R.D. Laing has shown us, this is the essence of the schizophrenic experience. The individual caught in this situation "cannot make a move, or make no move, without being beset by contradictory and paradoxical pressures and demands, pushes and pulls, both internally from himself, and externally from those around him."[18] But Laing has also shown that the individual's apparent sickness is but a reaction to the real sickness of society. Using the metaphor of the journey, he has argued that the healthy individuals, the true "priests," are those who have made this journey and returned. Soyinka was aware of this same idea when he spoke of the Palm-Wine Drinkard returning "wise *only* from the stress of experience."[19] Later he treated the subject in his play, *Madmen and Specialists*, where the "madman" holds the vision of a healthy society and his son, a doctor, is bent on cutting up the society. For us, as well as these characters, the world is completely turned on end. Outside it is dying of its own corruption, while in the inner world of the schizophrenic lies the seeds of regeneration both for the individual and society.

Here is one of the most important keys to understanding the distinction between the ethical and mythic consciousness. One of Achebe's novels, *Arrow of God*, has significant mythic elements and seems to be informed by the rhetoric of myth. The protagonist is a traditional priest, Ezeulu, who goes mad as a result of his conflict with his society. But the madness is seen as insurance of the society's continuity, as a lesson that "no man however great was greater than his people; that no man ever won judgement against his clan."[20] Sekoni, the engineer in Soyinka's *Interpreters* also goes mad, but here we never lose sight of the real madness in society. Though he is eventually killed in a car accident, Sekoni emerges from his insanity as an artist whose vision remains a force among the other interpreters, even after his death. We come to know Ezeulu in much more detail than we ever know Sekoni, but in the rendering of their respective conflicts we see Ezeulu's conflict externalized and rejected and Sekoni's conflict internalized and transformed into a positive and accepted force.

As we might expect, these two different types of conflict are reflected in the language and the ways in which space and time are manipulated. Where the conflict is externalized, we are in the world of objective phenomena, and accordingly the language is aimed at verisimilitude; where it is internalized, we enter a subjective realm, the language reflecting states of mind. Amamu, the lawyer of *This Earth, My Brother*, finds he must serve almost in the traditional role of carrier, a scapegoat who cleanses the community by carrying out all the accumulated evil and by voluntarily being sacrificed. Almost in a syncretic sense Amamu is a Christ figure wanting to let the cup pass from him, but knowing he must accept it. In a highly lyrical manner Awoonor catches this conflict by employing the rhythms of the traditional drum:

> The seventh night, deep deep night of the black black land of gods and deities they will come out. First the drums to-gu to-gu to gu to to to-gu if they insist and say it must be by every means. If they insist then I shall die the death of blood I shall die the death of blood....

> Sometimes I rode on the back of one of the smaller ghosts gidiga gidiga, rode through centuries I cannot recall. Mother, didn't I tell you I hated the sun, father didn't I tell you I hated the sun....[21]

Soyinka is a complete master at using language in a subjective manner for dramatic effect. In *The Trials of Brother Jero* he intensifies the comic situation inherent in Chume's relationship with the trickster Jero by having the messenger's confusion always revealed to us by his shifts from standard English into Pidgin. Samson, the passenger tout in *The Road*, makes similar shifts into Pidgin, though in this case the shifts indicate his possession by the dead lorry driver, Sergeant Burma, and recollections of his own past. We can also see how, in the opening chapter of *The Beautyful Ones Are Not Yet Born*, Armah captures the malaise of "the man." The long, detailed description of the bus ride and the man's arrival at his job reflect the utter oppressiveness of his existence, the continuous and inescapable landscape of real and metaphorical filth.

A result of this use of language in an impressionistic and often expressionistic fashion is the relative nature that time assumes. The chronological element, if not entirely confused, is at least subordinated to the space in which the conflicts take place. While aspects of this have already been explored in several articles, a thorough comparative study has yet to be done.[22] Nevertheless, it is apparent that without a mechanism for taking us out of so-called real time the writer would not be able to establish a mythos where aboriginal time prevails.

My main concerns in this brief introduction have been first to indicate that the work of Soyinka, Awoonor, and Armah needs to be seen less as a recent development in African literature than as a mainstream, the continuity of which can be traced back to Amos Tutuola, and secondly to offer a conceptual framework with which we can approach their aesthetics. In their use of myth, language, and demonic and apocalyptic imagery they have much in common, but my typology, as I indicated in the preface, is based on a structure that is not rigid, but is a continuum. Armah is very close to the ethical half of the continuum; Achebe, in *Arrow of God,* comes very close to the mythic. Armah, for example, draws on traditional myth far less than Soyinka. In fact, *Why Are We So Blest?* could be seen as anti-myth, an artistic exploration of the racial ideas in Frantz Fanon's *Black Skin, White Masks* and *The Wretched of the Earth,* and as such, an attack on "la mystification." Nevertheless, it still falls within our definition of myth, and the language and imagery are used in the ways we have been considering. Armah makes an unqualified attack on the myth of white supremacy (myth as lie), but replaces the lie with the myth of the revolution, of the last becoming first (myth as truth). How we view a given myth is not the question here, though that question could be resolved by pointing out the different levels of meaning on which the word "myth" operates. What is important is that even Armah's most recent work is mythic in the sense that it is structured more around the metaphors of myth than around the more strictly linear argument of an ethical writer; in other words, it is structured around paradox as opposed to analogy. Thus Armah extends into a novel Fanon's metaphor of the need for rivers of blood to fertilize the desert, where Achebe would write an extended simile about specific historic aspects of the colonial condition.

While Soyinka and Armah are working along the same axis, they may often be at different ends, the fantastic and prophetic poles that E.M. Forster has written of in *Aspects of the Novel.*[23] More than anything else these positions have to do with authorial tone. At the fantastic end are those works where the authorial presence asserts itself quite forcibly, creating a fundamental sense of confusion and resultant humor. At the prophetic end we find a more humble authorial presence directly concerned with establishing unity, avoiding humor, and creating only incidental confusion. Armah and, to some extent, Awoonor fall at this end of the axis and Tutuola at the other, while Soyinka continually shifts his position, being the prophet in *Idanre*, the fantasist in *The Trials of Brother Jero*. As often as not he shifts within the structure of one work, hence the serio-comic tone of *A Dance of the Forests, The Interpreters*, and *Madmen and Specialists*.

Regardless of these differences, their common sensibility leads us into worlds with which we may no longer have any daily contact. To the extent we can leave our rational baggage behind as we enter, we too may return wiser from the stress of that experience.

Armah's Mythic Hero: A Man Betwixt and Between

A lot of early criticism of African literature was aimed at identifying themes and showing how the themes were developed through the interaction of characters. Aside from the anti-colonial theme, perhaps no theme has been singled out for more commentary than the theme of culture conflict, or more dramatically, "the clash of cultures." Discussion will inevitably focus on the protagonist who is caught in this conflict, an individual who is caught "between two worlds." The "worlds", of course, are the value systems of the West and traditional Africa. The "between-two-worlds" commentary has been useful in opening up discussion on Chinua Achebe, Ama Ata Aidoo, Mongo Beti, Cyprian Ekwensi and a number of other African writers who write out of an ethical consciousness. For a long time, however, such commentary has been overdone with these writers; even worse, it has been misdirected at the works of those writers working from a mythic consciousness.

We can thus readily understand the context of Wole Soyinka's prefatory note to his play, *Death and the King's Horseman*. There he angrily denounces those who wish to focus on a simple clash-of-cultures theme in his work: "I find it necessary to caution the would-be producer of this play against [this] sadly familiar reductionist tendency, and to direct his vision instead to the far more difficult and risky task of eliciting the play's threnodic essence." To be sure, Elesin, the main character of the play, is a man "between two worlds," but they are the distinctly Yoruba worlds of the here and now and of the ancestors. Conflict between African and European value systems does have something to do with the setting of the play, but the central dramatic conflict can be entirely understood in terms of Elesin's particular position betwixt and between the living and the dead.

Ayi Kwei Armah's novels, like Soyinka's play, are built around historical frames, and thus we can easily move in the direction of an ethical, even a literal analysis of thematic structure. Essentially, all his novels deal with individuals caught in the web of economic, cultural and political forces dominating colonial and post-colonial Africa. To the extent, however, that we try to see these forces in terms of some European-African axis, we oversimplify and misread what Armah is doing. As Soyinka effectively pointed out in the prefatory note mentioned above, such an approach is crassly Eurocentric for it "presupposes a potential equality *in every given situation* of the alien culture and the indigenous, on the actual soil of the latter" (Soyinka's emphasis).

The works of Joseph Campbell point in a direction that might lead toward a more solid understanding of character, conflict and structure, not merely in Armah's novels, but also in other West African writers who share a mythic consciousness. Following C.G. Jung's theories about archetypes and Arnold van Gennep's theory of *rites de passage*, Joseph Campbell developed his thesis concerning the universal structure of myth. According to Campbell, all myths can be regarded as variations of a monomyth in which "a hero ventures forth from the world of common day into a region of supernatural wonder: fabulous forces are there encountered and a decisive victory is won: the hero comes back from this mysterious adventure with the power to bestow boons on his fellow man." Campbell represents the nuclear unit simply as a process of separation, initiation and return and has brought together an almost incredible amount of material from a large number of diverse cultures to support his thesis. He appears to have formulated much of this thesis at the expense of cultural differences which might be equally pertinent to any study of myth, yet I have found useful his definition of a mythic hero as one "who has been able *to battle past his personal and local historical limitations* to the generally valid, normally human forms. Such a one's visions, ideas, and inspirations come pristine from the primary springs of human life and thought. Hence they are eloquent, *not of the present, disintegrating society and psyche, but of the unquenched source* through which society is reborn. The hero has died as a modern man; but as eternal man — perfected, unspecific, universal man — he has been reborn. His solemn task and deed therefore ... is to return then to us, transfigured, and teach the lesson he has learned of life renewed" (pp. 19-20, italics mine). I have added special emphasis to the idea of the hero as one who transcends mundane space/time referents, for I am concerned less with the relation of the hero to Campbell's pattern of the monomyth than to the phase of initiation, what van Gennep calls the condition of liminality. Moreover, though the hero is "reborn," it is never vaguely as a "universal man," but specifically as a person in a given culture.

Ayi Kwei Armah's second novel, *Fragments*, contains what appears to be a perversion of the monomyth. Baako, the hero, is educated in the United States, an area which his people see as "a region of supernatural wonder." He returns to them with "a decisive victory" — namely, his degree — which gives him "the power to bestow boons on his fellow man." Baako himself does not perceive his journey in this light, but his family and friends do. The power he sees himself as possessing is a spiritual one, having nothing directly to do with the material benefits his people desire. Simply recognizing variations of the monomyth in Armah's work is not a useful exercise, but it is significant that much of his writing deals with characters who live on the margins of society in opposition to the values by which those inside society live their lives. In *The Beautyful Ones Are Not Yet Born*, "the man" confronts the futility of being good in a corrupt world. In *Fragments*, Baako confronts the futility of existing as a bearer of a spirituality the world has lost, and Modin, in *Why Are We So Blest?*, confronts it in revolutionary action. To paraphrase James Joyce, each of these heroes goes forth to encounter the reality of experience and forge in his soul the uncreated mythos of his race. For heuristic purposes I will regard these characters as mythic heroes, examining closely the nature of their liminality in relation to Armah's symbols and images. To do this, however, I will first need to clarify my terminology and discuss the relationship among myth, ritual and liminality.

Victor Turner has done some brilliant studies of liminality, going far beyond van Gennep's seminal work. For Turner, liminality is a key to understanding the way men structure their society and their myths. In the liminal phases of ritual, he says, we observe that "social relations are simplified, while myth and ritual are elaborated. That this is so is really quite simple to understand: if liminality is regarded as a time and place of withdrawal from normal modes of social action, it can be seen as potentially a period of scrutinization of the central values and axioms of the culture in which it occurs."[2] While confining most of his own work on liminality to the study of the liminal period in initiation rites, Turner recognized that liminality can be found in any individual or societal change from one state to another. Moreover, liminal *personae*, whom he calls "threshold people," can be found existing in a permanent or semi-permanent condition vis-à-vis a society.

In its need for structure and order, society rejects that which is unclear or ambiguous. The liminal figure is the very epitome of paradox, being one who is no longer classified in his old state and not yet classified in a new one. Thus, according to Turner, the subject is "structurally, if not physically, 'invisible.' As members of society, most of us see only what we expect to see, and what we expect to see is what we are conditioned to see when we have learned the definitions and classifications of our culture."[3] Insofar as they are dead regarding their former state, liminal *personae* are surrounded with symbols of death and decomposition, and to the extent that they have not yet been incorporated in a new state, they are also surrounded by symbols of birth and resurrection. The existence in this period of womb/tomb duality gives rise to metaphysical speculation. "Liminality," Turner says, "may perhaps be regarded as the Nay to all positive structural assertions, but in some sense the source of them all, and more than that, as a realm of pure possibility whence novel configurations of ideas and relations may arise" (p. 97).

Despite its being "a realm of pure possibility," the potential danger of liminality to the stability and continuity of any society is extremely high. The average farmer or worker cannot function under the stress which ambiguity and contradiction create. Were he, for example, to spend his time speculating about alternative life styles, his family would starve. Of necessity he must function within an extremely rigid conceptual framework within which everything has its place. The ambiguous is thus seen as an element of pollution. As Mary Douglas explains in her book *Purity and Danger*, "the idea of society is a powerful image. It is potent in its own right to control or to stir men to action. This image has form; it has external boundaries, margins, internal structure. Its outlines contain power to reward conformity and repulse attack. There is energy in its margins and unstructured areas."[4] In a tradition-oriented society the danger is minimized and the energy is tapped by means of ritual control. Thus there emerges ritualized rebellion, which, rather than breaking down the social structure, reinforces group solidarity and the society's image of itself. In modern technological societies that lack this ritual process, there develops the possibility of actual revolution.[5]

The idea of liminality seems to exist in direct opposition to the concept of a structured society, but the situation is much more complex than this opposition. Turner appears to confuse the issue in his terminology of "structure" and "anti-structure," but if we follow his work closely, we see that he is referring to complements and not opposites. Each realm, in fact, has its own structure by which the other realm, through differentiation, is able to define its own boundaries. This process is ongoing and continuous, and hence structure as well as anti-structure cannot be conceived of in static terms. Were we to conceptualize these structures as separate and abstract ideas, we could represent society as the absolute zero of change and energy, and liminality as pure energy and representing chaos, but — since there is continual interaction — such an extreme model is meaningless. We need to keep this interaction in mind when Turner tells us he will "in the fashion of Lévi-Strauss, express the difference between the properties of liminality and those of the status system in terms of a series of binary oppositions or discriminations."[6] It is the aspect of discrimination, and not opposition, that is useful in looking at the characteristics of these two realms of existence.

The relevance of Turner's ideas to any consideration of Armah's work should be readily apparent. Leaving aside for the moment Armah's heroes, we can see that the structure, or more accurately, the anti-structure of the societies he has rendered in each of his novels is a photographic negative of a well-ordered society. Without any idealization, in *Arrow of God* and *Things Fall Apart*, Chinua Achebe has depicted societies in which we could conceive of living; in *The Beautyful Ones Are Not Yet Born* we see a society from which we could desire only to escape.

The unbridled energies of anti-structure may be a useful source of cultural energy for society as we know it, but at the same time unbearable for the ordinary man. A person experiences liminality not because he wants to, but because he must.

The situation becomes involuted when we see that Armah's heroes are at the limen of what are essentially liminal societies. In other words, seen objectively in relation to the mundane world they are anti-heroes, inversions of what we would expect in a hero. But if we look at them subjectively, and in relation to their fictional societies, they can be seen as having positive heroic virtues in the mythic sense of possessing, or being possessed by, regenerative powers for their society. In many respects they are like Murano, the zombie-like character in Wole Soyinka's *The Road* and an almost idealized liminal *persona*. The main character of the play, the Professor, says of Murano: "When a man has one leg in each world, his legs are never the same. The big toe of Murano's foot — the left one of course — rests on the slumbering chrysalis of the Word. When that crust cracks my friends — you and I, that is the moment we await. That is the moment of our rehabilitation."[7] Murano has penetrated the limen, made contact with the ineffable, and is now speechless. In absolute humility and total commitment he exists as a servant to the professor, but remains hidden from the sight of all the other characters in the play. Even a random borrowing from Turner's series of discriminations would corroborate this picture of Murano as a socially invisible, but spiritually powerful individual. The most salient discriminations are as follows: "Transition/state ...; Equality/inequality; Anonymity/systems of nomenclature; Absence of property/property; Absence of status/status ...; Absence of rank/distinctions of rank; Humility/just pride of position; Disregard for personal appearance/care for personal appearance ...; Unselfishness/selfishness; Total obedience/obedience only to superior rank; Sacredness/secularity ...; Silence/speech...; Continuous reference to mystical powers/intermittent reference to mystical powers ...; Acceptance of pain and suffering/avoidance of pain and suffering; Heteronomy/degrees of autonomy."[8]

We are now in a position to see how the concept of liminality can illuminate the imagery and symbolic structure of Armah's work, for his protagonists differ from Murano only in degree, not in kind. Moreover, as they metaphorically inhabit the same twilight zone of society's margins, we might expect them to be surrounded by the same shadowy landscape. Murano would come to see the Professor only at dusk or at dawn, and Armah's *The Beautyful Ones Are Not Yet Born* significantly opens as dawn is about to break. The setting and the protagonist's confrontation with the bus driver serve as a paradigm for the whole novel, and perhaps for all of Armah's work.

The protagonist is on his way to work, moving along a surreal road in an all too real bus: "The light from the bus moved uncertainly down the road until finally the two vague circles caught some indistinct object on the side of the road where it curved out in front. The bus had come to a stop. Its confused rattle had given place to an endless spastic shudder, as if its pieces were held together by too much rust ever to fall completely apart."[9] The hero's anonymity is maintained throughout the novel; we never know him by any other name than "the man," but here, prior to even that distinction, we see him as one sleepwalker among many who seemingly exist only as material for the conductor to exploit:

> But what could a conductor take, even from a body that has yet to wake, when all this walking corpse holds out is the exact fare itself, no more, no less? Much better the days after pay day, much, much better. Then the fullness of the month touches each old sufferer with a feeling of new power. The walkers sleep still, but their nightmares in which they are dwarfs unable to run away and little insects caught in endless pools, these fearful dreams are gone. (p. 2)

In a few short paragraphs Armah has developed a very suggestive, though straightforward metaphor for the colonial and post-colonial political situation in Africa. The bus is the modern, yet corrupt machinery of a new African state; the passengers are the exploited masses; and the conductor is a politician whose power is contingent on his ability to victimize the masses. Altogether they are carried forward toward some vague, undefined destination. Up to this point the conductor is in control of his business; then Armah deftly executes a reversal, and the metaphor suddenly becomes more richly complex. The conductor is counting his take and is particularly fascinated by the smell of a bill. Again and again, in a rather compulsive manner, he lifts the bill to his nose: "It was a most unexpected smell for something so new to have: it was a very old smell, very strong, and so very rotten that the stench of it came with a curious, satisfying pleasure" (p. 3). It is not even necessary to go into the Freudian ramifications of this to understand the sense of shame that quickly overtakes him. When he looks around the bus to reassure himself that he has been alone, he confronts a pair of wide-open eyes staring at him. The man, one of the sleepers, has apparently caught him in his childlike play and seen the excremental basis of his power. The fear that then possesses the conductor is a foreshadowing of the fear that will later possess the politician, Koomson, after the coup.[10] More importantly, however, we are given insight into the potential power which the sleeper, the liminal *persona*, paradoxically holds from his position of weakness. As we can see from Armah's cryptic interjection of the italicized line *"And so words and phrases so often thrown away as jokes reveal their true meaning"* (p. 4), the power is akin to that which a court jester holds over a king.

The sleeper has become a watcher, a guardian of the conductor's lost sense of what his function should be on the bus:

> ... perched on his seat in the back of the shuddering bus, the watcher did not stir. Only his eyes continued their steady gaze, and the conductor felt excruciatingly tortured as they drilled the message of his guilt into his consciousness. Outrage alternated with a sweaty fear he had never before felt. Something, it seemed to him, was being drained from him, leaving the body feeling like a very dry sponge, very light, completely at the mercy of slight trying gusts of wind. (p. 4)

In a real, physical manner, the conductor experiences a catharsis, though the very idea that someone has been watching him also strips away his sense of reality. He attributes to the man's stare a degree of supernatural power and has even heard voices of accusation while consciously aware that the man has said nothing.

The conductor gets control of the situation by convincing himself that the man is, after all, human like himself and thus open to being bribed. Once again there is a reversal of power as the conductor draws closer to the man, ready to bribe him. He then explodes with indignation on finding the man asleep with spittle oozing out the corner of his mouth. The god-like accusator, sacred just a moment before, has now become a vile object, a "bloodyfucking sonofabitch! Article of no commercial value!" (p. 5). After more verbal abuse from the conductor, he is thrown off the bus and called an "Uncircumcised baboon," a "Moron of a frog" (p. 9) by an irate taxi driver who barely misses hitting him.

Later in the novel the man is actively engaged in an almost mystical pursuit of holiness, but it might seem absurd to conclude from the opening pages that he is a holy man, a kind of shaman priest. Quite simply, he is more acted upon than acting. Indeed, though we can sympathize with his plight, we see him in the repulsive condition of being covered with his own spittle. In our minds, as well as in the conductor's, there exists the tendency to equate him with the rubbish on the streets. We at first respond to him and the fiction on a very literal level. However, because of the incident of the spittle and the ensuing name calling, the man's role as a priest is confirmed on a symbolic level since he has become a scapegoat. Both the ascribed supernatural power and the animality mark the man as one outside the normal structure of society. Edmund Leach in "Animal Categories and Verbal Abuse" has shown that the manner in which man differentiates himself from the sacred is essentially akin to the manner in which he differentiates himself

from animals, or even more basically, from dirt. Whatever does not clearly
fit into man's categories for things in the physical environment in which he
lives becomes taboo and at once "sacred, valuable, important, powerful,
dangerous, untouchable, filthy, unmentionable."[11] For example, we produce
excrement and though it is an extension of ourselves, it becomes separate,
having an ambiguous identity. Thus it is made a taboo object. As Leach
explains, the sacredness of a given person, object or situation is commonly
marked off by language inversions. The collar of a clergyman in England is
called a "dog collar," playing on the inverted spelling of the word "God"
(p. 27). The ritual killing of a king, literally a negation of life, takes on
symbolic meaning as an act enabling regeneration, the affirmation of life.
The physical and verbal abuse the man receives in the opening chapter of
The Beautyful Ones Are Not Yet Born literally sets him apart while
metaphorically confirming his sacred position in relation to the social norms
epitomized by the conductor. Set apart from the moral and spiritual
corruption, he becomes a potentially regenerative force.

The rest of the novel is a powerful and eloquent thematic elaboration
and exploration of the man's role as priest and the attendant paradox of
being a part of, yet separate from, the structure of society. He is continually
offered bribes, but his refusal to take them causes his family to look upon
him as "a chichidodo bird," a bird that hates excrement but feeds on the
maggots that grow in it. Out of this paradox grows the *agon*, the conflict and
the agony without which the man could not function as a symbol of
regeneration. Were separation possible, the man and his society would go
their separate ways, but their fates are inextricably bound together.

From the point of view of society, the man represents a negation of the
dominant values. Thus he is a polluting agent, a danger to the existing social
order. As we have noticed, however, we are made aware of a symbolic
inversion whereby the society in its perverted materialism is seen as the
locus of a spirituality necessary for the society's regeneration. The cancerous
tissue of a sick person will react to a cure in exactly the same way any
healthy tissue will react to a disease. In both cases the tendency is to expel
that which is foreign to the organism. Because he stands alone, the man is
continually in doubt as to whether or not he is a disease. He is quite
conscious of his own isolation, and he is even at times excessively proud of
his personal morality. Nevertheless, his diffidence regarding the ultimate
sanity of this morality is so absolute that he never thinks of the possibility
that he might be a cure. An analogy taken from R.D. Laing shows that the
point of view is of crucial importance:

> From an ideal vantage point on the ground, a formation of planes may be
> observed in the air. One plane may be out of formation. But the whole

formation may be off course. The plane that is "out of formation" may be abnormal, bad or "mad," from the point of view of the formation. But the formation itself may be bad or mad from the point of view of the ideal observer. The plane that is out of formation may also be more or less off course than the formation itself is.

The "out of formation" criterion is the clinical positivist criterion. The "off course" criterion is the ontological.[12]

By the copious accumulation of demonic imagery we are continually made aware of the fact that the society is "off course," but as the man's vantage point is different from ours, this awareness is one that he must grow into.

The result we might expect of such symbolic inversion is dramatic irony, for at the beginning of the novel we know much more than the man. Harold R. Collins, in fact, has argued that *The Beautyful Ones* is ironic fiction.[13] For Collins the scatological imagery is symbolic of the man's bondage and leads us to look down on the man as well as his situation. There is a *non sequitur* in this reasoning, however, since it does not necessarily follow that in being aware of the nature of his bondage we will be aloof from the man. His situation, in fact, is circumscribed as *the* human condition. A certain amount of distance is necessary for us to understand the configuration of circumstances that surrounds the protagonist, but whatever irony results from this understanding is aimed at the society and not the man. The man actually carries a tragic potential, for we are made to feel the dignity of his struggle with forces that overwhelmingly contrive against human dignity. He is not *a* man or everyman, but *the* man, the only human being, the only person in the context of the novel who is struggling to maintain his humanity.

Before going on to look at the progression of the conflict between the protagonist and society in *The Beautyful Ones*, and in Armah's other novels, I would like to consider an essential problem in dealing with Armah's work. Virtually every page he has written is pervaded with negatives: the society in its corruption and the protagonist in his despair seem to epitomize Carlyle's "Everlasting No." While I have already touched on the positive implications of the liminal protagonist, namely that nay saying implies yea saying, I wish to examine these implications in relation to the larger patterns of experience that Armah's work communicates.

Starting with the idea that the ability to use a symbol or word to indicate something demands an understanding that the word or symbol is not the thing, Kenneth Burke has brilliantly argued that the negative is "perhaps the one great motivational principle that man, in his role as the language-using animal, has added to nature."[14] For the Western mind trained to think in terms of a positive/negative dichotomy with the emphasis always on the positive, this thought seems to turn the world on end. On the other hand, the African sees positive and negative not in terms of opposition, but in terms of complementarity. Turner has discussed complementarity in his studies of liminality, and the Yoruba trickster, Eshu, provides a ready example, one simultaneously thought of as a creative force (his sexuality) and a destructive force (his creation of chaos).[15]

"One uses metaphor," Burke says, "without madness insofar as one spontaneously knows that the literal implication is not true."[16] Although no one would deny Burke's statement, we often get so involved in a given fiction that we tend to forget to see the reality behind the fiction. "Hence, despite the freedom of the rational discount, there may be sheer necessity in the trend of the images as such. Insofar as terms, metaphors, 'models,' fictions generally are positive, they may compel us despite our genius for the negative; that is, we may not 'discount' them enough, not fully recognizing how imaginally positive they are" (p. 462). The situation is familiar enough to critics of British literature in the paradox of Satan being Milton's most fully realized character while simultaneously embodying the very antithesis of the ideals towards which Milton's rhetoric moves us. The analogy, however, has limited value, as there is no such absolute duality in Armah's work.

Nevertheless, the sheer profusion of demonic imagery can function rhetorically in persuading us to take that imagery at face value. In her introduction to *The Beautyful Ones Are Not Yet Born*, Ama Ata Aidoo found it "difficult to accept in physical terms the necessity for hammering on every page the shit and stink from people and the environment" (xii). Ultimately, of course, there is no way of proving that Armah should not be read literally, but to do so means that we must deny not only the rich symbolic complexity of his work, and thus his poetic genius, but also his African sensibility, the very particular way in which he sees the world as dynamic configurations of complementary opposites. In other words, we can look at the landscape of the man, the madness of Baako, or the sadistic torture of Modin as correlating directly with the real world and inducing us to accept an essentially nihilistic philosophy; or, we can look at these negations as symbolic action directed against an existing order, as essentially revolutionary, and hence inducing us to accept an apocalyptic orientation. If we accept Armah's images as symbolic action, it does not mean that we must totally discount their literal implications. The torture of Modin at the hands of the French soldiers can, and in fact should, be seen as a very real extension of white racism. But if we simply look at these images without also rationally discounting their literal reality, understanding that the work is fiction and not life, we can see them only as a monotonous, though grotesque, catalogue of negatives and fail to catch the vitality they have on an artistic level.

Keeping in mind the symbolic value of the negative in Armah's work, we can return to my assertion that the liminal *personae* of his novels are mythic heroes who transcend their particular historical limitations to bring the seeds of regeneration to their societies. That we never see how regeneration is effected is not important to the integrity of the work, for the tacit assumption of society, and by extension the artist, is that the ritual process enacted by the hero is the only way society can be rejuvenated. I have been primarily concerned with the liminal aspect of this process, but will now look at the larger pattern of separation, initiation, and return.

Armah's first three novels are variations of the same basic theme of the necessary symbiotic relationship between the liminal *persona* and society, and are structured by continual reiteration of these two contrasting but complementary symbols. The eloquence with which Armah controls his work, namely the compelling manner in which he tells his story and charges his symbols, leads us around the pitfall of monotony, the formal danger of any such repetition. Moreover, there is a logical progression in his early work from very general to very specific studies of man's relation to corruption. In *The Beautyful Ones* the symbols are the least specifically defined, the struggle being between an unnamed man and the malaise induced by material corruption. In *Fragments* the struggle is more sharply delineated in terms of an artist and his confrontation with the perversion of the old myths of his society. In *Why Are We So Blest?* the struggle is focused very clearly on a black intellectual's relationship with the corrupting power of the white racism around him which he has internalized as suicidal self-hate.

The opening pages of *Beautyful Ones* serve as a paradigm of Armah's central thematic concern, but in the structure of this novel the confrontation with the conductor also serves another symbolic function in separating the protagonist from society so that he can begin his mythic journey. Before the long philosophical interlude in the middle of the novel where the man converses with Teacher, there is a whole series of confrontations that establish this separation. From his home to his job, through the day, and back to his home, the man runs a course during which the fears of the conductor, a clerk, a timber merchant, Koomson, and the man's wife are ritually transformed into the man's anguish. The community makes him a scapegoat, a point underscored by the profusion of demonic imagery that is sandwiched between each encounter. It is from this landscape that he desires deliverance, but he is increasingly bound to it as one who must symbolically bear the burden of the corruption and carry it out of the society. In terms of symbolic action this role is fulfilled in his acceptance of his brotherhood with the night-soil men as he helps the politician, Koomson, escape after the coup.

On arriving at work the man finds the night clerk asleep and attempts to wake him: "At first there was no response, but the man kept a gentle pressure on the clerk's shoulder, increasing it till he woke up. The sleeper woke up in the grip of a brief, strong terror. As he came up from his easy darkness his face lost its softness and became strained ..." (pp. 14-15). The man's smile reassures the clerk, for he is not one to inform on anyone, aware himself of the effects of "the dead nights when long whole hours could go by pierced only by the departing sounds of good trains, lone and empty" (p. 15). In fact, the day shift is not very much different from the night shift for all the "suffering sleepers" (p. 20) who "seemed to sweat a lot, not from the exertion of their jobs, but from some kind of inner struggle that was always going on" (p. 20). At noon the man takes his lunch break and steps outside into the smell of "steamed grease" and "overwarm stench" (p. 22) and into a landscape of "unconquerable filth" (p. 23). As he sits by a bridge, however, he seems to intuit for a moment his own relationship to all the filth surrounding him and to "the gleam," the false promise of material success. A small stream of clear water trickles through a crack in a roughly made dam, pushing aside the mud and exposing the pebbles where it falls: "He drew back his gaze and was satisfied with the clearness before the inevitable muddying. It was the satisfaction of a quiet attraction, not at all like the ambiguous disturbing tumult within awakened by the gleam. And yet here undoubtedly was something close enough to the gleam, this clearness, this beautiful freedom from dirt. Somehow, there seemed to be a purity and peace here which the gleam could never bring" (p. 23). The flash of insight is soon gone. Back at work he listens to a message rattle across the telegraph, "Why do we agree to go on like this?" (p. 26). It is a message to which he has no answer.

Later, while working overtime, he confronts the timber merchant and can give no reason for refusing the bribe the merchant offers. The ennui he had experienced in contemplating the plight of the night clerk has now sharpened into a painful anguish, for he takes the guilt of the timber merchant and turns it inward: "The man was left alone with thoughts of the easy slide and how everything said there was something miserable, something unspeakably dishonest about a man who refused to take and to give what everyone around was busy taking and giving: something unnatural, something very cruel, something that was criminal, for who but a criminal could ever be left with such a feeling of loneliness?" (p. 31). By the moral standards of those around him he is a criminal, an outsider, but what is most important, he accepts their accusations of his criminality. In seeing himself apart from the corrupt masses, he must deny something of his own humanity. Later, in one of the most poignant scenes in the novel, the man tries to break through this barrier of loneliness by a simple act of physical contact with his wife. He has come home late and finds her in bed asleep. When he reaches over to touch her, he is revolted by the scar on her womb and quickly withdraws from her, both outwardly and inwardly. Like the biological decay which is necessary for the sustenance of new life, her scar is but a symbol of the necessary cycle of birth and death. One generation is born and another begins to die. The man has not yet come to the point where he can accept an aesthetic of the total cycle of life.

On his way home from work he runs into an old schoolmate of his who has successfully pursued "the gleam." Koomson and his wife, Estie, do not at first recognize "the invisible man of the shadows" (p. 37), but when they do see him, they are simply annoyed at being held up from a theatre engagement. To put the man off, Koomson hastily agrees to come to dinner at the man's house,[17] but when the man shakes hands with Estie, her hand "is withdrawn *as quickly as if contact were a well-known calamity*" (p. 38, italics mine). Like a neophyte in a traditional rite of passage the man has become an object of taboo, invisible for all practical purposes and thus dangerous.[18] The anguish of the man accordingly grows even more acute. As he rides home on the bus, he is at the nadir of his symbolic journey, and Armah presents the longest and most intensely scatological passage in the novel. The passage should be quoted in its entirety, for it shows a complete inversion of the promise of material salvation ("the gleam"); the images are a correlative to the man's period of separation:

The man gets in, choosing a seat by a window. The window turns out to have no pane in it. No matter. It is hardly a cold night. When the bus starts the air that rushes in comes like a soft wave of lukewarm water. The man leans back against his seat and fingers recoil behind his head. He does not look back. It is possible, after so much time up and down the same way, it is possible to close the eyes and lay back the head and yet to know very clearly that one is at this moment passing by that particular place or the other one, because the air brings these places to the open nose. Even at night there is something hot and dusty about the wind that comes blowing over the grease of the loco yard, so that the combination raises in mind pictures of thick short men in overalls thickened with grease that will never come off; blunt rusty bits of iron mixed up with filings in the sand; old water that has stopped flowing and confused itself with decaying oil from broken-down boilers; even the dead smell of carbide lamps and electric cutters. After the wall of the loco yard, the breeze blowing freely in from the sea, fresh in a special organic way that has in it traces of living things from their beginnings to their endings. Over the iron bridge the bus moves slowly. In gusts the heat rises from the market abandoned to the night and to the homeless, dust and perpetual mud covered over with crushed tomatoes and rotten vegetables, eddies from the open end of some fish head on a dump of refuse and curled-up scales with the hardening corpses of the afternoon's flies around. Another stretch of free sea line. More than halfway now, the world around the central rubbish heap is entered, and smells hit the senses like a strong wall, and even the eyes have something to register. It is so old it has become more than mere rubbish, that is why. It has fused with the earth underneath. In one or two places the eye that chooses to remain open can see the weird patterns made by thrown wrecks of upended bicycles and a prewar roller. Sounds arise and kill all smells as the bus pulls into the dormitory town. Past the big public lavatory the stench claws inward to the throat. Sometimes it is understandable that people spit so much, when all around decaying things push inward and mix all the body's juices with the taste of rot. Sometimes it is understandable, the doomed attempt to purify the self by adding to the disease outside. Hot smell of caked shit split by afternoon's baking sun, now touched by still evaporating dew. The nostrils, incredibly, are joined in a way that is most horrifyingly direct to their end. Across the aisle on the seat opposite, an old man is sleeping and his mouth is open to the air rushing in the night with how many particles of what? So why should he play the fool and hold his breath? Sounds of moist fish frying in the open pans of dark perennial oil so close to the public lavatory. It is very easy to get used to what is terrible. A different thing; the public bath, made for a purification that is not offensive. Here there is only the stale soapsuds merging in grainy rotten dirt from everybody's scum, a reminder of armpits full of yellowed hair dripping sweat down arms raised casually in places of public intimacy. The bus whines up a hill and the journey is almost over. Here are waves of spice from late pots of familiar homes, spices to cover what strong meats? (pp. 39-41)

Paralleling the real journey home is a metaphysical journey down into the very bedrock of existence where the dirt is "fused with the earth underneath." The question about the man playing the fool and holding his breath is not in this sense a rhetorical one, for it poses the primary question with which the man must come to terms. Were he just *a* man, he could accept the corruption, but he is aware that much greater demands are being made of him, even though he is unaware of the nature of the role for which these demands are made. When he arrives home the question is again brought before him, this time by his wife when she calls him a chichidodo. From the strangers to the old schoolmate to his wife, guilt has been forced on him in a series of concentric rings turning all his pain inward.

Bearing this guilt of family and community, the man steps out of his house and into an evening that "was a dark tunnel so long that out in front and above there never could be any end to it" (p. 46). The first phase in the ritual passage of the hero, his separation from society, is complete. The tunnel he enters, the womb from which he must be reborn, is at the threshold of his second phase, his initiation. It is his period of retirement from the mundane world, a time when he simultaneously must learn and contemplate the role he must fulfill on his return. The three chapters devoted to this period of instruction span the course of one evening at Teacher's house, but within this unit all sense of time, place and point of view become inextricably confused. As Gareth Griffiths has noted, "Teacher is clearly identified with the old sources of African culture, the non-European, the non-technological sources, the world of the dead gods where spirit and matter are interfused."[19] In effect, the man has made the heroic crossing into mythic time.

Griffiths' comment is perceptive, but I take exception to the idea that Armah has implied that the gods are dead. Teacher has also made the heroic crossing and is unable to make the second crossing, the return. He wishes only individual salvation and is thus, as Griffiths has noted, in his own way just as corrupt as Koomson. This refusal to return is connected with Teacher's loss of Manaan, the woman who, with her gift of *wee* brought second sight to Teacher. Her beauty, her regenerative powers, and her association with the water make her appear as Mammy Water, a goddess central to most West African mythologies.[20] True, we are told she is destroyed, but in the end we realize her destruction is no permanent loss. After making the second crossing and fulfilling his role, the man recognizes her on the beach, even though he has never seen her before.

Teacher is crippled by the idea that "there is no salvation anywhere," or at best, "only within the cycle of our damnation itself" (p. 55). Despite this knowledge, the call of society is too strong for the man to reject society and remain withdrawn like Teacher. He returns to his wife, still overcome by his inability to alleviate her suffering, but in bed he falls asleep and has a dream of "blinding lights, wild and uncontrolled, succeeded by pure darkness, from which the recognized self emerges. The man sees himself, very small, very sharp, very clear. Walking with an unknown companion, scarcely even seen, in the coolness of some sweet dust, leaving the dark, low hovels behind" (p. 99). He and his female companion see large white shining towers off in the distance and they are both "happy in the present and happy in the image of the future in the present" (p. 99). When he is separated from this woman by the blinding lights, the dream suddenly changes into a nightmare. Before he completely loses her, however, he notices that she is not blinded by the lights: "Through the insufficient protection of his fingers he can see her, her eyes shining with the potent brightness of huge car lights, returning the power of the oncoming lights" (p. 99). The woman would seem to be Manaan, the water goddess; the man has dreamt of the loss that Teacher has already experienced. That "anguish of severance," however, also has a locus in the man's psyche, for he must experience it in the living nightmare, the daily routine to which he will awaken.

When the coup finally occurs, the man is able to fulfill his role in carrying corruption out of the community. There is no absolute sense of purification in his leading Koomson away, for in the end the man realizes that the army is continuing what the politician had begun. Yet that brilliantly ironic escape through the latrine and along the gutters of the city does answer this question posed by the man: "The future goodness may come eventually, but before then where were the things in the present which would prepare the way for it?" (p. 158). Where indeed, but in the ritual process, in the actions of the man. Even the man's wife can now accept him, if only for the practical consideration that he has not been and never will be reduced to the contemptible figure of the frightened Koomson.

After getting Koomson safely out to sea, the man dives from the boat and swims back to shore. His own escape is not possible, since he feels his center is in the society, however corrupt it still is. The dive is the penultimate act, the ritual purification following his passage out of and back into the world of men: "He stayed there as long as he could, holding his breath. He held his breath so long that he began to enjoy the almost exploding inward feeling that he was perhaps no longer alive" (p. 176). Finally the man must be reborn, a process which involves his coming up and breathing the polluted air of the corrupt world. On reaching the shore he falls asleep. When he awakes he sees Manaan moving toward him. Her face "was not young, and it looked like something that had been finally destroyed a long time back. And yet he found it beautiful as he looked at it" (p. 177).

In West African religion the gods draw their strength from the worship of men, just as men in turn draw their strength from the gods. Man can thus create or destroy gods; there is no concept, as in the West, of a deity having an existence independent of man. Manaan has been neglected by man, and in that neglect lies the cause of the madness by which the man finds her possessed. Her madness is a correlative to the corruption in society. As she plays with the sand, there is meaning in the mad words she utters "with all the urgency in her diseased soul, 'They have mixed it all together! Everything! They have mixed everything. And how can I find it when they have mixed it all with so many other things?'" (pp. 177-78). The man's involvement in the ritual process was implicitly an act of faith in this goddess of regeneration. Her existence has been extended by this action, but it still remains for the Beautiful Ones, yet to be born, to restore her and the community to a healthy state.

Fragments is structured around a much more specific theme. Picking up where he concluded *The Beautyful Ones*, Armah probes the question of the relationship between society and the sick god, between society and perverted myth. If we approach the novel with Western-oriented aesthetics, we will see the rather universal theme of conflict between society and the artist, but if we go deeper we will find a clear culture-specific manifestation of this configuration. Even at the so-called universal level, ground must be cleared in order to handle this rather complex novel.

We tend to think of alienation as a uniquely modern, Western phenomenon, a by-product of the industrial revolution. As we moved from an agrarian to a post-agrarian, urban-centered culture, we suffered a loss of traditional values and thus experienced a concomitant crisis in our identity. The country boy moving to a city did not know where he was in terms of a recognizable pattern of expectations in his relationships with the people he met, and so he could no longer be sure of who he was. Victorianism was a rear guard fight against this loss of stability, but punctilious behavior in the face of inner disquiet served only to intensify the problem. We then effected a philosophical reversal in which we saw the loss of traditional values in positive terms, for the loss gave man absolute freedom in the ordering of his existence. Alienation was seen as a necessary step in the realization of that freedom.

All of this is so well known that it would hardly warrant the above repetition or any further elaboration were it not for the particular bearing it has on the criticism of African literature. Existentialism no longer receives the great flurry of attention it received during the fifties, but intellectuals have been conditioned by the dialectics of existential thinking. Observing the changes brought about in traditional African societies by the intrusion of Western technology, one could easily make comparisons with the effects that technology has had on us. Moreover, such comparisons have been necessarily encouraged by those négritude writers who wanted to foster the idea of an existent unified sensibility in Africa prior to the white presence. This idea is still of central importance to the critical outlook of some followers of négritude, but there appears to be no evidence to support the thesis that there were no alienated individuals in the traditional societies. The traditional griot, in fact, was often a marginal figure.[21]

At any rate, Gerald Moore has argued that at the heart of *Fragments* is the problem of accommodating a writer who must "interpret his purpose to a society which refuses any romantic tolerance to those who isolate themselves from it, even for the sake of creative objectivity."[22] Moore has a point, but he has not really stressed the central issue. Granted, "Africa does not possess the mythology of the lonely, neglected and misunderstood genius in his garret" (p. 73), but it does possess equivalent mythologies as manifested in the concept of liminality. The problem, then, is not so much one of accommodation as it is one of direction, of orienting the conflict inherent in the artist-society relationship toward the regeneration of the society. *Socially* the artist and society have always been at odds, perhaps more noticeably in Africa than in the West, but *culturally* the artist and this conflict have been at the center of the social structure, continually charging it with energy. In other words, the question raised concerns the way in which the writer can reassert this cultural centrality.

Fragments deals with this question in a structure built around the third phase of the hero's ritual passage, the return. On his way back home from a course of study in the United States, Baako decides to make a stopover in Paris for a few weeks, but a feeling of ennui compels him to change his plans and return to Ghana immediately: "within himself what he was aware of was vague: an unpleasant but not at all sharp sensation that everything he had done in about the last half year had been intended as a postponement, a pushing away of things to which he felt necessarily called" (p. 82). The way his desire to return relates to the frame of the novel, the opening and closing chapters given over to Naana, Baako's grandmother, makes it clear that this desire is much more than simply a case of homesickness. It corresponds to what Campbell has termed "the magic flight" where the hero is "explicitly commissioned to return to the world with some elixir for the restoration of society ... [and is] supported by all the powers of his supernatural patron."[23]

According to West African religion the beginning and end of an individual's power reside in his lineage, his ancestry. It is thus no coincidence that the Akan word for grandmother or grandfather, *Naana*, is also the word for ancestor and grandchild. When Baako departs for America it is his grandmother who makes sure the proper ceremony is performed to have the ancestors vouchsafe his journey. His uncle Foli wishes to cheat the ancestors of the necessary libation, and we are told that Naana's "blood was poisoned with the fear of what would happen if Foli's greed for drink was allowed to break the circle and to spoil all the perfect beauty of the libation" (p. 19). As Foli does not wish to give even her any of the liquor, she responds: "We give our ghosts to drink, or am I a liar? And what is an old woman but the pregnancy that will make another ghost?" (p. 20). After then getting a large glass of alcohol, she pours it over the doorway where Foli had offered up a few drops.

The African conceives of death as a passage from this world into the spiritual world where the individual gains in his ability to bestow power to those left behind. Reasoning by analogy, Baako's relatives and friends see his journey as a kind of death. In describing Baako's departure Naana compares Baako and the other passengers with ghosts:

> Then we went outside to a long white fence behind which we stood with others like us who had come to weep for a departing one, and after a long time we saw the line of people, many white people but also others who were black, go like gentle ghosts into the airplane. When it swallowed Baako in his turn, I could look no more. I did not turn to see it as it began to go into the air, though Foli was by me telling me to look, because like a child he saw only beauty in the going of the thing. The heavy sound made me fear for Baako. But I remembered how perfect the words had been for his departure and his protection, and I was

happy inside myself that I had taken the drink from Foli and given the ancestors their need. The circle was not broken in any place. (pp. 24-25)

The idea of death implicit in this conception of Baako's journey is further reinforced in the dirge-like tone of Naana's reflections. The chapter headings throughout the novel, "Naana," "Osagyefo," "Iwu," "Obra" (ancestor, redeemer, death, life) are, in fact, key words in Akan dirges.[24] Moreover, the prayers that Naana says for Baako bear a noticeable resemblance to the dirge. The manner of supplication in the following excerpt from a dirge recorded by J.H. Nketia is formally not very much different from Naana's prayer which we also give in part:

Send us something, Mensa,
Do send us something,
Alas, there is none to tell Grandsire
That death has broken down his state.
Alas, there is none to tell Grandsire
That litigation and strife has broken down his state.
If the Departed could send gifts,
They would surely send something to their children.[25]

And when he returns
let his return, like rain,
bring us your blessings and their fruits,
your blessings
your help
in this life you have left us to fight alone.
With your wisdom
let him go,
let him come.
And you, traveler about to go,
Go and return
Go, come. (p. 18)

Despite his ancestral patronage, Baako's return is no easy task. His mother, his sister, and the majority of those in his community expect him to return like Brempong, the "been to," who brings back material, not spiritual, gifts. Against the overwhelming power of this pattern of communal expectation, Baako increasingly comes to feel his own gifts are of no avail. Even as he steps off the airplane, the welcome that Brempong receives makes this all too clear:

It was not a mere game. Not to the welcomers he had seen this night. More insistently, Baako saw the ceremony working itself out: the straining crowd, the clothes, the jewels, the cascading drink, the worship of this new chief, the car, the words in the night. Did it matter whether there was real power or real joy as long as the human beings involved thought there was? So what if these words and ceremonies were the mere outward show of power and joy hiding impotence? Who was going to stand outside it all and say maybe the show was designed to hide impotence, but all it did was steep this powerlessness in a worsening stupidity? And who would stop laughing and praise-singing long enough to hear such words? (p. 96)

Baako tries to make his own return as inconspicuous as possible, but there is no way he can avoid the inevitable confrontation.

Everywhere Baako turns he finds that the old myths of his people have been perverted. There are two aspects of this perversion that Baako immediately runs into, and a third he must become aware of before he can function as an artist within the community. The first has to do with the artist's giving up or abusing his role vis-à-vis the myths of the society, the second with the society's use of the myths for material gain, and the third with the necessary realism behind the action of the society.

Boateng does nothing but sit around on an unpublished manuscript and complain about how corrupt society and his fellow artists are. Akosua Russell continually reads at poetry readings and republishes in anthologies one horrible poem she has written. Except for his own self-destruction with alcohol, Boateng is perfectly harmless, and satire is surely the best remedy for an overdose of Akosua Russell's poetry. While neither writer is directly responsible for the condition of society, both are guilty of complicity in not providing society with a sense of direction. On the beach with Juana, his lover, Baako begins to probe this problem as he compares the rich poetic quality of the original myth of Mammy Water and the musician with Russell's insipid version:

"The singer goes to the beach, playing his instrument. These days it's become a guitar. He's lonely, the singer, and he sings of that. So well a woman comes out of the sea, a very beautiful goddess, and they make love. She leaves him to go back to the sea, and they meet at long, fixed intervals only. It takes courage. The goddess is powerful, and the musician is filled with so much love he can't bear the separation. But then it is this separation itself which makes him sing as he has never sung before. Now he knows all there is to know about loneliness, about love, and power, and the fear that one night he'll go to the sea and Mame Water, that's the woman's name, will not be coming anymore. The singer is great, but he's also afraid, and after those nights on the shore, when the woman goes, there's no unhappier man on earth."

"It's an amazing story."

"The myths here are good," he said. "Only their use ... "His voice died. (pp. 174-175)

The net result of the misuse of myth and loss of cultural direction is that things become more valuable than persons. Neither the death of the lorry driver at the ferry nor the death of the child at the outdooring ceremony[26] was necessary, except for this reversal in priorities. As Naana says at the end of the novel, "The baby was a sacrifice they killed, to satisfy perhaps a new god they have found much like the one that began the same long destruction of our people when the elders first ... split their own seed and raised half against half, part selling part to hardeyed buyers from beyond the horizon ..." (p. 284).

Without society being confronted with its guilt and without having a scapegoat to carry the guilt away, there can be no re-orientation of the values. It is here that Baako, like the man, completes his heroic mission. Early in the novel this mission is symbolized in that long, gruesome description of the ritual-like slaying of the dog presumed mad by the men who surround and trap it. As Baako begins to meet his family and friends, a circle tightens around him, culminating in a chase where he is encircled and carried off to an insane asylum. On the surface, the ending has the same negative aura about it that the ending of *The Beautyful Ones* seems to have. Baako is still in the asylum, Naana is dying, and there is no tangible sign that things will change. In *The Beautyful Ones* the sum of the symbols is positive, though the parts are negative, a phenomenon not very much different from T.S. Eliot's "Wasteland," where the overall picture does not yield the despair one might find in the individual sections of the poem. To carry the comparison further, if *The Beautyful Ones* is Armah's "Wasteland" then *Fragments* is his *Four Quartets*. As Eliot moved into a more explicitly religious affirmation of life so has Armah in his second novel, for the note of death on which the novel ends prefigures a positive transformation. The final words of Naana even echo Eliot's "East Coker": "I am here against the last of my veils. Take me. I am ready. You are the end. The beginning. You who have no end. I am coming" (p. 286).

Armah's positive assertion has more than just a metaphysical basis. Before he is taken off to the asylum, Baako notices a correlation between the Melanesian cargo cults and the perversion of myths among his own people. At the heart of both nativistic responses lies a pragmatic sense of adjustment, a will to survive despite the impending threat from an alien culture:

So how far, how close are we to Melanesia? It can be seen as a pure, rockbottom kind of realism, the approach that accepts what happens at this moment in this place and raises it to the level of principle. A reality principle par excellence, this. Two distinct worlds, one here, one out there, one known, the other unknown except in legend and dream ... The main export to the other world is people ... the been-to has chosen, been awarded, a certain kind of death. A beneficial death, since cargo follows his return ... he will intercede on behalf of those not yet dead, asking for them what they need most urgently: rain perhaps if their crops are dry, an end to rain if there has been a punishing surfeit. Needs dictated by instant survival and subsistence requirements. (pp. 225-226)

The artist needs to draw on this "reality principle" as much as the society needs to draw on the energy inherent in the artist's spirituality. The artist cannot expect to be left alone dabbling in aesthetics for his own ends and neither can society expect to use the artist simply as an intermediary who brings back quick material gains from the world of the gods. At the one extreme are Baako's mother and sister who would sacrifice anything, however unconsciously, for the "reality principle." They make a sacrifice of the baby and Baako, a point underlined by the title of the chapter that deals with Baako's stay in the asylum and his remembrance of the outdooring ceremony in which the child is killed: *Iwu*, the Akan word for death. The following chapter, the penultimate one of the novel, deals with the obverse, *Obra* or life. Baako's recovery is imminent, for he will soon be leaving the asylum to live with Juana. More importantly, he rejects the other extreme represented by Ocran who divorces himself from society for the sake of his art. As Baako has come to realize, the marriage of artist and society is a marriage of opposites, inharmonious yet ultimately beneficial to everyone because of the tensions inherent in the relationship.

Why Are We So Blest? probes the relationship of the educated African to the masses. Through his education the African intellectual becomes a marginal figure separated from his own society, but never fully assimilated into the West. Being in touch with a new source of power, he has the potential to aid his society, yet this potential is continually frustrated by the control which the West maintains:

> Knowledge about the world we live in is the property of the alien because the alien has conquered us. The thirst for knowledge therefore becomes perverted into the desire for getting close to the alien, getting out of the self. Result: loneliness as a way of life.
>
> This loneliness is an inevitable part of the assimilationist African's life within the imperial structure. Because of the way information is distributed in the total structure — high information in the center, low information on the peripheries — overall clarity is potentially possible only from the central heights. The structures in the peripheral areas are meant to dispense low, negative or mystifactory information. (pp. 32-33)

While this argument is implied in his earlier novels, Armah never brings it to the foreground, nor does he state it in such explicitly syllogistic terms and carry it forward dramatistically (i.e., with symbolic action) to its logical, yet tragic conclusion.

There is no suspense at all concerning the outcome or the tragic victim. Armah obviously wanted nothing to interfere with the clarity and power of the tragic statement. The novel is narrated from three points of view, Solo, Aimee and Modin's, but it soon becomes readily apparent that Modin will be the scapegoat, a victim of Aimee's insatiable lust, of Solo's inaction, of the whole neocolonial enterprise including whites like Dr. Jefferson and *assimilados* like Jorge Manuel. Modin is the only character totally committed to getting back from the periphery to the center of his society, to making, as it were, the hero's second crossing. In the dining room at Harvard he spells out his commitment to Mike, an American who tries to talk him into taking personal advantage of his having made it into the ranks of the elite:

> "Modin, you're nobody's plaything. That's vulgar. The question is deeper than that. You're a scholarship student. There's justice in that. You belong here. The arrangement that brings you here has to be a good arrangement. In the Greek tradition you'd be a crossover. One of those who rise from the plains to live on Olympus. A hero. Part man, part god. Therefore more interesting than either."
>
> "Even staying in your mythology, you shut out the Promethean factor."
>
> "I guess that's a reverse crossover. No. I didn't want to shut it out. But it's unique. Besides, who has the idiotic ambition to go through the crossing twice: first a heroic, then a Promethean crossing? That's insane."
>
> "Only according to your mythology. There are other myths, you know."
> (pp. 101-02)

Although Moore wrote his article on "The Writer and the Cargo Cult" before the publication of *Why Are We So Blest?*, he had already begun to sense that Armah was working with "other myths." To find an answer to why Armah's heroes so willingly face annihilation, Moore explains, it is helpful to turn to Soyinka and his mentor, the god Ogun. Since Armah has been continually concerned with the hero's role in rituals of regeneration, Moore's comments are particularly apposite to an understanding of these rituals in the West African context. Ogun "first faced annihilation by casting himself into the gulf dividing man from the gods in the hope of uniting them once more ..." and the artist must ritually repeat this act in his work where he "breaks out of the cycle of repetition and so creates the possibility of new life, new order. Hence he cannot help being a disturber of the existing ones, which rest within 'the encrustations of soul-deadening habit.'"[27] Not only does this idea of ritual rebellion explain Armah's fascination with annihilation in all his novels, perhaps it also indicates why in the case of Modin he has carried the apparent morbidity further than ever. Though Modin is not an artist like Baako, he is a hero commissioned to make the second crossing; the elixir he carries is not his art, but his blood.

The slave castle in Accra is, in a double sense, made an apt symbol of the old order, of the African past as well as the Western colonial and neo-colonial superstructure. First used as the place where the slavers kept their slaves, then used as the colonial governor's mansion, and finally as Nkrumah's palace, Armah introduces it in both his earlier works,[28] but here it becomes a metaphorical extension of the middle term in his syllogism ("Knowledge about the world we live in"). In the slaving days there was always a "factor," an African who saw to it that the slaves were brought from the island to the coast and kept under tight control until the boats came to take them away. The African who has been educated in the ways of the West, a modern day "factor," thus becomes an extension of the minor term ("the assimilationist African"), the major term being the West itself ("the property of the alien"). In other words, knowledge about the modern world is controlled by the West. The factor, "the assimilationist African," is defined by this knowledge. The conclusion in the syllogism is inescapable — the factor is controlled by the West. Diagrammatically the relationships might be expressed in the following manner:

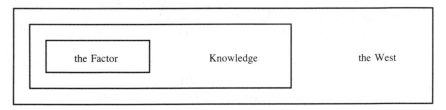

Modin, realizing that he is to be made a "factor," throws himself entirely against the system in order to break the inexorable cycle.

Armah owes an extremely large debt to Frantz Fanon; no other writer has had a comparable influence on the philosophical bases of his novels. Griffiths has already discussed this influence with respect to *The Beautyful Ones*[29] and I could easily do the same with *Fragments*. These two novels, however, accept Fanon's views concerning the psychological effects of colonization on the colonized while avoiding Fanon's revolutionary commitment to violence as the only way of destroying the colonial and neo-colonial presence in Africa. Fanon himself changed quite radically between

Black Skin, White Masks and *The Wretched of the Earth*, shifting his attention from an existential concern with freedom of choice to the problems of social determination and revolutionary demystification. Whereas the early Fanon felt that a solution to the colonial problem was possible through reason and a humanistic approach, the later Fanon, transformed by the Algerian War, came to regard "violence not merely as a political necessity, as the only viable means of prizing apart the iron fingers of colonial rule, but also as a form of social and moral regeneration for the subjugated peoples. The flowing blood transforms the colonial dust bowl into rich and fertile national soil."[30] In *Why Are We So Blest?* Armah embraces the revolutionary Fanon.

This Fanon believed the colonial order could only be destroyed by a systematic reaction of complete disorder. The first essay in *The Wretched of the Earth*, "Concerning Violence," capsulizes his outlook: "The naked truth of decolonization evokes for us the searing bullets and blood-stained knives which emanate from it. For if the last shall be first, this will come to pass after a murderous and decisive struggle between the two protagonists. That affirmed intention to place the last at the head of things, and to make them climb at a pace (too quickly, some say) the well-known steps which characterize an organized society, can only triumph if we use all means to turn the scale, including, of course, that of violence."[31] In the next paragraph he is completely unequivocal about the necessity of violence in changing the present order: "this narrow world, strewn with prohibitions, can only be called in question by absolute violence" (p. 37). The artist would apparently have no place in such a struggle, yet as Fanon shows in the essay "On National Culture" (pp. 206-48), his position is actually in the center, laying the groundwork for the struggle through the revolutionary demystification of his art. This is precisely the point made by Solo, the artist in *Why Are We So Blest?* :

> Why not simply accept the fate of an artist, and like a Western seer, close my eyes to everything around, find relief in discrete beauty, and make its elaboration my vocation? Impossible. The Western artist is blest with that atrophy of vision that can see beauty in deliberately broken-off pieces of a world sickened with oppression's ugliness. I hear the call of that art too. But in the world of my people that most important first act of creation, that rearrangement without which all attempts at creation are doomed to falseness, remains to be done. Europe hurled itself against us — not for creation, but to destroy us, to use us for creating itself. America, a growth out of Europe, now deepens that destruction. In this wreckage there is no creative art outside the destruction of the destroyers. In my people's world, revolution would be the only art, revolutionaries the only creators. All else is part of Africa's destruction. (p. 23)

Has Armah adhered here too closely to Fanon's normative perspective, becoming himself too much of a programmatic writer? Certainly there is a bothersome reductionism in passages such as the one just quoted. Nevertheless, Armah successfully avoids any diffusion of effects, leading us, even with these passages, directly to the desert where Modin's blood is spilled in a sadistic sexual assault. With Solo who follows this agonistic journey in Modin's notebooks, we too experience the catharsis that such violence necessitates: "The initiation was a quick death of the hopeful spirit. For days my body shook with the realization. Refusing to renew itself, rejecting sustenance, it threw out life already stored in it. All my apertures ran with fluid, living and dean [sic], escaping a body, unwilling to hold them: blood, urine, vomit, tears, diarrhea, pus" (p. 114).

Once again I take my orientation from Burke, whose remarks on the integral relation between the negative and property, and the similar relationship between the negative and personality cogently pertain to this analysis. He notes that

> insofar as a cult of virtue is guided by thou-shalt-not's, personality itself is compounded of negatives. Since personality involves *role*, and since roles necessarily involve enactment through the use of properties set by the given social order, note how personality can turn two ways. It turns in the direction of property, status, material resources, all things that have to do with the *implementing* of an act. And insofar as a given social order contains some measure of injustice, personality turns toward the *ideal transcending* of the social order by negations variously along the line between revolution and gradualist improvement.[32]

Achebe's Okonkwo, despite his suicide, clearly turns in the first direction while Armah's characters, implicitly in the first two novels and explicitly in the third, turn in the second direction. Here again is the position of Turner and Gluckman that rebellion or revolution is inherent in liminality (anti-structure), but now it is clearer why the apparently negative excesses are necessary in describing what one would think could be best handled as a clear blueprint for positive action. The question could be closed by simply asserting that the artist is under no obligation to write political pamphlets, but Western critics have become hoarse from this call for poetic purity. The negatives, the grostesqueries, serve as symbolic injunctions to contemplate what could be, but clearly is not.[33] The rhetoric of such indirection is inevitably more devasting than a direct assault. Art, insofar as it is the manipulation of symbols for rhetorical purposes, is nothing if not indirect.

The Proverb, Realism and Achebe: A Study of Ethical Consciousness

More people have read Chinua Achebe than any other African writer. This is no less true outside the continent than it is within it. And this is constantly reflected in the fact that more critical attention is paid to his novels than to the work of any other writer. Find someone who has read but one African literary work, and the odds are that the work will be Achebe's *Things Fall Apart*. The reasons for this are not hard to surmise. Achebe writes in a style that is at once accessible to the individual who knows nothing of Africa and intensely compelling to even the most knowledgeable Africanist. He was one of the first writers to effectively dramatize the most important historical, political and cultural issues facing Africa, and he has remained among the best. Moreover, he is a consumate artist; he always tells a good story.

One result of his accessibility and popularity is that Achebe has become something of a standard against which other African writers are measured. Often when writers like Soyinka and Armah are attacked for their obscurity, or their use of scatological imagery, there is the implicit, if not explicit comparison with the "model" writer, Achebe. In saying this I wish to take nothing away from Achebe's well-deserved reputation. In fact, the act of pre-judging what a writer should do has led to problems in interpreting Achebe as well as Soyinka and Armah. Approaching the mythic consciousness is indeed much more difficult than approaching the ethical consciousness, and thus most of my attention in this book is focused on the former. Still, I would maintain that if we can approach the ethical in a clearer manner, we will have far less trouble in approaching the mythic.

By turns Achebe has been both praised and condemned for his didacticism. Regardless of how it is judged, perhaps the least controversial statement anyone could make in the field of African literature is that Chinua Achebe is a didactic writer. By his own statements and through his work, Achebe clearly shows his belief in the role of the artist as teacher. The pejoration of the word "didactic" in Western criticism, however, makes this statement rather misleading for many readers. Achebe's artistic concerns are with presenting a holistic view of the ethos of his people in an entirely vital, dynamic mode that is expressive of his culture in terms of form no less than content. His works progress in a linear manner and are set in an historical framework that reveals the persistence of cultural continuity despite internal and external threats to the society. Yet, as Soyinka noted, there is never a mere photographic rendering of the world he gives us. We confront an ethical consciousness, an authorial presence that leads us into the societal structures of Ibo life and proceeds in a realistic, linear and historical manner, while revealing the depth and breadth of strategies open to the individual and society for coping with reality. Achebe's works are didactic, but not in the manner of a facile, two-dimensional realism where all ethical choices are clear cut.

Kenneth Burke has suggested that complex literary works can be considered "proverbs writ large."[1] On more than one level Achebe is clearly engaged in writing proverbs. As Burke has explained, the proverb is a very primary unit through which we can see art as equipment for living. Proverbs name and encompass ranges of strategies or attitudes for handling recurrent situations. A strategy, if it is worth anything, must be functional and realistic — in other words, it must size things up rather accurately. Above all, the proverb must have vitality: "The point of issue is not to find categories that 'place' the proverbs once and for all. What I want is categories that suggest their active nature. Here is no 'realism for its own sake.' Here is realism for promise, admonition, solace, foretelling, instruction, charting, all for the direct bearing that such acts have upon matters of welfare."[2]

Few who have seriously looked at Achebe's work would argue with the aptness of Burke's comment on the proverb as a description of the activity Achebe has been engaged in. That Achebe artistically employs proverbs in his writing is not even the central question; it merely underscores my point about the complexity of the ethical consciousness reflected in his work. Proverbs are reflective of the values of a society, and the proverbs that Achebe employs are important elements in the whole system of values that *Things Fall Apart* reflects, elements as it were of a very large proverb. So careful is Achebe in putting the elements together, that we have an empirically valid statement about Ibo society at a given period of time, the 1890s. In other words, we have a work that is not only a distinctive piece of literature, it is also an important piece of meta-history, meta-ethnography, and meta-theology. I will look at the way Achebe reveals the human tragedy of an individual, Okonkwo, who cannot come to terms with the values of his society, that is to say, the strategies for surviving in that society. It is possible to understand the more encompassing tragedy, that of the group, in terms of the historical circumstances of European colonialism, but colonialism can only be seen as a catalyst for what happens to Okonkwo. To try to explain his tragedy outside of the meta-ethnographic and meta-theological framework Achebe provides, is not simply to misread the work, but to rob Okonkwo of his tragic dignity and explain what happened to him in terms of historical determinism.

For the non-African reader the subtleties and complexities of Achebe may indeed be rather difficult to perceive at first. The clues are there, however, and careful reading can lead to an understanding of a great deal that is distinctly African, though comprehensible within Western terms.

In a monograph entitled *Oedipus and Job in West African Religion*, Meyer Fortes explores the way fate and divine justice operate in West African religion.[3] The title sounds arrogantly ethnocentric, but Fortes is careful to avoid any superficially descriptive comparisons of the kind Sir James Frazer made. Instead, he considers the stories of Oedipus and Job from an analytical perspective and shows how they together form a useful paradigm for understanding the paradoxically contradictory and complementary concepts of prenatal fate or destiny, and supernatural justice in West Africa. I will show that this paradigm is one we can also extract from Achebe's *Things Fall Apart*. The point is not to reduce an aspect of Achebe's work to a Eurocentric archetype, for we are actually pulling two rather disparate ideas together to create a metaphor that will facilitate an understanding of a religious strategy artistically rendered by an African writer. A tighter argument might be made by taking an emic approach and first going into Ibo religious thought, but the justification for my etic approach lies in what such exegesis will reveal about the accessible pattern in this novel.

A common observation by Western critics has been that *Things Fall Apart* is very much like a Greek tragedy. Okonkwo, like his Greek counterpart, appears to be brought down by a fatal flaw that is beyond his control. Without any doubt Oedipus is the victim of Destiny; personal responsibility or guilt has nothing to do with what happens to him. We also find that Okonkwo's *chi*, his personal god, has quite a lot to do with his destiny, but we are stopped at the very beginning of the novel from pursuing a descriptive comparison for we are told that a man can, in part, shape his own destiny: "If ever a man deserved his success, that man was Okonkwo. At an early age he had achieved fame as the greatest wrestler in all the land. That was not luck. At the most one could say that his *chi* or personal god was good. But the Ibo people have a proverb that when a man says yes his *chi* says yes also. Okonkwo said yes very strongly; so his *chi* agreed. And not only his *chi* but his clan too, because it judged a man by the work of his hands."[4]

Having learned that a man can assert control over his *chi*, we learn a few pages later that the *chi* controls the man. Okonkwo is compared to "the little bird *nza* who so far forgot himself after a heavy meal that he challenged his *chi*." (p. 28) As there are limitations on how strong the "yes" can be, we are left with an apparent contradiction that seems to raise questions about the nature of Okonkwo's tragedy. How much can he be held responsible for his end and how much can be attributed to an overpowering Destiny?

In order to answer this question I must make a closer comparison of the structural parallels in the lives of Oedipus and Okonkwo. The summary Meyer Fortes gives of Oedipus's life clearly shows where these parallels lie. Oedipus enters life with an ominous foreboding of an evil Destiny as he is rejected by his parents who physically cast him away. Only for brief moments in his life does he ever escape being an outcast; ultimately his fate overwhelms him.

> His tragedy can be described as that of a man blindly seeking to achieve his legitimate place in society, first as son, then as husband, father and citizen against the unconscious opposition of an inborn urge to avenge himself by repudiating his parents, his spouse, and his children. When in the end, he succeeds to this fate he shows his revulsion against himself by mutilating his own eyes and so blotting out his relationship with his kind and his society. He dies in exile, almost like a ghost departing from this world rather than like an ordinary man.[5]

With a few changes of detail, Meyer Fortes could have been talking about Okonkwo. By material standards Okonkwo's father, Unoka, is an outcast in Umuofian society, and by any spiritual measure, he dies one: "He had a bad *chi* ... and evil fortune followed him to the grave, or rather to his death, for he had no grave" (p. 16). Okonkwo spends his life trying to avoid his father's fate only to succumb to a death that also severs him spiritually from his society. In the course of his life, while attempting to repudiate the "feminine" characteristics of his father, he is respectively alienated from his father, one of his wives, his son (Nwoye), and finally his clan. He treats the memory of his father with contempt; he beats Ojiugo during the Week of Peace; he is horrified by Nwoye's attraction to Christianity; and he is physically exiled when he accidentally kills a young man. His suicide, moreover, is a clear correlative to Oedipus's self-mutilation.

Granted, I am still operating on a rather tenuous descriptive level, but behind both men there is definitely a strong force of Destiny controlling their lives, their parents and their children.[6] With Oedipus this control is complete and with Okonkwo it is partial, though in both cases "it serves to exonerate both society and the sufferer by fixing ultimate responsibility on the ancestors and on a pre-natal, that is pre-social, event."[7] No careful reader of *Things Fall Apart*, any more than a character within Umuofian society, could hold Okonkwo to blame for his fate, despite the fact that a good argument can be made for the idea that there are implicit authorial criticisms of both Okonkwo and his society. Within that society we are shown that a man can have either a good or a bad *chi* — Okonkwo's life is simply controlled by an evil Destiny.

Yet such knowledge about a man's fate can only be known for certain after the fact. Moreover, neither the novel, the society, nor Okonkwo's life is all that simple. As Bernth Lindfors has very cogently shown, a very large proportion of the proverbs used by Achebe in *Things Fall Apart* have to do with achievement.[8] Many of these proverbs confirm the idea that in Ibo society a man is not necessarily foredoomed by an evil *chi*. Providing he acts in the appropriate manner, he can say "yes" to a *chi* that says "no": "the sun will shine on those who stand before it shines on those who kneel under them" (p. 7); "if a child washed his hands he could eat with kings" (p. 8); "a man who pays respect to the great paves the way for his own greatness" (p. 16); "as a man danced so the drums were beaten for him" (p. 167).

These proverbs encompass strategies for individual equity that are antithetical to the closed system of prenatal destiny we find in the story of Oedipus. They are, however, rather incisive leads into another dimension of the religious framework of Okonkwo's society — a dimension that can be understood in terms of the patterns of divine justice we find in Job.

Nothing has been pre-established for the course of Job's life. He is free to choose between good and evil, and whatever consequences result from his choices are the rewards and punishments of an omnipotent God. Though personified, and ultimately just and merciful, this God cannot always be comprehended in terms of what the individual perceives as just. Job never admits, nor does he need to admit, any

> guilt in the sense of responsibility for actions that are wicked by ordinary human standards. What he admits is having placed himself on a footing of equality with God, judging for himself what conduct is righteous and what wicked. This wrong relationship was his sin ... Job's sufferings are like severe measures of discipline that a father might use to correct a son who, while exemplary in his conduct, was getting too big for his boots and arrogating to himself a status equal to his father's; and Job's salvation might be compared to the son's realizing and accepting his filial dependence."[9]

As we are dealing with a paradigmatic and not a simple descriptive comparison, it might help to momentarily reverse perspectives. Job, in other words, can be seen as one who wrestled with his *chi*, realized his mistake before it was too late, and took the necessary steps to rectify his relationship with his God. Again, the idea here is not in some missionary-like manner to find one-sided "universal" correspondences, but to show that the Western reader should be able to get into the aesthetic complexity of Achebe's work. No injustice to the integrity of the work need be committed by this artificial

atomizing so long as we see the process only as a key to a holistic understanding of a work that in its totality is very unlike the stories of either
Oedipus or Job.

The parallel between Job and Okonkwo that is significant to us is the
idea that the ancestors, just as Job's God, can be angered or pleased in such
a way that they either confirm or override an individual's Destiny, bringing
him disaster or good fortune. In discussing this in relation to the religious
thought of the Tale, Meyer Fortes makes three generalizations about Tale
ancestral belief that we can also draw out of *Things Fall Apart*.[10] These
generalizations concern

> axiomatic values from which all ideal conduct is deemed to flow. The first is the
> rule that kinship is binding in an absolute sense. From this follows the second
> rule, that kinship implies amity in an absolute sense. The third rule is the funda-
> mental one. It postulates that the essential relationship of parent and child,
> expressed in the parent's devoted care and the child's affectionate dependence,
> may never be violated and is, in that sense, sacred. It is indeed the source of the
> other rules.[11]

Thus, when Okonkwo is exiled from Umuofia he must flee to the village of
his mother. He must accept his relatives there, and they are bound to accept
him in complete friendship. Moreover, they are seen almost literally as
living extensions of his mother.

Beyond any strict legalistic adherence to these values it is imperative
that one have a proper attitude towards the moral relationships that follow
from them. Like Job, Okonkwo is an upright and honest man, guilty not of
any willfully unjust actions, but of an unbending self-righteousness in his
relations with his gods, his ancestors and his kin. Moreover, he cannot
accept the suffering he is forced to bear. While in exile he is angrily
castigated by his kinsman, Uchendu:

> You think you are the greatest sufferer in the world. Do you know that men are
> sometimes banished for life? Do you know that men sometimes lose all their
> yams and even their children? I had six wives once. I have none now except that
> young girl who knows not her right from her left. Do you know how many
> children I have buried — children I begot in my youth and strength? Twenty-
> two. I did not hang myself, and I am still alive. If you think you are the greatest
> sufferer in the world, ask my daughter, Akueni, how many twins she has borne
> and thrown away. Have you not heard the song they sing when a woman dies?
>
> > "For whom is it well, for whom is it well?
> > There is no one for whom it is well." (p. 122)

Though Job's relation to his god is unilaterally contractual and Okonkwo's relation is a bilateral one of mutual dependence, the attitudes of both men pose a threat to the religious fabric of their society. God had a bet with Satan that had to be won; Umuofia had its very survival at stake in its confrontation with the white man. This survival of gods, ancestors and kin was more important than the inflexible will of one man: "What the ancestors demand and enforce on pain of death is conformity with the basic moral axiom in fulfilling the requirements of all social relationships; and these are the counterpart, in the domain of kinship, of the obligations posited between persons and their ancestors in the religious domain."[12]

The first thing we learn about Okonkwo is that "his fame rested on solid personal achievements" (p. 3). It is noteworthy that this is followed by our seeing that "he had no patience with his father" (p. 4). Considering the value placed on personal achievement in his society, Okonkwo certainly had no obligation to have patience with his father, who had no rank at all in the society. But there is a more fundamental kinship value that Okonkwo ignores. In a very subtle manner Achebe introduces this tension between individual and communal values and carefully orchestrates its buildup. The proverb that "age was respected ... achievement ... revered" (p. 5) lays emphasis on achievement, but indicates a balance between respect and reverence that Okonkwo ignores. His father praises him for his proud heart, but warns him of the difficulty in failing alone (p. 23), advice that Okonkwo is unable to accept. When a joke is made about a man who refused to sacrifice a goat to his father, Okonkwo is uncomfortable, ironically because it reminds him of his father's poverty and not of his own neglect of his father's memory. An old man commenting on Okonkwo's success quotes the proverb "Looking at a king's mouth ... one would think he never sucked at his mother's breast" (p. 24). The proverb is not used here in any derogatory manner, but is one more sign to the reader that Okonkwo lives much of his life as if he had no kin.

All this is revealed within the first few chapters. The subsequent action sharpens our insight into the tragic ordering of values that should be complementary, but in Okonkwo become completely oppositional. Communal and individual values must be in carefully ordered balance. In his extremist actions Okonkwo shows "no respect for the gods of the clan" (p. 28). Though he may feel contrite, as he did after beating his wife during the Week of Peace, he never shows it. The group itself must adjust and change when it is threatened by its customs; it expects no less of the individual. This point is indirectly, but firmly underlined by Ezeudu's recounting of the heavy punishments that were once exacted whenever the Week of Peace was broken. After a while the custom had to be altered as it destroyed what it was intended to protect.

Without going very far into a Lévi-Straussian type of structural analysis, it is very obvious that we have here yet another aspect of Okonkwo that can be understood in terms of the Oedipal paradigm, namely the underrating of blood relations.[13] Unlike Oedipus in his incestuous relationship with his mother, Okonkwo never overrates blood relations. Yet comparable to Oedipus's parricide is Okonkwo's rejection of his father and all things feminine. Okonkwo continually acts in a manner that leads to an absolute rejection of his autochthonous origin. In his participation in the killing of Ikemefuna and in his reluctant acceptance of his exile in his mother's land, he shows a willful refusal to submit to the Earth Goddess; in his beating of his wife during the Week of Peace and in his accidental killing of the boy during Ezeudu's funeral, he commits overt offenses against the goddess.

During a feast at the end of Okonkwo's exile, an old kinsman rises to give a speech to thank Okonkwo for the great banquet. Very discreetly, however, he gives a talk on the strength of kinship bonds, which while a general warning to the clan, must also be construed as a specific warning to Okonkwo: "A man who calls his kinsman to a feast does not do so to save them from starving. They all have food in their own homes. When we gather together in the moonlit village ground it is not because of the moon.... We come together because it is good for kinsmen to do so" (p. 152). The words, in effect, are beyond Okonkwo's comprehension. When he returns to Umuofia, he is entirely out of step with his clan. A clear, inexorable logic thus leads him to the ultimate offense against the Earth Goddess, his own suicide.

The logic, however, was inexorable only because of Okonkwo's unbending will. Had he submitted to the will of the clan, a will dictated by survival, he too might have avoided a tragic end. Okonkwo's daughter, Ezinma, is born with an evil Destiny. A diviner is consulted and he informs the family that the child is an *ogbanje*, a spirit that continually returns to the mother's womb in a cycle of birth and death. Once the proper ritual measures are taken, the evil *chi* is propitiated and survival from its threat is insured. The implication is clear — Okonkwo never fully propitiates his *chi*.

What Meyer Fortes had noted in a general way we can see very specifically, namely an Oedipal predisposition figuratively transformed into a Jobian fulfillment.[14] Okonkwo is a strong man, but he has limited vision and is caught in the singleminded pursuit of his ambitions and escape from his fears. Only in the end, after he has killed the messenger, does he achieve some tragic recognition: "Okonkwo stood looking at the dead man. He knew that Umuofia would not go to war. He knew because they had let the other messengers escape.... He wiped his matchet on the sand and went away" (p. 184). But even then, Okonkwo sees only the futility of his own course of action. Complete understanding would entail the perception that "the system as a whole is impregnable, particularly since the criterion invoked is ritual service, not conduct that can be judged by men themselves. Whatever the ancestors do must therefore be, and is, accepted as just, and men have no choice but to submit."[15]

Two scenes that the Western reader is likely to find annoyingly inexplicable can be easily understood in relation to the function they serve in underscoring the need to submit to ancestral control. No reason is given for the Oracle's decision that Ikemefuna must be sacrificed — nor is any reason given for the Oracle's decision to take Ezinma to Agbala's cave for an evening and then bring her home. A boy appears to be senselessly killed and a young girl taken on a seemingly meaningless journey. The point is, however, that man's understanding cannot encompass the ancestor's justice. When Okonkwo attempts to interfere with the Oracle's decision and prevent her from taking his daughter, the priestess warns: "Beware Okonkwo! ... Beware of exchanging words with Agbala. Does a man speak when a god speaks? Beware!" (p. 91).

We can see, then, that while prenatal destiny and divine justice appear to be completely oppositional, even antithetical concepts, they are in fact complementary aspects of a logical, well-balanced system in which masculine and feminine values as well as individual and communal values are incorporated without any sense of contradiction. Okonkwo's tragedy is that he fails to recognize this. Like the tortoise in the folktale narrated by Ezinma's mother, Okonkwo tried to have everything his own way. His greed may not be as devious as that of the tortoise, who calls himself "All of you," but in the same fundamental sense of selfish desire he sets himself against the group. Likewise, he rejects everything that is feminine in his own nature and others; the group is left with no recourse but to reject him. On the other hand, the imposition of Christianity and the incursion of the European colonial administration afford a great shock to the system, but they do not shatter it.

To return to Burke's idea of novels as proverbs writ large, we can see that *Things Fall Apart* names a strategy for dealing with change. Divine justice and prenatal destiny, the basic components of this strategy, are also the woof and warp of an extremely flexible social fabric. Okonkwo, in his political conservatism and obsession with status, poses a threat to the fabric. Existing almost entirely on a physical, material plane, and concerned solely with maintaining the status quo, Okonkwo gets into a death lock with his *chi*. The strategy, and mainly the component of prenatal destiny, insures for society that survival is accepted over stasis. It is worth taking note that the last proverb in *Things Fall Apart* is about the bird who is always on the wing: "Men have learnt to shoot without missing their mark and I have learnt to fly without perching on a twig" (p. 183).

The Riddle, Myth and Tutuola: A Study of Mythic Consciousness

Criticism, if it is worth anything, should ultimately propose models that help to explain, clarify, or simply give the reader a handle on whatever is going on in a given creative work. A disproportionate amount of the criticism on Tutuola has been directed at assessing his literary value, at the question of whether Tutuola is "extraordinarily good, extraordinarily bad, or extraordinarily lucky."[1] The fact, however, that Tutuola is generally more highly regarded in the West than in Africa is quite significant — not because, as has been asserted on one side, Africans have willfully refused to recognize a native son who is a literary genius, nor, as has been asserted on the other side, because Europeans have been naive and patronizing in their praise of a man who has simply written down stories that many young Yoruba children could tell, but because it demonstrates that perceptions, or more specifically, aesthetics, are relative and culture based. Knowing that the story of the "beautiful complete gentleman" is commonplace in West Africa does not necessarily lessen one's enjoyment in reading Tutuola's interpretation of it any more than knowing that phrases such as "he would not have to listen before hearing" or "bad-bye function"[2] are nonstandard English, or possibly transliterated Yoruba, ruins the freshness and vitality of these figures of speech. At the same time, for one who already finds Tutuola commonplace or tedious, learning that his tales conform to some monomythic pattern will do little to change that opinion.

The difficulties we face in dealing critically with Tutuola are legion. His works are as difficult to pin down as the monsters he writes about. In talking about the form of these stories, we have no label we can easily use. For convenience they are commonly referred to as novels, but arguments have also been advanced that the form is that of the extended folktale, the prose epic, or the romance. The structure no less than the language of these works is often confusing, the characters as well as the settings are more often than not fantastic, and the situations we and the characters are presented with are always problematical. While there is a great deal of disagreement over the assessment he should be accorded, it is clear that the words, images and even the sense of what Tutuola is saying more often than not violate our prevailing notions of propriety, Western or African.

This violation of a sense of propriety points to a rather significant aspect of Tutuola's work that has not yet been fully explored, namely the rhetorical stance of the author and the relationship between the authorial voice in these works and the audience. The rhetoric, of course, has been mentioned by the critics who have recognized that Tutuola is more like a fireside raconteur than a conscious literary artist, but the implications have not been pursued. His rhetoric is that of a riddler; he generates confusion, transgresses propriety, and inverts our normal perceptions of the real physical world, leaving us with the sheer joy we derive out of participating in that confusion as well as the astonishment we get on emerging from fictional chaos and finding the world re-ordered.

In the preceding chapter I noted that Kenneth Burke has argued the idea that complex literary works can be seen as "proverbs writ large." However, not all complex literary works are written in a realistic mode, nor do they, like the proverb, necessarily function in any realistic manner. It might help us to extend Burke's idea and think not only of "proverbs writ large" but also of "riddles writ large." Proverbs are often structured around a metaphor, but if the proverb is to function when used in a social context, the analogue to the real situation must be readily apprehended by those to whom the proverb is directed. In contrast, whatever is being described in a riddle must not be very apparent. All the clues may be there, but the description must lead the audience away from any easy answer. The riddle thus tends to be problematic rather than normative, confusing rather than clear. It creates artificial conflict and opens speculation, whereas the proverb smooths over conflict and closes further thought. Even when a proverb is metaphorical in its form, it must function as a simile, showing clearly that one thing is like another. The riddle, however, must always function metaphorically, drawing together apparently incongruous elements, a point first noted by Aristotle in his *Poetics*: "For the essence of a riddle is to express true fact under impossible combinations. Now this cannot be done by any arrangement of ordinary words, but by the use of metaphor it can."[3]

This is also the very nature of what Tutuola is doing in each of his works. *The Palm-Wine Drinkard, My Life in the Bush of Ghosts*, and all the other books are, in effect, riddles writ large. Tutuola spins us into a world where the impossible is always possible. There is always just enough of the world and language we recognize for us to follow what he is doing, but he continually startles us by rearranging the pieces in ways we never imagined. As a riddler he cannot be second guessed, for he is always creating his own grammar.

Tutuola's works, like myth, explore the riddles of existence. In *The Palm-Wine Drinkard*, he deals with the very primary question of death. In *My Life in the Bush of Ghosts* the riddle we confront is hatred. A young boy, not old enough to know what is "good" or "bad," learns what hatred does as he is driven into a bush of terrors. Simbi, in *Simbi and the Satyr of the Dark*

Jungle, leaves her wealthy family to discover and "experience the difficulties of the 'Poverty' and of the 'Punishment,'" in short, to fathom the meaning of suffering. The young lady in *The Brave African Huntress*, like the Drinkard, is one who has "sold death." Here, however, the end is to explore the nature of bravery. The "entertainments" narrated by the Yoruba chief in *Feather Woman of the Jungle* explore the mystery of wealth. Finally, in *Ajaiyi and His Inherited Poverty*, we have another look into the mystery of suffering, though this time from the perspective of one born into it. In all these works the characters must, at some point, confront death. Simbi, for example, starts off her adventure heading down "the Path of Death."

The *Palm-Wine Drinkard* starts off as if there is going to be a plot centering around the Drinkard's search for his dead tapster, but as soon as we get past the first few episodes we realize that situation becomes more important than narrative development. The capture of death and the remarkable escape from the "Skull's family house" have almost no significance in terms of bringing the Drinkard closer to his tapster, though these and other episodes have a great deal of rhetorical impact as dramatically and cleverly resolved conundrums. Our attention is drawn away from any ultimate or final resolution and focused on the manner in which the Drinkard extricates himself from each of the successive agonistic moves. As in a riddling session, we derive pleasure from this pattern of tension and relief, since "what in everyday life proves disruptive, in play form is able to create fun and pleasure. (This is simply a restatement of a bylaw of aesthetics that threatening motives, when re-enacted in artificial form, create a sense of pleasurable control and completeness which is absent in everyday life.)"[4]

Noting again that I am looking at *The Palm-Wine Drinkard* from a rhetorical and not a formal perspective, I would point out that such a pattern (i.e., of tension and relief) is not limited to riddling sessions. Nevertheless, this pattern, coupled with the overriding presence of death, the ultimate riddle, the ultimate source of confusion and disorder, does distinguish it. Between his departure in search of his dead tapster and his return to his village, the Drinkard has some nineteen or twenty adventures.[5] In all but two he faces the threat of death, and as we shall see later, the two exceptions add to my argument. Death, *the* riddle without an answer, must not simply be confronted and overpowered. The Drinkard is able to do this at the outset, but it does not get him to his tapster. He must first come to understand and resolve the enigma that death represents; then and only then can he "sell his death" and "lend his fear." This involves an understanding of death not in the biological sense as an absence of life, but in a mythic sense where death is seen as a necessary complement to life, and as an event that infuses life

with value. Just as the resolution of a riddle is predicated on shifting modes of perception (in many cases simply shifting the way we perceive a certain word is being used), myth is able to resolve the life/death contradiction by playing off an alternative reality against our sensory reality.[6] In other words, unless one sees into another order of things, namely a mythic order, death remains in its realistic frame as an annihilator of order and inducer of chaos.

To the extent that one of the basic functions of myth is to explain the primary contradictions of existence, mythic narrative tends to have the rhetorical structure of a riddle. In both the riddle and in myth there is a meaningful play between sense and nonsense. "Sense," in effect, comes out of "nonsense." The Drinkard feels confident at the outset of his journey that, armed simply with his own wit, he can recover his dead tapster and thus, in effect, plumb the secrets of death. He soon meets Death, but his victory does not prove to be much of a help to him. He must plunge deeper into a world where natural laws do not operate, and, in fact, he finally winds up in a town where natural order is entirely inverted. Here, in the "Unreturnable-Heaven's Town," he and the wife who joined him shortly after his adventure began, must undergo a most incredible series of agonizing tortures. First they have their heads shaved, rather, scraped with broken bottles. Then they have pepper rubbed into their bare scalps and their heads burnt with fiery rags. As if this is not enough, their heads are scraped again, and the two are buried up to their heads out in an open field. They are flogged and then tortured by the presence of food they cannot touch. Finally, an eagle is left to peck at their heads. But this is only the first day's treatment — they undergo a similar series on the second day.

With this experience the Drinkard's initiation into the world of myth is halfway complete. He is dead, as it were, to the world of physical reality. Now he must learn to cope with riddles — he must learn to make sense out of nonsense.

The first episode not dealing with any direct confrontation with death significantly comes at this point, literally halfway through the story. The Drinkard and his wife recuperate in the hospital of the Faithful-Mother, and at the end of this rest continue on their way, having now "sold their death." The wife, generally quiet up to now, takes a more active role, serving as a mentor who instructs her husband through the use of riddles. As the two leave the Faithful-Mother, they immediately meet another female figure who leads them into a frightening "Red-Town." On approaching this town the wife predicts that their adventures there will only be "fear for the heart but not dangerous to the heart" (p. 73). The wife, of course, already sees the implications of their having "lent fear" and "sold death."

At other crucial points the wife predicts and teaches through her riddles. When they are close to death among the Red-people she tells her husband

"This would be a brief loss of woman, but a shorter separation of man from lover" (p. 78), a prediction that comes true when she is transformed for a short period into a tree along with the Red-people and their town. Later, she warns that "The Invisible-Pawn" will be a "Wonderful hard worker, but he would be a wonderful robber in future" (p. 86). Again, the Drinkard only realizes the significance of her words after he finds that the pawn takes far more than he gives.

The "mixed town" episode, which occurs just prior to the Drinkard's last adventure before returning to his village, appears to be a total digression from the series of adventures the Drinkard has recounted. Certainly from any formal critical perspective, the episode does not seem to fit into the overall pattern of a particular genre. If we look at the rhetorical unity of the work, however, its position is clear. While in a real sense the Drinkard has been engaged in a search for his dead tapster, he has in a metaphysical sense been engaged in developing a certain attitude toward and understanding of death.

While telling of the "mixed town" the Drinkard relates two dilemma tales involving death and calls on the reader to render a judgement in each of the cases. In the first, a debtor and a bill collector have a fight and kill each other while performing their respective jobs, owing money and collecting money. A third man, doing his duty as a neutral onlooker, kills himself to see how the conflict is resolved in heaven. We are asked to decide who is responsible in this conflict where everyone was doing what he should have been doing. In the second narrative, a man who has three wives dies. They all perform special tasks in bringing him back to life. One, however, must be given to a wizard for his work in reviving the dead man. Again we are asked to make a judgement.

In its problematical structure the dilemma tale is in many respects very much like a riddle, and is an equally significant form of verbal art in Africa. As William Bascom has pointed out, however, it differs in that it involves choices and not answers.[7] In his own process of coming to terms with death, the Drinkard himself has been involved with a series of choices, the most important being his very decision to undertake the journey. The choice necessarily comes before the discovery of an answer. In effect, what the Drinkard is telling us is that he can give us no answer to the riddle of death; we must find it ourselves through first making the proper choices in our lives. The Drinkard has at this point completely made the transition from neophyte to teacher and can return to the real physical world.

On telling us that he came back to his village to find a great famine, the Drinkard interrupts his narrative to explain through myth the causes of famine. The myth relates how two friends, Heaven and Land, fought over the possession of a mouse they had killed. Because of their greed they could not resolve the conflict and went back to their homes. Heaven then punished

Land by withholding rain and thus bringing famine into the world. Having himself in a sense unlocked the mysteries of life, the Drinkard has returned with a boon that will provide an answer to the problem the people face. His answer, in the form of a magical egg that will produce food on command, proves too fragile an item for the people to handle. They break the egg and in their greed bring punishment upon themselves. Having been properly punished, the people are then in a position to learn from the Drinkard the proper sacrifice and course of action necessary to stop the famine and restore life to the land.

Achebe uses a close variant of this same myth in *Things Fall Apart*.[8] However, considering Achebe's particular use of this myth in symbolically supporting the structure of the novel,[9] it is again clear that he is engaged in the process of writing proverbs, not merely in the literal sense that he uses them, but in the metaphorical sense that his novels provide a clear moral orientation. Tutuola, on the other hand, engages us in the process of resolving riddles. In *The Palm-Wine Drinkard* the riddle is death, a riddle whose answer we find to be eclipsed only by our own insufficiency. The Drinkard addresses us directly as we watch him make his choice and move from his own insufficiency to fulfillment, from chaos to order, and through death into life. In a parallel, but foreshortened process, we see an entire community go through the same experience at the end of the book.

Tutuola's language, whether or not it is the accidental or unconscious transliteration of Yoruba expressions, or use of Nigerian vernacular English, lends itself very effectively to these "riddles writ large." Tutuola's Drinkard journeys into the mysteries of death and returns to tell his tale of this other reality. The very fact that there are no direct correspondences between that world and our physical reality necessitates the bending of our perceptions, not merely by what is said, but by the manner in which it is said. The unimaginable horror of the inverted utopia that the Drinkard goes through is thus far better expressed by the term "Unreturnable-Heaven's Town," than by any conventional expression he might have employed. As a linguist has shown in a paper on Tutuola's language, the very word "Drinkard" is a felicitous choice as it conveys a sense of present and on-going time as opposed to the standard term "drunkard."[10] The past has no reality in the Drinkard's experience, for he has stepped into mythic time, co-terminous with past, present and future.

Had Tutuola bent his language any more, he would have been totally unintelligible, but almost always it operates on the level of metaphor. To the extent that it does this, it approximates the riddle in its effect. This is not ex-actly what Aristotle would call the perfection of style, but then we need not accept his value judgement. It is, however, worth returning to Aristotle's *Poetics* here, as his comment on diction does clarify what I have been saying about Tutuola:

> The perfection of style is to be clear without being mean. The clearest style is that which uses only current or proper words; at the same time it is mean.... That diction, on the other hand, is lofty and raised above the commonplace which employs unusual words. By unusual, I mean strange (or rare) words, metaphorical, lengthened — anything, in short, that differs from the normal idiom. Yet a style wholly composed of such words is either a riddle or a jargon; a riddle if it consists of metaphors; a jargon if it consists of strange (or rare) words. (p. 29)

Tutuola employs large numbers of strange words, but mainly in contexts where the metaphorical effects of these words can be seen or felt. Almost always there is enough balance between the familiar and the strange that we can follow him, confident that we are being led by a genius. He riddles and we peer into chaos; he resolves conundrums and we see order restored. Nothing, however, is made perfectly clear, and in the end we are left with enough questions to respect the mystery and beauty, no less than the humor, this riddler conveys.

Kofi Awoonor's *This Earth, My Brother* as an African Dirge

The formal structure of Kofi Awoonor's *This Earth, My Brother* is probably as puzzling to the African reader as it is to the non-African reader. In strictly formal terms the book is more like a prose poem than a novel, though for purposes of general discussion it is not worthwhile quibbling about the label. Despite the extremely thin narrative thread which runs through it, *This Earth* relates to a tradition of expressionistic experimentation that can be traced from James Joyce to the present, though it is questionable how far this alone would lead anyone. Nor is it necessarily helpful to learn that the author himself has insisted on his work being thought of as a poem.[1] The final judgment will of course be left to the reader. But classification *per se*, whether by the artist or his critics, is a rather useless game if it fails to reveal perceptions into the situation the artist has presented, and there is little beyond the obvious that a formal analysis of this novel will yield to the critic who does not take into consideration the formal elements that come from Eweland as well as those which come from England.

Perhaps no other prose writer in Africa, aside from Tutuola, has written a work which so thoroughly defies conventional Western criticism. The cul-de-sac that Gerald Moore found in Tutuola is, more than anything, an apt description of the critic's problem where the critic is unwilling to keep in mind the traditional literature these writers are so close to. Certainly Awoonor does not write from exactly the same naive sensibility as Tutuola, for their educational backgrounds are vastly different, the former having earned his doctorate in comparative literature and the latter not having gone beyond primary six. Yet in discussing his poetry, Awoonor has said that he has been influenced primarily by the tradition of the Ewe song, "especially the Ewe dirge, the dirge form, the lament, and its lyrical structure with the repetition of sections, segments, lines, along with an enormous, a stark and at times almost naive quality which this poetry possessed."[2] In fact, the images, motifs, and themes we find in the novel are very close to those Awoonor has employed in his poetry. He himself has written that "You must see *This Earth* and my poetry as constituting the same continuous poetic statement about man and society. My concern is not ... to provide a picture of a particular society at a particular time, but rather to provide through a series of selected images, the idea of the continuous process of corruptibility which the human society without strength and vision can be locked in."[3] The assertion that *This Earth, My Brother* is a prose poem may thus have some critical relevance, providing I show how Awoonor has built it on the structure of a dirge or a lament.

Before moving into this specific analysis, however, I would like to briefly consider some of the elements that *This Earth*, as an expression of a mythic consciousness, shares with the works of Armah and Tutuola. Scatological imagery, insanity, and death loom in a large manner as key pieces in an ongoing process of symbolic inversion. As in a riddle, what you first see is not necessarily what you get. Once again, decay is not just the end of life, it is also the beginning. The reader's vision is transformed to see from a mythic perspective, to see that in the beginning is the end, and in the end is the beginning. However serious the end, the means and the way are often ludicrous (humor is something Awoonor shares with Tutuola far more than Armah). Moreover, Amamu, like one of Armah's or Tutuola's heroes, is clearly a liminal figure. Property, status, rank and personal appearance mean little to him. In silence he is totally obedient to a sacred and mystical calling. In humility, and without the slightest regard for the pain and suffering it will cost him, Amamu makes what amounts to a heroic crossing.

This Earth, My Brother is obviously not a dirge in the traditional African sense any more than it is a conventional English novel. And even though, for the sake of analysis, I will look at the internal structure as the structure of a dirge modified to fit the external shell of a novel, the two aspects function dialectically to forge a formal synthesis that supports the thematic synthesis. The work integrates forms from two traditions, African and European, but Awoonor always puts the latter tradition in the service of the former. The protagonist, Amamu, is a man between two worlds, two traditions, and he is striving to effectively put the European side of his self in the service of his African side. Hence the rather bizarre cover to the American edition of *This Earth* which shows an African lawyer with only half of the white wig traditionally worn by English barristers. On the most general level the dirge is a celebration of man's conquest of death, but this dirge is also an attempt to move beyond the deadly constrictions of cultural conflict.

Keeping in mind the formal and thematic syntheses, I will first look at the relationship of time and character in the novel in terms of its dramatistic basis, specifically in terms of ritual action. In order to show how this relates to the West African dirge I will then draw on J.H. Nketia's analysis of Akan funeral dirges.[4] While the Akan are a linguistic group distinct from the Ewe, they are culturally similar in many respects and in particular as regards their dirges.[5]

As there is no simple narrative pattern, the pervasive tone of the lament holds the novel together and asserts its presence with more force than the actual characters. Character, in other words, is made subservient to the lyrical structure (and, as we shall also see, the ongoing process of transition). Thus it is not so important who Amamu is, as what he represents within this framework. His position as a specific person is no more important than the characters of Lycidas and Adonais in the elegies by Milton and Shelley, for it is the expression and the transcendence of grief that become important to us. Here even more so, since it is ultimately neither the death of Amamu, nor the symbolic death of a country, Ghana, which holds our imagination. These specific events serve only as reference points to focus our attention on the man and his land as individual and collective carriers of a long history of suffering. Beyond this we are left with the unstated, but implied efficacy of any such ritual move, namely individual and collective rebirth.

E.M. Forster has said that it is impossible for the novelist to abolish time from his work.[6] Perhaps this is true, yet the novelist can fracture time so completely that it ceases to be an important aspect. Rather than telling a story which proceeds in any chronological fashion, Awoonor has painted in a very cubistic manner a certain landscape from a number of different angles. We could piece sections together to give the book more chronological coherence, but that would almost totally destroy the poetic assertion which is being made. Amamu's anguish is not simply an individual's suffering, but the agony of a land, its people, and their gods, and none of this can be understood as something which is localized in time in any historical sense. What we have instead is mythic time, time that we can relate to most directly through ritual. In an essay, "The Fourth Stage," Soyinka has discussed how in the African world view the element of eternity is something from which the individual does not feel estranged. The individual in Africa "is not, like European man, concerned with the purely conceptual aspects of time ... life, present life contains within it manifestations of ancestor, the living and the unborn."[7] Rather than making distinctions in time he makes distinctions in areas of existence. Moreover, he is painfully aware that there are great gulfs between these areas which must be bridged by ritual and sacrifice. The person most sensitive to these gulfs must necessarily be a kind of priest, in short, a man such as Amamu. Amamu has been educated as a Western lawyer, but his ritual (traditional) role as a priest-like individual figures much more prominently in the novel.

Divided into fifteen chapters in which the main narrative line is developed, the book has a poetic introduction, almost an invocation, along with eleven poetic interludes which follow the first eleven narrative chapters. Awoonor himself explains the central importance of the poetic sections:

> ... there was a publisher's error in this. I wanted the chapters to slide on into the poetic interludes which would be indicated by the use of italics. But they

decided to separate them, and this imposed a more rigid structure than I wanted. More importantly, it makes the poetry seem to be a comment on what has gone before, though it actually moves into a lot more important area than what has just been said in the story. In fact, the story plays a secondary role to the poetry rather than the other way around.[8]

Towards the end these interludes are no longer necessary as the narrative line and the poetic assertion are fully merged.

The introduction sets the tone into which all the succeeding chapters tend to modulate, and functions, moreover, as a kind of poetic invocation. The protagonist has just passed through a period of loss and separation and is describing that trial which was a moment of pain for others as well as himself. Like the worshippers on the beach, he is singing "A low moan, mournful song of death and loss."[9] The immediate cause of sorrow is the separation from his woman of the sea, but beyond this are adumbrations of the decay which pervades his land, "this house whose fences were falling" (p. 6). Only at the end will we learn that he is already dead, that he is speaking here as an ancestral voice, though we are provided with a clue that makes sense only in relation to his reunification with his woman of the sea: "And I was alone. But not for long" (p. 8). This spiritual reunification further adumbrates an ultimate salvation for his land, since he is better able as an ancestral force to effect the changes he had not the power to effect while living.[10]

In the opening chapter we are given a feeling of the great age of the land and the decay that pervades it. The road overseer is presented as a symbol of that decay, "a veritable picture of human lethargy translated into power at its most resigned and unconcerned pivot" (p. 10). The time is during England's colonial rule of Ghana, but as I have already indicated, the specific time is not very important; it is the colonial situation in general that Awoonor is protesting against, not just British colonialism. He is establishing the recurrent dunghill image, an emblem of the land and a symbol of disorder and human corruption. Out of this setting comes the potential savior, Amamu. Chapter 1a, the first poetic interlude, is a song to his birth, the pain of that birth and the hope that it offers. A heavy drum rhythm accentuates the contrasting elements that will frame his life, the necessary "death of blood" and his birth as a hunter "in the wild butterfly field in the wild field of sunflowers" (p. 20). For all the beauty that he may discover, it is necessary that he be a priest and a carrier, a sacrifice to end the cycle of suffering in his land.

The second chapter reveals Amamu as a fully grown man, an established lawyer in Accra. We move through part of a day with him seeing the corruption with which he is beseiged as well as the suffering he feels as the result of witnessing the mechanical life the average man is forced to live.[11] In effect we see him taking on his role as a carrier. He assumes the anguish of the policeman who stands for years on his pedestal going through an "eternal marionette show" (p. 24) and of Richard, the barman, who knows only to serve "his new masters ... and dream of his native land five hundred miles away" (p. 26). The interlude is then packed with invectives hurled against the "Fart-filled respectable people ... [who] continue where the colonialists and imperialists left off" (p. 36). Yet as the dunghill imagery is intensified, so is the hope for a Christ who will "let us return to the magic hour of our birth for which we mourn."

The rest of the book consists of images which are extensions of and variations from those presented in the first two chapters. In terms of narrative structure this makes the book sound rather facile, but as we will see, the relationships are extremely complex. Chapter three extends our perception of the situation in which Amamu grew up by showing in detail life in a colonial primary school. We are again taken forward and see the respite which Amamu has found in his relationship with his lover, Adisa. Images of suffering and joy, destruction and creation quickly and effectively alternate to form a single plaintive lyric. These alternations are paralleled by the successive moves backward and forward in time, and finally we see through a number of details, such as the missing center tooth, that Adisa blends into Dede, Amamu's cousin who died when she was twelve. Together they represent his woman of the sea, Mammy Water, the mythic figure, a metaphysical, unifying force. In an interview in *Transition* Awoonor has commented that

> They are aspects of Amamu's consciousness .... Adisa is a warm womanly woman. The essence of womanhood. The essence of Africa in a way: or one aspect of Africa. Adisa is like Africa, like the little girl who is raped and dies before she has even been initiated into the puberty rites. All that lives on is her tiny mite of woman's wisdom. And so we see her again as the mermaid, the woman of the sea .... I was trying to incorporate the imagery of that myth into another symbol of Africa. Somewhere she does exist as the final repository of wisdom .... She knows what I must do, what Amamu must do, what we all must do. And I must go with her in order to acquire this knowledge and survive the truncation of the soul that society imposes. Unless we follow this path to wisdom, the Dance of Death will continue, onward and onward.[12]

This female figure, then, is a link between the reality of death as loss and the ultimate transformation that death represents. Here is the very essence of the mythic consciousness. As Kenneth Burke has written: "In the sense that discursive reason is dialectical, the mythic image may be treated as figuring a motive that transcends reason. It may also make claims to be 'religious,' since it presumably represents man's relationships to an ultimate ground of motives not available for empirical inspection."[13] Not only in his use of this woman, but also in his extensive use of scatological imagery Awoonor is pointing towards the same "ultimate ground of motives" as Armah. The death of Amamu, an apparent suicide, seems to be a negation of everything that is good in the society. On a symbolic level we usually look for a positive transformation in the death of a villain, not a good person. As with all sacrifice, however, the symbolism becomes inverted and the victim who represents the greatest loss to the community stands out as the most efficacious offering. Add to this the fact that amongst the Ewe suicide is the greatest sin one can commit against the earth, the ultimate act of rebellion,[14] and we can clearly see Amamu's death in terms of a negation of the *present* social order. The act is progressive, forward looking in its orientation. From a historical perspective Okonkwo's death in Achebe's *Things Fall Apart* was symbolic of the necessary *specific* transformation that his people had to undergo; likewise the death of Amamu, when seen from a mythic perspective, is symbolic of the *recurrent* transformations necessary to the health of any society.

Amamu's destruction is foreshadowed in the lunatic priest, Paul Dumenyo, whose sin of the flesh turns him into a scapegoat to be stoned by young children. Both Amamu and Dumenyo are victims of a hypocritical society that has been torn apart by culture conflict, but they are also both carriers of the collective guilt of that society, thus functioning in the same sacrificial role. Neither one is at first a willing carrier, and both pray "to let the cup pass away," though in the end they are forced to accept this in the calmness of their insanity.

In the opening lines of the chapter following the one about Paul Dumenyo, we see Amamu prepared to accept his fate. "He was very calm this morning. There was a sudden quiet that surrounded him, like the peace of all times ..." (p. 136). The day quickly slides into evening when he goes out to a high-life bar where he experiences a love-act ritual in the music of the band. But this is merely a prelude to his own final marriage to the woman of the sea. "Diminishing afternoon in the darkness of after-love a cruel mocking laughter strangles the only love left" (p. 169). Between the time he hears the music and the time he meets the woman of the sea, he must experience the nadir of despair as initiation into complete understanding of his role. His anguish must be the anguish of his people. The sardonically twisted line from T.S. Eliot reveals both the scatological and eschatological nature of this process ("Fear death by shit trucks."), while the lines from Kierkegaard and the refrain from Marlowe, "Despair and Die," assert the alienation he feels.[15] The continual references to the late Nigerian poet, Christopher Okigbo, are to one who has already completely experienced this anguish and gone through the final *rite de passage*, death.

The flashback to the return from England of Amamu's wife and the humorous vignette of the party, function as elaborations on the absurdity of the world in which Amamu must live. As a child in the cemetery recounting for the other children the circumstances around the death and burial of his cousin, Amamu had a naive understanding of a world that had order, but the dirges he remembers echo out beyond the limitations of his childlike perceptions which finally "vanished into the fast fading twilight" with his friends.

Amamu's search for his servant, Yaro, involves the assumption of yet another's anguish and the purgatorial wanderings through the slums of Nima, "the eternal dunghill," serving as a stone to put a fine edge on his awareness. Along with this new awareness comes a bitterness which is reflected in the intensive use of irony. The university is described as a "new Jerusalem in Nima's green and pleasant fields" (p. 195), an ironic allusion to William Blake's "Preface" to *Milton,* and we are told of "a senseless roundabout which used to be [named] for the man they threw out, now for the abstraction for which they threw him out" (p.196).[16] For the third time in the novel we see how the magic of a lawyer's words can open all doors as Amamu helps Yaro see his brother who has been apprehended by the police. Earlier with the traffic officer, and another time with the customs officer, Amamu's magic had worked. But it now comes too late, for the brother has already died from the beatings he received from the police.

The final poetic interlude brings all these ironies together as a series of invectives hurled against all those people who have had a hand in ravaging the land, Africans as well as colonial administrators. The steady beat of one newspaper-like statement after another is counterpointed by understatement and intermittent personal reportage: "We have many beautiful places in the country to which tourists, especially Americans, who will pay to see anything, can be lured with the appropriate posters and publicity material .... When I told them that young Africans left secondary schools speaking Latin and Greek they thought it was one of those fantastic African lies. All Africans are congenital liars. Othello was a liar" (p. 208). Though more intense here than elsewhere there is a continuous injection of humor throughout *This Earth.* And this humor, just as the joking in an African funeral celebration, goes well beyond comic relief in a potentially tragic situation. The intensity of both the ludic and the serious elements in such close proximity to one another takes us deep into the heart of a ritual process. We are drawn into that center where everyday rigid distinctions between disorder and order, death and life are transgressed, even abrogated, and where, in effect, man can squarely face the problem of temporary/ temporal existence and bridge the ontological gap inherent in his existence.[17]

Framing this ritual celebration, however, is Amamu's journey, mythical in the sense that Amamu makes the heroic crossing out of society with the intention of winning the revitalizing boon held by his woman of the sea and thereby gaining communal as well as individual salvation. Literally crossing the Volta on a ferry at Tefle, Amamu figuratively moves across that traditional area between states (the areas of the living and the dead) before making his final frenzied run to the sea.[18] But his move occurs only after the accumulated anguish of the protagonist appears to be beyond what any one man can bear, beyond any assuagement: "Our sadness itself, based upon that distant sadness which is the history of this land, defies all consolation" (p. 208). Having gone to the depths of despair the poet turns the dirge into a poignant supplication to the woman of the sea to release the land from this perpetual anguish: "For now believe me, the land is covered [with] blood, and more blood shall flow in it to redeem the covenant we made in that butterfly field, and under my almond. For you I renounce the salvation of madness and embrace with a singular hope, your hope" (p. 211). Counterpointing the earlier refrain of "Despair and Die," we have the softer plea "return the miracle." Dramatic action and poetic assertion merge as Amamu becomes literally possessed by ancestral rhythms:

> His headache had come again this evening. Throbbing, violent, as if many drums and gongs and rattlers were playing there. There was a jerkiness, a pumping regularity in all things as he watched them. The walls seemed to shiver in different lights.... It rested for a while in a violent glimmer. He had never seen a light like this before. The drums and the gongs and the rattlers had resumed their play in his head with a regular syncopation. They were playing a weird drum beat of this childhood.... The drums went into a slow funeral beat of mourning. Faintly a voice emerged singing a dirge. (p. 213)

Able now to see what he must do, Amamu follows the rhythms which lead him back to the sea.

As with Armah's Baako, Amamu's madness is only seen as madness by a prosaic world unable to partake of his poetic vision.[19] The true insanity is the distorted idea of reality which blinds the more prosaic world from the clear view that Amamu achieves in the moment that he is possessed by the ancestral rhythms. The pain of the initiation passes as he becomes one with that vision: "It seemed suddenly that the centuries and the years of pain of which he was the inheritor, and the woes for which he was singled out to be carrier and the sacrifice, were being rolled away, were being faded in that emergence. Here at last ... was the hour of his salvation" (p. 227).

According to Soyinka, the separation of gods and men since time *ab origine* has created a sense of anguish in both parties, though "it was the gods ... who first became aware of their own incompletion. Anguish is therefore primal transmission of the god's despair, vast, numinous, always incomprehensible."[20] Though he is concerned with the creative process of acting and the manner in which it enables man to be released from destructive despair, Soyinka's argument may be seen to apply to the creative process in general and to Awoonor's work in particular. If we follow Soyinka's criticism further, we can see how Awoonor has bridged "the infernal gulf ... with visionary hopes," for it is only through music, "the sole art form which does contain tragic reality,"[21] that this bridge can be achieved. It is, after all, through the drum that the ancestors are able to communicate with the living.[22] After a death this anguish must be most acute, for the living are immediately confronted with the reality of the gap between themselves and their ancestors. At the tragic moment, namely the moment of this intense anguish, the poet (and often he is a drummer) is called upon to serve as a mediator, thus militating against despair by means of the communication he is able to effect in the dirge that he sings.

As we have noted, the death of the protagonist has already occurred when the story opens. On a literal level the book is a dirge sung about his death. Not death in the Western sense of an event, but death as an ongoing process to be celebrated, a journey toward complete awareness. On this level it is also a dirge for the woman of the sea, whose death at an early age first made Amamu aware of the anguish of severance. This moves us into an allegorical level, since this woman is not merely his cousin but a mythic figure whose fertility is in direct opposition to the effete landscape through which Amamu moves. She personifies the awareness that Amamu moves into and the land so desperately needs. Thus, while the dirge is celebrating this life force, it is lamenting the land that is without that force and dying a death quite different than the death of Amamu: "the nation is dying on its knees, dying in its own defecation" (p. 209).

More than just the dirge is going on here, but the dirge can be seen as the structure within which the events of the novel occur. Likewise, during a funeral celebration a number of things are happening while the dirge is sung: "customary greetings and return of greetings, expression of sympathy by word of mouth and a handshake, the serving of drinks to visitors, the narration of the circumstances of the death and later events to visitors, conversation among visitors, music and dancing with accompanying comments, congratulations or even jokes and laughter ... arguments or quarrels here and there."[23] Knowledge of what occurs during a Ghanaian funeral celebration is not entirely necessary to an understanding of Awoonor's expressionistic mode of presentation, and yet it does help to explain why he has pulled together such an abundance of disparate elements: the poet sings to us and we become his audience in a mimetic recreation of a funeral celebration.

The four main themes of the dirge are easy to find in *This Earth*. References to the ancestors, references to the domicile of the ancestors and the deceased, references to the deceased, and reflections and messages are numerous.[24] The first two of these themes are immediately taken up in the opening chapter in the descriptions of Deme, Amamu's home town, and Mr. Attipoe, Amamu's uncle. In this place of his ancestors Amamu has received two legacies. The legacy of corruption, which his uncle, the road overseer, represents, is the most noticeable, but it is a legacy that Amamu is to transcend in his role as a carrier, his second legacy. During the outdooring ceremony where Amamu is to receive his name, the family priest calls forth the ancestors and a pledge is made to them that the child will be "their torchbearer and servant all his life" (p. 15). He is, in other words, to live his life as a priest.

Actually the opposition here is not as clear as it would at first appear. The greatness of Amamu's lineage is partially established with the references to his grandfather, whom he is said to resemble: "He was a tree on which they all leaned and under whose shade they all took shelter. Nyidevu, the canoe-upturning hippo, the hippos of Agave tried to upturn the canoes heaped with sand. Their necks snapped in the attempt" (p. 15). But the legacy he receives from his uncle is not entirely negative. Nketia explains that deeds of the ancestors which are seemingly uncomplimentary are often mentioned in dirges because the character trait implied in the deed is considered more important than the deed itself (p. 24). Thus, the intelligence and cunning of Attipoe are seen as positive attributes, though this involves no overt approbation of the manner in which he used them. More simply put, a man cannot be truly great unless his ancestral lineage is broad enough to encompass many different types of men.

As the novel progresses we see Amamu's role spread out beyond a relationship to his own ancestors to include all the ancestors of the land. Moreover, the legacy of corruption is not merely a localized corruption, but a corruption of the entire land. We have noted that the narrative aspect of the novel is minimal, and to the extent that the expressionistic mode is used here to shatter this temporal element, we have an increased awareness of space. We are not so aware of when things happen chronologically, as where they happen. At each place we see Amamu, he is confronted by another facet of corruption, and the slums of Nima, the National Club, the colonial school, as well as Deme, are all part of this landscape.

The mention of the qualities of the deceased individual are intended to establish the significance of the loss of the individual to those who were close to him as well as the community. Our understanding of the sensitive nature of the protagonist increases in direct proportion to our expanded awareness of the landscape in which he moves. The references to his special qualities, however, are rarely as direct as they are in a dirge. His integrity, for example, is established in the second chapter where we see him in direct contrast to the various regulars of the National Club, and is effectively confirmed by his refusal to allow his vision to be compromised by the corruption which surrounds him.

It might reasonably be argued that the three themes I have so far discussed are of a general nature and could be found in any novel, but it is their specific combination with a series of reflections and messages that clearly relates the contents of this novel to the contents of a traditional dirge. As Nketia has pointed out, the reflections are on the plight of those who are left behind, and the messages are requests for aid and comfort from the dead (p. 44). Thus the mourner might make general comments on the death: "What were your wares that they are sold out so quickly?" or "This death has taken me by surprise" (p. 47). In addition he will add phrases which express more directly his own personal anguish and the loss to the community: "There is no branch above which I could grasp" or "I am in flooded waters. Who will rescue me?" (p. 47). The reflections in *This Earth, My Brother* are similar and, in fact, make up a large part of the poetic sections:

> I do not know where they buried my birthcord. (p. 18)

> Home is my desolation, home is my anguish, home is my drink of hyssop and tears. (p. 38)

> In the gray truce of those hours we will win a temporary respite. In our penance hour, we shall pack our bags ready for a long journey homewards. (p. 147)

> A nation is doing a death dance now in a banquet hall of its imaginings.... (p. 148)

> Anger is futile, for death maybe is the only reality. (p. 207)

Aside from the reflection on the dying nation, these all could have come from a traditional dirge. The reflection on death as a journey, however, is particularly noteworthy. Nketia has said that

> throughout the singing of the dirge, the conception of death as a journey with its implication of inevitable physical separation is not lost sight of. All the mourner's wishes for a good journey, her wish not to be left alone, her

expressions of sorrow for the loss sustained and of her anxiety for the future are thought of because death makes physical separation unavoidable. This thought may culminate in yet another wish — the wish for continued fellowship when the deceased reaches his destination in the underworld. (p. 48)

Amamu's journey into and through his society symbolizes this journey, the final *rite de passage*. The messages even more than the reflections support this interpretation as they are direct addresses to those with whom he desires to be reunited:

Mother, didn't I tell you I hated the sun, father didn't I tell you I hated the sun, the little one was never found they must journey to god's house and purchase him with offerings, must buy him with sacrifices look after him well, mother. (p. 19)

Dear one, hold on, for I come. (p. 77)

My woman of the sea, I am leaving for the almond tree where I first met you. I shall be there when you rise.... (p. 210)

Without a thorough knowledge of the Ewe language, or at least the linguistic structure of the Ewe dirge, I am very much restricted in what I can say about how *This Earth, My Brother* bears similarities to the dirge in terms of the language patterns. Nevertheless, the most distinctive prosodic features of the Ewe as well as the Akan dirge are the numerous types of repetition that occur. Each dirge is individuated by its own system of repetitions which control meaning as well as rhythm, and range from alliteration and assonance to repeated collocations and repetitions of entire sentences. We see such use in the first of Awoonor's poetic sections as well as all the subsequent interludes, and even, though to a lesser extent, in the narrative sections. The following is one of the finest examples of the way he interweaves such a complex of repetitions:

The seventh night, deep deep night of the black black land of gods and deities they will come out. First the drums to-gu to-gu to-go to to to-gu if they insist then I shall die the death of blood I shall die the death of blood. They will march through every lane drums echoing across no one can tell where they are now, no one can tell. They will pause for entrance into thunderhouses the silence of crickets nocturnal wail of bullfrogs taking over from as near as Kosivi's ground water tank. If they insist insist and say it must be by every means, if they insist then I shall die the death of blood. The echo recedes into distant farmlands the sole witnesses of the journey the restlessness of gods if they insist if they say it must be by every means then I shall die the death of blood. (pp. 17-18)

Words, phrases and sentences are rhythmically bound together by the insistent, drum-like repetition of d's, t's and b's. The reiteration of adjectives and key phrases as well as the parallel construction effects an intensification of that rhythm.

It is not merely a rhythm for musical effect, but a rhythm which also carries a lot of meaning. As would most scapegoats, most carriers, the protagonist would have his cup pass from him, but the drums, the voices of the ancestors, have already decided that he will "die the death of blood." His statement "If they insist" is thus counterpointed by an implicit ancestral rhythm saying "we insist, we insist." By the end of the book Amamu has given himself entirely over to the demands which the ancestors have made upon him. When he begins to return to the sea he follows the intense rhythm of a dirge, hearing drums move into "a slow funeral beat of mourning." As there are no more worldly things distracting him, he no longer needs the firm insistence of the ancestors. Only one soft voice calls out to him: "It was a distinct female voice singing a dirge about the day of death, of trees withered, of leaves fallen from the evergreen baobab, of a desert storm, of skulls crossing a wide impenetrable expanse of forest soaked in the desert rain. Then a voice began to talk about the searcher who finds, the searcher who finds in the wilderness the death that will kill him, the sorrow of the pallbearers, the pity he will have for them who will carry his body to the grave" (p. 213).

Seeing *This Earth, My Brother* as an Ewe dirge, however transformed by the artist, establishes the coherence of the work as a whole and the vision which is the basis of that coherence. Past and present are locked in a tragic cycle which goes back to a primordial anguish of severance. Through his death, Amamu is able to serve as a mediator who can break the cycle for the future. The vision is a mythic one, but framed in a lament that might be sung to any great man in the Ewe community. Though this clarifies much that is going on in the novel, it certainly makes it no less complex. In fact, as Forster said about *Moby Dick*, as soon as we begin to feel the music in it, the work suddenly becomes amazingly difficult.[25]

Having looked at the specific ways this novel is a dirge, I would like to return to some general implications. Liminality and the liminal individual are among the clearest marks of a mythic consciousness. The dirge, as an expression of the ultimate human transition, serves as an ideal vehicle to explore the transformation of a land, a society and an individual. To the extent that we focus just on the subjects, the death of the individual or the society, the work is indeed depressing. Yet the subjects here have meaning within the context of the dirge, within a statement about a process, a transition. Death, as we have seen over and over again, is merely the ultimate symbol of transformation. It is the riddle that appears to be an end, and from a literal and realistic perspective, it is an end. From a figurative and mythic perspective, it is but a passage to a beginning.

The perceptions we are given in myth are always riddles that defy our sensory perception of reality. Amamu, as a world traveler and successful lawyer, is seemingly the quintessential Western-educated African. To the extent that he moves away from that role he is judged first strange, then mad by those around him. From a realistic perspective his actions seem to be a nonsensical rejection of his Westernization. Nowhere in the novel, however, does Awoonor show us anything that would reduce Amamu's situation to a simple Westernization versus tradition theme. Amamu is no more involved in rejecting any aspect of his being than he is in rejecting life itself. He comes to see life in mythic terms, and this involves acceptance of a traditional role, even affirmation of the ritual journey he must undertake.

The Function of Yoruba Cosmology in Wole Soyinka's *The Interpreters*

In much of his work Wole Soyinka has drawn elements, motifs and subjects very extensively and directly from oral tradition and mythology. Of the writers I am considering perhaps only Tutuola has done this more clearly. I am, however, less concerned with how readily one can identify specific traditional motifs in a given work, than I am with the ways, and also the ends toward which, the author establishes mythic patterns. These patterns subvert the accepted or ordinary way of looking at reality. They break down the boundaries and forms within which society operates. The immediate effect is that the mythic consciousness assaults the reader, defying his expectations. Though I have talked of theme, there is a very important sense in which the mythic consciousness works against theme and unity. Tutuola leads us through a process, his Drinkard's confrontation with the riddle of death, and not toward an end. We might remember that at one point in *The Palm-Wine Drinkard* the narrator asks the audience, his readers, if they have the answers. The riddle thus subverts closure. In looking at the novels of Armah, I focused on the liminality of the hero. The very act of situating a figure between boundaries raises questions as to what those boundaries are. The demonic imagery pushes the questioning process even further. In Awoonor's novel a prophetic voice guides us across the spatial form of the work and into ritual action. The form and the action move us outside of the chronological/temporal frames of our ordinary lives.

With each author, I have looked mainly at selected features of the mythic consciousness: the riddle, anti-closure and death in Tutuola; liminality and demonic imagery in Armah; spatial form and ritual action in Awoonor. In the case of Wole Soyinka I wish to consider all these features in relation to the specific elements he draws from Yoruba cosmology in his novel, *The Interpreters*. It is a work that has been given surprisingly little critical attention, perhaps because it is so thoroughly problematic. What is the center in this work? Is there one? The reader is made dizzy as he is moved vertiguously away from any core. Ostensibly the novel is about a group of young individuals (the interpreters) who are actively engaged in their critiques of society. They are continually raising questions about what goes on around them. (Are they serious or just playful?) The work, however, simply ends without concluding. Along the way, however, the interpreters have had to confront madness and even death. They are, of course, situated at the very edge of their society. (Is this by their own volition or are they caught up in patterns of action above and beyond them?) Chronological development is hard to follow because of sharp ruptures in the narrative. What we finally get are bits and pieces across time, forming a mosaic of the interpreters' collective lives and actions.

Soyinka has said that "a concern with culture strengthens society, but not a concern with mythology."[1] The statement is confusing since a society's mythology is part of its culture. Moreover, Soyinka himself seems very concerned with mythology in his own work. The apparent contradictions, however, rapidly fade in light of the context in which the statement was made. Attacking the modern African writer, especially those writers involved in the philosophy of *négritude*, Soyinka argued that the artist failed his primary responsibility in allowing the present direction of Africa to be created by politicians: "When the writer woke from his opium dream of metaphysical abstractions, he found the politician had used his absence from earth to consolidate his position" (p. 18). The main thrust of this 1967 address to the African-Scandinavian Writers' Conference in Stockholm was an unqualified condemnation of myth-making isolated from the realities of the artist's culture. The role of the artist, Soyinka argued, is not to make myths, but to interpret them, not to give society an identity, but to make it aware of its essence, however much that essence has been obfuscated by the politician's rhetoric: "The test of the narrowness or the breadth of [the writer's] vision ... is whether it is his accidental situations which he tries to stretch to embrace his society and race or the fundamental truths of his community which inform his vision and enable him to acquire even a prophetic insight into the evolution of that society" (p. 17). Soyinka goes on to say that the *négritude* writers have vitiated their own work with an excessive fascination with the past: "Of course, the past exists now, this moment, it is co-existent in present awareness. It clarifies the present and explains the future, but it is not a fleshpot for escapist indulgence, and it is vitally dependent on the sensibility that recalls it" (p. 19).

When he discussed "mythology" in Stockholm, Soyinka was thinking along lines quite different from the operational ones I set up in the opening chapter of this book. He was attacking the reification of an ideology geared at entrenching an elite in their position of power — what Marx and Fanon would have called "mystification." Soyinka told the Stockholm audience "The writer must, for the moment at least (he persuades himself), postpone that unique reflection on experience and events which is what makes a writer — and constitute himself into a part of that machinery that will actually shape events .... He therefore took his place in the new state as a privileged person, placed personally above the effects of the narrowness of vision which usually accompanies the impatience of new nations ..." (p. 15). Yet in calling for a broader vision, a concern with culture and not with private mythologies, Soyinka is calling for a return to the real roots of a society, those myths from which a culture draws its sustenance. What he refers to as the writer's vision is the interpretation the writer articulates through his work. Much like the British writers Thomas Carlyle and D.H. Lawrence, Soyinka maintains that the gods may die or change their appearance, but the essential "godness" remains. Soyinka is perhaps closer than either of these writers to the myths with which he is working, and throughout *The Interpreters* we can sense this in the pervasive element of time *ab origine* that enters with his Yoruba pantheon.

Soyinka may have been treading on thin ice in his address to his fellow writers. It is at least questionable whether he is not very often pushing his own very private mythology. Is Eshuoro in *A Dance of the Forest* simply a god that Soyinka has created for his own ends, or is he in fact a reinterpretation of the essences of Eshu and Oro based on Soyinka's artistic comprehension of the Yoruba people and their gods?[2] While there is no simple answer to this question Soyinka has covered himself well in emphasizing the dangers in any myth-making and the need for the artist to be aware of a reality that comes from the people, not from the illusions of an isolated elite. Where criticism is warranted he is not exempting himself, but only giving a warning much as Bandele in *The Interpreters* gives to Kola and the others: "Just be careful. When you create your own myth don't carelessly promote another's, and perhaps a more harmful one."[3]

Despite his apparently ambivalent feelings about the uses of mythology, no other contemporary African writer has shown such a broad and thorough concern for the relationship of mythology to art, the artist and society. In many of his earlier works Soyinka probes into aspects of this relationship, and in *The Interpreters* he attempts to give a rather comprehensive picture. He was already moving in this direction in *A Dance of the Forests*, but perhaps the stage provided too small an area for him to fully explore the essence of Yoruba cosmology, despite his being a consummate dramatist. In shifting to another genre, the novel, he found the additional space he needed. Kofi Awoonor is fond of saying that there is not one novel here, but five or six novels, each with its own plot and protagonist.[4] We might go even further and say the novel is made up of a number of small plays, for in all Soyinka's work the play *is* the thing. In the radical sense of drama, Soyinka is always attempting to explore the above relationship in terms of the ritual process, never to define it in terms of a fixed meaning.

The protagonists in this process are all liminal *personae*, they are ultimately governed by a morality in which a sense of balance and order is the highest virtue, and they are involved in an open-ended debate concerning their roles. In the course of this chapter I will consider each of these aspects, namely character, theme, and structure, in relation to the picture of Yoruba mythology that emerges in Soyinka's novel.

Two images, water and the bridge, dominate *The Interpreters* and bind together a rather large and often disparate group of individuals. The images are closely related, but for now I will simply consider the relation of the latter image to the roles the characters play. Significantly, the bridge is the central image in Kola's painting, but also the most difficult one for him to realize. When he is able to find his bridge, a model for Esumare, the Yoruba god of the rainbow, Kola is able to complete the painting. Each one of the interpreters is, in his own way, cut off from the rest of society and needs to find a point of contact where his interpretive qualities will be effectively realized.

Egbo in his violence, Sagoe in his philosophy of Voidancy, Sekoni in his madness, and even Bandele in his inscrutability are all freaks, or at least very strange when judged by the standards of the mundane world. They all have qualities that associate them with the gods of the Yoruba pantheon almost in an allegorical manner: Egbo, loving palm wine and adventure, is Ogun, the god of carnage and creativity; Sagoe, often infantile, yet always the witty trickster, is Eshu, the god of chance; Sekoni, an electrical engineer who must bear overwhelming suffering, is Shango, god of lightning; Bandele, who is always in control of life, is Obatala or Orisa-nla, the god of creation. But this can easily be overdone for it is as men, not gods that they figure in this novel. To the extent they have characteristics of the gods, they also may be seen as priests who have the responsibility of serving the gods that possess them.[5]

Soyinka's essay "The Fourth Stage," subtitled "Through the Mysteries of Ogun to the Origin of Yoruba Tragedy,"[6] offers extensive insight into the philosophical questions Soyinka deals with in his novel. Though *The Interpreters* is not a tragedy, the main characters, much like the protagonists of Armah's novels, carry a tragic potential, for as individuals marginal to society they are all potential scapegoats. Though most of them have to bear only a certain amount of ostracism, we see that the society's rejection of Sekoni actually causes him to become demented. Only by understanding this can we really come to terms with their individual roles in relation to the larger design of the novel, and in particular to the centrality of the bridge imagery. Soyinka elaborates on the well-known point that in the Yoruba world view there are three areas of existence: the realms of the ancestors, the living, and the dead. Respectively, these areas are the past, present and future, but as I have already pointed out in discussing Awoonor's novel, these areas are seen in synchronic terms, not diachronically as in the West. They are separated, however, by an immeasurable gulf, a fourth area of existence, "the no man's-land of transition between and around these temporal definitions of experience."[7] Metaphorically, Soyinka has called this "the fourth stage" for he sees those who plunge into this area as actors who ritually bridge the gulf. And in this sense Soyinka uses the words "artist" and "actor" interchangeably. Both are able to obtain from "the numinous territory of transition ... fleeting glimpses by ritual, sacrifices and a patient submission of rational awareness...."[8]

The problem posed by the existence of this transitional area is essentially the same for those who exist in each of the three areas: "the deities stand in the same situation to the living as do the ancestors and the unborn, obeying the same laws, suffering the same agonies and uncertainties."[9] There is almost nothing here of the distinction which is made in the West between man and God, for the gods all have historic and anthropomorphic dimensions, and all men reflect aspects of the gods. According to Soyinka's interpretation of Yoruba mythology, our concept of self and time has been fragmented. Atunda, a slave of the first deity, rolled a large boulder down on the back of his master, smashing him into a multiple godhead, namely the present pantheon.[10]

Following the model we are given in "The Fourth Stage," we should look at the primary quality of an "actor," the ability to face total dissolution of self. Ogun, and hence Egbo as well, are prototypic in this respect:

> To recognize why Ogun was elected for his role (and the penalty of horror which he had to pay for his dare) is to penetrate the symbolism of Ogun both as essence of suffering and as combative will within the cosmic embrace of transitional gulf .... nothing but the will — for that alone is left untouched — rescues being from annihilation within the abyss. Ogun is embodiment of Will and the Will is the paradoxical truth of destructiveness and creativeness in acting man. Only one who has himself undergone the experience of disintegration, whose spirit has been tested and psychic resources laid under stress by the most inimical forces to individual assertion, only he can understand and *be* the force of fusion between the two contradictions. The resulting sensitivity is also the sensitivity of the artist....[11]

Though couched in different language this is basically the same argument that Joseph Campbell makes about the hero, or that R.D. Laing makes about the schizophrenic individual. For Egbo the necessity of facing such dissolution is closely aligned with his will to become a "force of fusion" between the past and the present: "The spectre of generations rose now above him and Egbo found he would always shrink, although incessantly drawn to the pattern of the dead. And this, waiting near the end of the journey — was it not exhumation of a better forgotten past? Belatedly thinking, who am I to meddle? Who? Except — and this counted for much — that he knew and despised the age which sought to mutilate his beginnings" (p. 8).

Egbo's parents drowned when he was still very young. His father had spent his life as an evangelical Christian minister, and though his aunt tried to raise him as a Christian, Egbo was always drawn to his pagan past, especially the grove of Oshun where he would often go and lie by the bank of the river. Jokingly, but with admiration, Kola referred to him as "the first genuine throwback of [his] generation" (p. 10) and, indeed, the first time we meet Egbo at the night club with his friends we are led into a flashback to Egbo's pilgrimage to Osa. His mother had been a princess of Osa, and now that his grandfather is old, Egbo is considering giving in to the urgings of the Osa Descendants Union, accepting his line of inheritance and becoming the next ruler of the creek town. The question of power intrigues him, and this is certainly why he is working in the Foreign Office of the Civil Service. However, he realizes during his pilgrimage that his problem is much larger than anything that can be resolved through choosing between the traditional politics of his grandfather and those of a modern state: "I have, I sometimes suspect, strained objectivity to its negative limits. What choice, I ask myself, is there between the ugly mudskippers on this creek and the raucous toads of our sewage-ridden ports?" (p. 11).

In other words, Egbo is struck with the realization that his grandfather with his control of a large network of smuggling routes is not essentially different from the Chief Winsalas and Sir Derinolas who supplement their income with bribe money. The problem is "the collapse of humanity"[12] and the source of rejuvenation cannot come from a political strategy alone. At this point Egbo is just bewildered, though Kola reads him incorrectly in interpreting Egbo's refusal to accept his inheritance as willful apostasy. Sekoni, already having experienced the anguish of standing before the gulf that Egbo now faces, is the only one who does understand him. In turn it is only Egbo who catches the essence of Sekoni's metaphysical stutterings:

"Sekoni, what do you say? If the dead are not strong enough to be ever-present in our being, should they not be as they are, dead?"

"T-t-to make such d-d-distinctions disrupts the d-d-dome of c-c-continuity, which is wwwhat life is."

"But are we then," Egbo continued, "to continue making advances to the dead? Why should the dead on their part fear to speak to light?"

"That is why wwe must acc-cept the universal d-d-dome, b-b-because ththere is no d-d-d-direction. The b-b-bridge is the d-d-dome of rreligion and b-b-bridges d-d-don't jjjust g-g-go from hhere to ththere; a bridge also faces backwards."

"There should be more Alhajis like you, Sheikh," Egbo said. "You violate the silence but yours insists on a purpose." (pp. 6-7)

Just as Egbo sought to find some mythical boon in his journey to his ancestral home, Sekoni had gone to England and taken a degree in electrical engineering believing he could return to his country armed with the power to reorder it: "Sekoni, qualified engineer, had looked over the railings every day of his sea voyage home. And the sea sprays built him bridges and hospitals .... And the logic of nature's growth was bettered by the cabalistic equations of the sprouting derrick, chaos of snakes and other forest threads by parallels of railtracks, road extravagances and a nervous electronic core" (pp. 24-25). But frustrated by an ossified bureaucracy and finding his experimental power station allowed to rust as a political favor, he went mad. On his recovery he made a pilgrimage with his father to Mecca and brought back a boon more powerful than his engineering degree, the sensitivity to deal constructively with the forces that had torn him apart. Even though he is soon killed in an auto accident, he leaves behind an artistic statement that epitomizes the spiritual quest the interpreters are pursuing: "Sekoni began sculpting almost as soon as he returned. His first carving, a frenzied act of wood, he called 'The Wrestler'. He had not asked Bandele or anyone to sit for him, but the face and the form of the central figure, a protagonist in pilgrim's robes, was unmistakably Bandele. Taut sinews, nearly agonising in excess tension, a bunched python caught at the instant of easing out, the balance of strangulation before release, it was all elasticity and strain" (p. 105).

Sekoni's death is, symbolically, a ritual sacrifice, for it is his death that brings the interpreters together again, causes them to take stock of their own lives and perhaps redirect their action. It would certainly seem more than coincidental that he is killed on the road, the common domain both of Eshu and Ogun, respectively the mentors of Sagoe and Egbo. The relationship of Egbo and Sekoni is particularly close, just as the relationship of Ogun and Shango. Soyinka's notes to "Idanre" put the idea of sacrifice in perspective: "Today Ogun of the metallic lore conducts Sango's electricity. The ritual dance of the union is seen sometimes during an electric storm when from high-tension wires leap figures of ecstatic flames. This is the ideal fusion — to preserve the original uniqueness and yet absorb another essence."[13] Consider also that the rainy season is Ogun's season and the passage announcing Sekoni's death becomes clear:

> The rains of May become in July slit arteries of the sacrificial bull, a million bleeding punctures of the sky-bull hidden in convulsive cloud humps, black, overfed for this one event, nourished on horizon tops of endless choice grazing, distant beyond giraffe reach. Some competition there is below, as bridges yield right of way to lorries packed to the running-board, and the wet tar spins mirages of unspeed-limits to heroic cars and their cargoes find a haven below

the precipice. The blood of earthdwellers mingles with blanched streams of the mocking bull, and flows into currents eternally below earth. The Dome cracked above Sekoni's short-sighted head one messy night. Too late he saw the insanity of a lorry parked right in his path, a swerve turned into a skid and cruel arabesques of tyres. A futile heap of metal, and Sekoni's body lay surprised across the open door, showers of laminated glass around him, his beard one fastness of blood and wet earth. (p. 167)

In addition to the rain, the images of blood, bridges and metal serve to confirm the connection between the sacrifice and Ogun.

The connection is purely symbolic, yet Egbo, being the one most overwhelmed by grief at Sekoni's death, reacts like Ogun after his blind slaughter of his men.[14] Fleeing to his sanctuary in the rocks by the bridge that spans the Ogun River, Egbo sought to find solace in his tears.[15] Despite his grief, Egbo never experiences the anguish borne by Sekoni in his moment of madness, though the leitmotiv that comes to be associated with Egbo ("like a choice of a man drowning") indicates he is on the brink of such anguish, and it is, in fact, on this note that the novel ends. Egbo is caught in the dilemma of needing contact with the past in order to give meaning to the present, but also needing to avoid the seductive hold of the past in order to act. Passing by the place where his parents had drowned Egbo shouts down to the water a defiant call about his own present situation, "not another Egbo so soon, you nymphomaniac depths" (p. 11).

Egbo's ambivalence about the past is reflected in his reaction to Owolebi, the large woman dancer in the high-life bar: "She had no partner, being wholly self-sufficient. She was immense. She would stand out anywhere, dominating. She filled the floor with her body, dismissing her surroundings with a natural air of superfluity. And she moved slowly, intensely, wrapped in the song and the rhythm of the rain. And she brought a change again in the band, who now began to play to her to drape her in the lyric and the mood .... The song, a cry and a legend of the past, brought back [Egbo's] own commitments and he tensed" (pp. 20-21). Though he momentarily checks himself because she and the song are reminders of his dilemma, the woman represents someone in the realm of the sacred to Egbo, and hence he reacts violently to the caricature which Kola draws. After Kola has altered the drawing and the incipient fight is thwarted, Sekoni cryptically verbalizes Egbo's thoughts about Owolebi: "Re...member, a woman is the D-d-dome of love, sh-she is the D-d-dome of Religion ..." (p. 24).

This episode, along with the trip back to Osa, prepares us for the conflict that Egbo faces in his triangular involvement with Simi and the young co-ed. Simi, like Owolebi and Osa, represents his maternal roots, infinitely warm, gentle, and dangerously seductive. When Egbo meets Simi and is drawn into her world, he makes, in effect, the crossing into mythical time. His affair with her is analogous to what Campbell has called "The ultimate adventure ... a mystical marriage of the triumphant hero-soul with the Queen Goddess of the World."[16] His dilemma is symptomatic of his refusal to return and his affair with the co-ed is the situation that draws him back into the mundane world, though as the book ends this is not very clearly resolved.

What of the boon that he gains? As Campbell tells us, "The mystical marriage of the queen goddess of the world represents the hero's total mastery of life; for the woman is life, the hero its knower and master ... [He is] made capable of enduring the full possession of the mother-destroyer, his inevitable bride. With that he knows that he and the father are one: he is in the father's place."[17] The elixir is thus the spiritual wisdom gained by the hero. This goes a little further than Sekoni's metaphor of the Dome, but the statements are essentially the same. The very liminal, semi-inarticulate Sekoni is a complement to the earthy, physically involved Egbo. They are, as it were, body and soul of one being.

Soyinka is a difficult writer to pin down. Much like that other great mythic writer, Joyce, he is working on many levels at the same time, and where he is concerned with penetrating the limen and dealing with the numinous we will be as consistently frustrated as we will be excited by the perceptions he offers. Nevertheless, though we might have difficulty handling the arcanum set before us by Sekoni, we can see it dramatically realized in Simi and Egbo. The appellation assigned to Simi, *ayaba osa, omo Yemoja*[18] (Mammy Water) clues us in to her role, and Soyinka elaborates:

Those who boasted that Simi gave them her love, that she lived for them, could never get the world to accept it, for Simi was cast in the mould of distance, and it made her innocent. As if there never had been contact between her and the world, and these men with whom she slept experienced nothing but desperation, for they must see afterwards that they had never touched her. To recapture the act was, in the dare of Simi's cold liver gaze, a sacrilege. And so men could not tire of her whom they had never possessed, and the illusion maddened them, began a craving they could never end. (p. 55)

After Egbo attains her, possessing her in his first night of love-making, he takes the train from Ibadan to Lagos and gets off at Olokemeji, where the tracks cross the Ogun River. There he spends the night, a neophyte passing through the final phase of his initiation:

So now, for the first time since his childhood ascent into the gods' domain, Egbo knew and acknowledged fear, stood stark before his new intrusion. For this was no human habitation, and what was he but a hardly ripened fruit of the species....

And morning came, baring lodes in rocks, spanning a gridiron in the distance; it was a rainbow of planed grey steel and rock-spun girders lifting on pillars from the bowels of the earth. Egbo rose and looked around him, bathing and wondering at life, for it seemed to him that he was born again, he felt night now as a womb of the gods and a passage for travellers....

He left with a gift that he could not define upon his body, for what traveller beards the gods in their den and departs without a divine boon. Knowledge he called it, a power for beauty often, an awareness that led him dangerously towards a rocksalt psyche, a predator on Nature. (pp. 135-36)

Kola and Sagoe in their joking relationships with the world at large tend to represent positions antithetical to those of Egbo and Sekoni. This is certainly an oversimplification, for Kola and even Sagoe, have their moments of seriousness just as Egbo and Sekoni have their moments of levity. Nevertheless, the observation is generally valid and is reflected in their behavior in the high-life bar of the first chapter. I noted that there was immediate polarization when Kola drew the caricature of Owolebi. What Kola and Sagoe took to be extremely funny, Sekoni and Egbo saw as sacrilege. Eventually a compromise is subtly reached and the tensions resolved when Kola amends the drawing and all share the levity, but Kola and Sagoe's "blasphemy" serves an important function in establishing the very religious tone of the book. As Edmund Leach has put it, "Any theory about the sacredness of supernatural beings is likely to imply a concept of sacrilege which in turn explains the emotions aroused by profanity and blasphemy."[19]

Egbo's reaction to the caricature is but a foreshadowing of his more violent reaction to Kola's "Pantheon." Especially outraged at what Kola has done with Ogun he calls the portrayal "an uninspired distortion.... He has taken one single myth, Ogun at his drunkennest, losing his sense of recognition and slaughtering his own men in battle; and he has frozen him at the height of carnage" (p. 253). Later, having heard of Joe Golder's involvement with Noah's death, Egbo glares at the painting, again feeling "that he was trapped on it, for ever, with the primal slime of all creation" (p. 258). What at first appears to be simply a very personal reaction to the way he has been used as a model goes down to a much deeper source of insult. Before he even studies his own portrait, Egbo says on seeing Lazarus portrayed as the rainbow deity that the painting has captured a view of life he cannot accept, "an optimist's delusion of continuity" (p. 253), a view where the idea of resurrection is given primary importance.

It is one of the unfortunate weaknesses of the novel that we never get to see clearly Kola as a character, despite the importance of his role. As it is we must see that role defined indirectly, more through his painting and his relations with others than himself. If we consider the configuration of Egbo's aversion to Lazarus, Noah, and Joe Golder, as well as his aversion to Kola's painting and his close relationship with Sekoni, an image of that role will emerge. Sekoni, a Muslim, went through a crisis situation, found himself as an artist, and expressed his struggle in a carving he called "The Wrestler." The central figure, dressed in pilgrim's robes, is apparently engaged in an agonizing combat with spiritual forces. In contrast to the spiritual quality of Sekoni's carving, there appears to be something sacreligious about Kola's work for the models are all freaks, and this is reflected in the painting: Lazarus, the albino who professes to have physically died and been born again; Noah, the thief who almost becomes a religious convert; Usaye, the albino girl who is nearly blind; Joe Golder, the mulatto homosexual; Simi, the prostitute; and all the interpreters. No wonder that the controlling idea here is the resurrection, an idea which has Christian implications and thus offends Egbo's pagan sensibility. Despite the cogency of this to his own recent experience as a neophyte, Egbo seems far more in tune with Sekoni's idea of life as an ongoing struggle. But Sekoni's work is informed with his Muslim experience no less than Kola's painting is informed with the syncretic Christian-pagan experience of Lazarus. Kola is thus a foil to Sekoni, and what Egbo feels about his painting is perhaps more like ambivalence than clear antipathy.

In the chapter on Armah I discussed how the negative implies the positive. Here, Ogun's destructiveness implies his creativity, though this does not help us to fully understand the function of the smallpox God, Sopona (Usaye), Erinle, hermaphroditic god of the hunt (Joe Golder), or even Esumare, the rainbow deity (Lazarus). Once again Leach's comments are helpful:

> Religious belief is everywhere tied in with the discrimination between living and dead. Logically, *life* is simply the binary antithesis of *death*; the two concepts are the opposite sides of the same penny; we cannot have either without the other. But religion always tries to separate the two. To do this it creates a hypothetical "other world" which is the antithesis of "this world." In this world life and death are inseparable; in the other world they are separate. This world is inhabited by imperfect mortal men; the other world by immortal men (gods). The category god is thus constructed as the binary antithesis of man. But this is inconvenient. A remote god in another world may be logically sensible, but it is emotionally unsatisfying. To be useful, gods must be near at hand, so religion sets about reconstructing a continuum between this world and the other world. But note how it is done. *The gap between two logically distinct categories, this world/other world, is filled in with tabooed ambiguity. The gap is bridged by supernatural beings of a highly ambiguous kind ...* [emphasis added]. [20]

Peter Morton-Williams fully substantiates this idea in relation to the Yoruba in his analysis of Yoruba cosmology. He shows that there are three types of divinities: those of *Ilẹ̀* (earth), *Ilé Aiye* (world), and *Oke Ọrun* (sky), each type respectively further from man.[21] The idea of God, with the Western connotation of distance, does not really fit any of the deities in Kola's "Pantheon." Only Olódùmarè, the Supreme God (Obatala is the head of the other deities, the *orişa*), has complete distance from man.[22] His distance is such that no one would think of attempting to represent him, and hence he is absent from Kola's painting.

The way in which this gap is bridged can have at its motivational base either a comic or a tragic source, or both. In discussing Soyinka's essay on Ogun and examining the liminality of Egbo and Sekoni, I have already examined the tragic base. Of paramount importance to Egbo is "the fact of sacrifice. Ritual immolation" (p. 196). Complementing this sacrificial element is the sacreligious element represented on Kola's canvas and acted out by Sagoe. Whether he is throwing plastic lemons at a cocktail party, pontificating on the value of farting when praying, or leading a government minister into considering the economic value of human excrement, Sagoe is always the perfect model of indecorum and the leading actor in Soyinka's divine comedy. In continually playing with the taboo he functions much like Eshu filling the primal interstice between man and the deities simply by making fun of the discriminations imposed on the sacred and the profane. It is indicative of his role as an Eshu figure that Sagoe steals the wreaths from Sir Derinola's funeral and gives them to the funeral of Lazarus's apostle.

Eshu is the great leveller. His comic pose militates against what Soyinka refers to as the tragic consequences resulting from "the first act of revolution,"[23] Atunda's rolling of the stone and the creation of the multiple godhead. He emphasizes the commonality between the gods and man by showing that neither are immune to the workings of chance.[24] Earlier I mentioned that Sekoni had been killed on the road, the realm of Eshu as well as Ogun. In any culture Sekoni's death would not be seen strictly as tragic because of its accidental nature, but the Yoruba cosmological system simultaneously allows for both the cathartic effect of his death as ritual sacrifice and a means to assuage the anguish of the survivors by having the death seen as the work of Eshu.

Sagoe, like Eshu, is a great player with words, bringing down the mighty with his satirical barbs. A passage from his bible, a dissertation on excrement, will suffice to show how he goes about this. Reminiscing about his youth and how he and his family thought of the king and queen of England as deities, he reveals how he brought them down to human proportions:

... I remember at this period of my childhood, and the door of our huge sprawling guaranteed eternal dugout, a portrait in colour of a pair of supra-human beings, ethereal, other-existential in crowns and jewels, in wide fur-borders, gold, velvet and ermine, with orbs and sceptres and behind them, golden thrones. These images in my child's eyes, and — lest any ideological significance be attached to the portrait's location, these portraits were present also in the parlour and in the bedrooms, for my people were staunch royalists — in my child's eye, these two figures could be no less than angels, or God and his wife. It was a critical phase in my introspection and if I had been in this country [the United States] where all the facilities are available, I would undoubtedly have graduated into a fulltime schizophrenic. For it became an obsession with me, the limitation of this delicate, unreal pair. Did they, or didn't they? As in a seance, the solution came with blinding simplicity. In one session of a purely Voidante nature, I realized finally the attitudinal division within this human function. They would be Voidantes; but Christ, never the other!

To shit is human, to voidate divine.

This was the Birth, the concrete formulation of Voidancy.... (p. 168)

Significantly, this is the passage Dehinwa reads to Sagoe after Sekoni's death, for it is in effect his credo, a refusal to accept a tragic vision of life.

In negating hierarchies through his blasphemous words and actions, Sagoe expresses the same basic optimism that we find in the resurrection motif of Kola's painting. This, however, is in direct opposition to the view held by Egbo and expressed by Sekoni in "The Wrestler" that life is an ongoing, anguished struggle. An examination of Bandele and his importance in giving the novel thematic unity will show the following underlying structure, since Bandele mediates between these two opposing factions:

As I indicated earlier, it is Bandele who mediates between the two parties in the incipient fight over the caricature of Owolebi. Bandele's intrusion is so stuble we might barely notice it. As Lasunwon, the lawyer, is about to drop the drawing on the wet floor, Bandele's arm reaches "from the dark corner, long and thin, *deceptively* frail" (p. 20, emphasis added), and slips the drawing from him. It is possible to read *The Interpreters* for the first time without being aware that Bandele is there. He says little and is always in the background, but the lines given to him almost always show him as calm, wise, powerful and impartially just. In a bar fight that did occur, Bandele sat quietly by watching the proceedings until the thug who had precipitated the fight knocked him over and pulled him into it. Within minutes the fight was over as Bandele caught the thug with some rope and trussed him up. The taut sinews of Bandele's muscles became indelibly fixed in Sekoni's mind, eventually re-created in the form of his powerful carving, "The Wrestler."

Bandele is interested in seeing that decisions are made, and that the individual accept moral responsibility for his decisions. During the trip to Osa, Egbo is uncertain about whether to continue on, and Bandele urges him to make up his mind, though he does this without any personal bias: "it was like Bandele to insist though motiveless" (p. 11). Although no overt comparison is made, Bandele is cast in the role of Obatala, who has "an exalted purity exciting man to be beautiful and to be strong. It is a positive vitality. It is patience brought to bear against darkness and hate."[25] But the drama enacted here is between men, not gods, and accordingly the comparison Soyinka makes is to the *ogboni*, the cult of the earth and justice. While the novel may end on Egbo's dilemma, the penultimate word is given by Bandele who pronounces judgement on the hypocritical group of professors who are concerned with "meral terpitude":

> He was looking at them with pity, only his pity was more terrible than his hardness, inexorable. Bandele, old and immutable as the royal mothers of Benin throne, old and cruel as the *ogboni* in conclave pronouncing the Word.
> "I hope you all live to bury your daughters". (p. 273)

Bandele's appearances are so brief that it is easy to scan them. The following, a survey of his actions and the descriptive words and phrases applied to him, shows just how clearly he is cast in the role of an Obatala figure:

patient	"Bandele wore his mask of infinite patience" (p. 42).
inscrutable	"Bandele was a total stranger, and becoming increasingly inscrutable" (p. 266).
strong	"Bandele came in again, a palace housepost carved of ironwood" (p. 266).

"And Bandele held himself unyielding, like the staff of Ogboni, rigid in single casting" (p. 266).

quiet, gentle See pp. 130, 172, 262.

defender of the past (to Egbo)

"You continue to talk of of the past as if it has no place with us" (p. 128).

comforter "To Bandele fell the agony of consoling Alhaji Sekoni ..." (p. 168).

takes care of Joe Golder after Golder accidentally kills Noah (pp. 256-58).

takes care of Simi, sensing her imminent rejection by Egbo (pp. 266-70).

mediator in the argument over Lazarus after Lazarus gives his sermon (pp. 191-98).

for the young co-ed and Egbo (pp. 262-64).

observer "Egbo turned angrily on him. 'What are *you* getting out of it [involvement with Lazarus]?' 'Knowledge of the new generation of interpreters'" (p. 193).

understanding of the parts they all are playing

"Is it not time for the freakshow?" (p. 265).

Bandele patiently observes and takes care of the strange band of interpreters. Not at all surprisingly, William Bascom has noted of Obatala that albinos, cripples, and dwarfs, i.e., are all sacred to him.[26]

Despite the abundance of ironic and satirical thrusts led by Sagoe and directed at virtually everyone and everything, the authorial presence remains extremely neutral. Bandele, it would seem, is closest to that presence and thus carries, more than any other single character, the thematic weight of the novel. The above phrases are of course taken out of context, and the Westerner confronting Bandele's personality for the first time probably will react to him much the way he would react to an *ogboni* bronze sculpture, finding him stiff, cold, and at times even ugly.[27] This reaction is likely to be exacerbated by Bandele's refusal to categorize anything as strictly good or evil; for if Bandele stands above everyone as a judge, the Western sensibility demands that the problems be adjudicated with a sense of equity in mind. Bandele, on the other hand, epitomizes Yoruba morality, being concerned more with the preservation of communal harmony than with categorical good and evil.[28] When the others are arguing about whether Lazarus is a fraud, Bandele asserts that the really relevant issue is the meaning he has brought into his congregation. Here as elsewhere Bandele is the cooling element in a potentially hot situation. Such "coolness," by extension is seen as a necessary counterbalance to the chaos of the present political scene in West Africa. It is the "coolness" expected of leaders such as Chief Winsala and Sir Derinola, but discarded by them when they become involved in corrupt political machinery.

Robert Farris Thompson has noted the relationship between the ideals expressed in Yoruba dance and mythology, and his comments aptly serve as a summary of Soyinka's thematic concern in *The Interpreters*:

> The equilibrium and poetic structure of traditional dances of the Yoruba in western Nigeria, as well as the frozen facial expressions worn by those who perform these dances, express a philosophy of the cool, an ancient, indigenous ideal: patience and collectedness of mind. Yoruba myths relate tales of disjunction, the dangerous jarring of elements that had been in balance, of the near-destruction of mankind by breach of trust. In one myth, the Yoruba god of divination locates the mediating principle in cool water; in another, a powerful man named Agirilogbon locates the mediating principle in a cool, healing leaf. There is nothing arbitrary about these myths: They all posit water, certain leaves, and other items as symbols of the coolness that transcends disorder and without which community is impossible. Ask a traditional member of this populous African society, "What is love?" and he may tell you, as one told me, "Coolness." [29]

Using the key figures in Soyinka's interpretation of Yoruba mythology, we can see that he has placed Obatala (literally "King of the White Cloth" and the quintessence of cool) as a buffer between the heat of Ogun's forge and the heat of Eshu's satire.

Society, pictured as being controlled by derelict politicians, is in need of being revitalized and reorganized. Egbo is intrigued with the idea of power and perhaps has the potential for being a new leader, though he has still to learn the lesson that Winsala and Derinola failed to grasp, namely that the past neither can nor should be discarded. Sagoe, as a young journalist, is equipped with the ability to clear the way for new leaders, levelling the old with his words. But he too needs the kind of maturity that comes with an understanding of the connectedness of things. It is precisely this wisdom that Bandele possesses and is the basis of his "coolness."

One of the most puzzling parts of the novel, Lazarus's sermon, is really quite clear when seen in relation to Bandele's "coolness" and the overall theme of chaos and order. Bandele is the only one who articulates what the others as cynics and apostates refuse to see as their primary motivation to come and hear Lazarus. The appearance of a man who has claimed to have risen from the dead is something of a shock to the entire group, coming as he does so shortly after the death of Sekoni. At a moment when their own faith in life is threatened with dissolution because of this loss, a man appears who believes he has met and conquered death. Lazarus tells them that he fell down and died in a strange village, was about to be buried by the townspeople, and emerged alive from his coffin transformed into an albino.

Unlikely as the story sounds, the interpreters all wish to go and hear his sermon, for he has promised to give the details of his transformation and rebirth. A polished raconteur, Lazarus begins with a story of Christ's battle with Death. Though he emphasizes the Christian concept of resurrection, the images are all his own: Christ hitting Death, giving him an uppercut like Dick Tiger and scattering his teeth "from Kaduna to Aiyetoro" (p. 179), or Death having his matchet cut in half by Christ's "shining sword of stainless steel" (p. 179). Having set the stage, Lazarus then recalls what it was like when he died. He was walking through a field of cotton and all the cotton pods began to quietly burst, surrounding him with cotton wool. When all movement of the cotton wool ceased he found himself being drawn into a heavy sleep. At this point he was attacked by an old man with a long white beard, a mouth full of cotton wool, and a walking-stick.[30] He tried to escape through a smooth black gate, but the cotton wool began to fill his own apertures while also weighing him down. Praying to God for deliverance, he suddenly saw the gate open before him.

More than the pain, the most salient aspect of Lazarus's death experience is the overwhelming whiteness. "Everything was white" (p. 181). Death, a very disordering experience for those left behind, is the very antithesis of disorder for the one who experiences it. Here it is absolute coolness, the cessation of all movement. Lazarus returning resurrected from this experience sees himself as having much to offer those whose lives are lacking any cohesiveness. He makes himself priest of his own church, converting thieves, thugs and murderers, in short, all the outcasts of society, and maintains control with the mystique that surrounds his knowledge of death. In a revivalistic moment following the sermon, we are told of Lazarus that "his possession was the violinist's, alien in a group of *agidigbo*, as if it was not he who would not submit his body completely to communal joy but an ordered force keeping him separate in his own spiritual capsule" (pp. 188-89).

The precise way in which the sermon affects Bandele is never fully spelled out, but it would seem certain from the way he reacts to others' cynicism that it has in some small manner enabled him to adjust to Sekoni's death. What is important to Bandele is not the particulars of the experience, but the pattern, the way in which Lazarus not merely survived a painful experience, but came out of it a transformed individual who was then able to pass on his newfound strength to others. In responding to Sagoe's question concerning whether or not he believed in what happened to Lazarus, Bandele says: "It didn't matter whether I did or not. But at least one thing was obvious, this man did go through some critical experience. If he has chosen to interpret it in a way that would bring some kind of meaning into people's lives, who are you to scoff at it ..." (p. 194). After first being led astray by his own misconception of Noah, Kola finally shares Bandele's perception when he makes Lazarus the symbolic harbinger of a new order, the rainbow deity, and thereby completes his painting.[31]

Earlier I spoke of the predominance of bridge and water imagery in *The Interpreters*. The concept of the bridge is the *sine qua non* of Soyinka's interpretation of Yoruba cosmology. Where harmony is the most important value, links are needed between the disparate states of existence, people and places in that universe. Each of the interpreters, no less than Bandele and Lazarus, functions as this kind of link. Water then, as the quotation from Thompson indicates, is symbolic of the harmony between these links. Significantly, the main action of the novel spans the course of a rainy season, and rain functions contrapuntally to the dissonance sounded by the "jarring of elements" in several crucial moments: the opening bar room scene with the argument over Owolebi and the flashbacks into the lives and conflicts of Egbo and Sekoni; the burial of Sir Derinola, his "final imposition on his countrymen," and the appearance of Lazarus; the death of Sekoni; the search for Noah and discovery of his apostasy. Moreover, in moments of personal crisis Egbo is always withdrawing either to "the safety and sense of Bandele's house" (p. 127) or "to the soothing run of the waters of Ogun" (p. 134), both places of "coolness."

A key agent in the maintenance of harmony is art, which within the system of Yoruba cosmology is metaphorically equivalent to water: "Art cools the earth and makes life viable."[32] The aspect of time in *The Interpreters* is marked not only by the duration of a rainy season, but also by the completion of two works of art, Sekoni's "Wrestler" near the beginning and Sagoe's "Pantheon" near the end. The very existence of these two works is an anodyne to the divisive elements that continually threaten the solidarity of the interpreters. When, at the end, the group meets to celebrate Sekoni and Kola's art, we see just how cohesive this force is. The rift between Egbo and Bandele over Egbo's affair with the young student has grown to the point that the two are near a serious confrontation:

Sekoni's exhibition had been opened in the afternoon to palm wine and roast meat from the black ram, and its congealing blood still stuck to Kola's studio floor. Bandele had said, "What do you need the ram for? Haven't you had your sacrifice?" And for a long moment, it seemed that Egbo would plunge the knife into his throat and they all stood, horrified, round the reek of blood and the convulsive vessel of the severed throat. But Egbo gave the knife a playful flick in his direction and a thin streak of blood marked Bandele across the shirt. Immediately the tension was loosened and laughter replaced the unmeaning moment of antagonism; even Bandele smiled, remembering that this, after all, was also for Sekoni. On Kola's canvas the paint was hardly dry on Esumare, but they carried it and hung it in the foyer of the theatre where Joe Golder would sing later that night. (pp. 264-65)

Thompson has written that "The time-resistant dances of the cool form a kind of prayer: May humanity be shielded from the consequences of arrogance and the penalties of impatience."[33] For all his self-control, Bandele is only human, and is as guilty here of impatience as Egbo is of arrogance. Fortunately "the prayer" is effective and the consequences are avoided. But art is no panacea for every problem, nor is Soyinka professing this to be the case. Yoruba art and mythology continually reaffirm ideals for man to live up to *despite the fact he continually fails to do so.*[34]

The Interpreters is structured in an open-ended manner having no thematic resolution. As in a riddle or a dilemma tale, we are left with a question and not an answer.[35] Sagoe is going to destroy his "Book of Enlightenment," Kola's painting is completed, and the conflict between Bandele and Egbo is resolved, but there is no closure regarding the alienation of the interpreters, the larger conflict they still have with society. The novel ends with Bandele pronouncing his curse on the pharisaical professors and Egbo struggling with his decision concerning the way in which he will commit himself to involvement with society. Regardless of the fact that he has completed his painting, the problem for Kola is not even how he will commit himself, but whether he will:

Fitfully, far too fitfully he had felt this sense of power, the knowledge of power within his hands, of the will to transform; and he understood then that the medium was of little importance, that the act, on canvas or on human material was the process of living and brought him the intense fear of fulfillment. And this was another paradox, that he dared not, truly, be fulfilled. At his elbow was the invisible brake which drew him back from final transportation in the act. It was typical that Egbo would volunteer to return with him to Noah, for Egbo did not hesitate to pursue the elusive, never sought to define even in their frequent futile arguments. (pp. 237-38)

Very much in the manner of an African dilemma tale, a problem is set forth, here the "collapse of humanity," the collapse of a viable social structure, and various solutions are debated. If the politicians have failed, who is then to pick up the pieces they have left behind? Equally important, what is to be done? Sagoe's refusal to pay a bribe to get his job with the newspaper results in his coming to a profound awareness of this dilemma. Seeing Chief Winsala drunk and lost in self-pity, and Sir Derinola confronted with an image of his own loss of self-respect, he is caught between his feelings of respect for their age and his abhorrence of their actions. Winsala himself realizes this as indicated by the string of proverbs he mutters: "*Agba n't'ara* ... it is no matter for rejoicing when a child sees his father naked, *l'ogolonto* .... The adulterer who makes assignations in a room with one exit, is he not asking to feed his scrotum to the fishes of Ogun?" (p. 96). But on the following day Sagoe finds that he has been given the job, and he learns that even unimpeachable politicians are vulnerable.

Bandele standing in the middle as a buffer, the interpreters argue with one another and with society, always getting, it would seem, nowhere. Having studied abroad, several of them returned home hoping to initiate change, yet in the end they find themselves literally where they were in the beginning. Egbo's dilemma at Joe Golder's recital is the same one he faced on the creeks at Osa. Yet this is only a facile evaluation of their circular journey, for although they have found no absolute solutions, the act of confrontation and debate has effected their maturity as individuals and as a group. The stresses and tensions they learn to cope with help to define their own image of themselves and to reinforce their feeling of solidarity. Most importantly, they learn of the power they wield as interpreters, individuals moving between their people and their gods. Acted out before us are the struggle of Sekoni's "Wrestler" and the resurrection of Kola's "Pantheon," rituals "to pierce the encrustations of soul-deadening habit, and bear the mirror of original nakedness."[36]

Liminality and the Priest-Like Role of the Personae in Awoonor's and Soyinka's Poetry: The Poet as Prophet

I would like to return to a comment I made at the beginning of the Armah chapter, namely that the idea of the modern West African writer as an individual who must continually move between two worlds, African and Western, often standing outside both, has become an unfortunate cliché. However apt it is in many cases, it is a convenient label that categorizes the writers while saying little about their work. As I have tried to show in my examination of three of Armah's novels, we may be misled in finding a ready answer to why there is so much alienation in their writings unless we think beyond the most superficial implications of this problem as faced by the West African writers themselves. Certainly it is a lot easier to see the alienation as coming from culture conflict than to look for it in perhaps a very autochthonous concept of the artist as a shaman who must distance himself from his society in order to gain powers helpful to his art and, ultimately, to his people.

This is meant less as a denial of the theme of culture conflict than as a caveat that too much emphasis on it can lead to rather narrow interpretations of otherwise complex works, and with poetry to virtually no understanding at all. The critic's excessive concern with culture conflict presupposes a very Eurocentric premise about the African's motivation for writing, namely that it lies primarily in a desire to confront the shock of Western contact with Africa. While it is possible to play such games with the novel, a European transplant, it is extremely difficult to do so with poetry. Not at all surprisingly, very little attention has been paid to West African poetry, and to date very few book-length studies of individual poets have been published.

When asked about the needs of a writer, Kofi Awoonor spoke about the necessity of a writer to live in a state of exile before he attempts to deal in his writing with the conflicts and anguish of his society. So long as he is drawn into the immediate reality of that anguish, his work will be distorted. Awoonor goes on to say that the exile need not be physical, but must at least entail psychological distancing from the people and things the writer is close to, a point which appears to be directly related to other comments he has made concerning his own interest in the theme in African literature of the cyclical journey where a priest-like man leaves his society only to return with the power to revitalize it.[1]

Looking at the poetry of Wole Soyinka and Kofi Awoonor, I will explore the way they have utilized this theme and some of the deeper ramifications of being between two worlds, the power that is gained and the threat that is posed by such existence. I will approach this problem by comparing the ways in which subject matter is organized and *personae* are developed in Soyinka's *Idanre* and Awoonor's *Night of My Blood*.[2]

It may help first to examine a single poem to see more concretely what the limitations are of looking at this poetry simply from the perspective of the culture-conflict position and the possibilities of an approach predicated in the idea of the poet/*persona* as a shaman priest. Awoonor's short, but powerful lament entitled "The Weaver Bird" is often read as a very strongly anti-colonial statement. Virtually every line confirms the idea of the bird as a symbol of the colonizers who came to Africa, were welcomed by the Africans, and were belatedly recognized as agents of destruction:

> The weaver bird built in our house
> And laid its eggs on our only tree.
> We did not want to send it away.
> We watched the building of the nest
> And supervised the egg-laying.
> And the weaver returned in the guise of the owner.
> Preaching salvation to us that owned the house.
> They say it came from the west
> Where the storms at sea had felled the gulls
> And the fishers dried their nets by lantern light
> Its sermon is the divination of ourselves
> And our new horizon[s][3] limit at its nest.
> But we cannot join the prayers and answers of the communicants.
> We look for new homes every day,
> For new altars we strive to re-build
> The old shrines defiled by the weaver's excrement. (p. 37)

However, Awoonor himself has expressed surprise at this interpretation, saying that he did not have the colonialists in mind when he wrote this poem, but rather was thinking specifically of Kwame Nkrumah.[4] Educated in the West, Nkrumah returned to his land as a savior, but after leading his people to independence he was thought to have led Ghana to the brink of economic destruction.

Both readings fit without any strain and even complement one another in supporting a larger, more abstract question the poem deals with concerning the nature of pollution in a society. Two types of external threats to social order are simultaneously examined, the threat of the outsider and the threat of one who has journeyed outside the order and returned. In neither case is there any sense of castigation of those who present the threat, and perhaps only a very minor amount of resentment that the society will now have to be re-ordered. But there is a sense of loss and bewilderment concerning the form that the order will take, coupled with an understanding that the weaver bird has had much to do with that future form ("Its sermon is the divination of ourselves ..."). The final image of defilement might at first seem to stand against the assertion that there is not any anger here, but there is nothing outside of what we might read into this image to support any other conclusion. Anger and anguish are two distinct emotions and the poem seems to be expressing the latter. Unless we wish to see the defilement simply as a contradiction or denial of the lament, we must see it as an objective correlative to the *persona*'s perception of an extremely ambiguous order.

We have here a poem about mutability and change. The relation of the West to this is incidental rather than fundamental in the same sense that the disquietude in Elizabethan England concerning scientific and political change is merely incidental to the perceptions regarding change that Spenser and Shakespeare deal with in their poetry. Where those poets, however, sought an ideal of purity based on the exclusion of the ambiguous, this poet is embracing the ambiguous as a necessary factor in growth. As we shall also see in Soyinka's poetry, the power which makes the ambiguous thing or polluting agent dangerous is the same power which can be transformed to a more positive end. It is the concern with the process of transformation that informs Awoonor and Soyinka's poetry with a very similar sensibility despite the very distinctive character that is also present in each one's work.

First, let me again clarify what I mean when I speak of the power of the ambiguous. In "The System Shattered and Renewed," the final chapter of *Purity and Danger*, Mary Douglas analyzes the cycle wherein dirt is first seen as being dangerous to order and finally as having power to revitalize it: "Dirt was created by the differentiating activity of mind, it was a by-product of the creation of order. So it started from a state of non-differentiation; all through the process of differentiating, its role was to threaten the distinctions made; finally it returns to its true indiscriminable character. Formlessness is therefore an apt symbol of beginning and of growth as it is of decay."[5] She goes on to explain that while "in its last phase ... dirt shows itself as an apt symbol of creative formlessness .... it is from its first phase that it derives its force. The danger which is risked by boundary transgression is power. Those vulnerable margins and those attacking forces which threaten to destroy good order represent the powers inhering in the cosmos. Ritual which can harness these for good is harnessing power indeed."[6]

The weaver bird committed a boundary transgression in defiling the shrine, but if he was destroying one order, he was also acting as a harbinger of a new one. The poetic statement is thus an expression of a ritual process, an attempt to harness the power inherent in this ambiguity. It is difficult to summarize the rather solid analysis that Douglas gives us without making it sound as if it is coming from one who is more of a mystic than an anthropologist. Perhaps her own metaphorical statement about the power of the ambiguous best reveals the very empirical approach she has taken: "... a garden is not a tapestry; if all the weeds are removed, the soil is impoverished. Somehow the gardener must preserve fertility by returning what he has taken out. The special kind of treatment which some religions accord to anomalies and abominations to make them powerful for good is like turning weeds and lawn cuttings into compost."[7] To extend the metaphor, neither Awoonor nor Soyinka sees a poem as a tapestry, an object which, however beautiful, is intentionally artificial and removed from the decay and other threats to such discriminations that we cannot avoid in life. It must, on the contrary, have a very organic relationship to the world. They tend their poetic gardens carefully, know the value of compost, and never try to separate the flower from the soil. For the Western sensibility this is particularly difficult to grasp, since in effect they are insisting that we cannot perceive the beauty of the flowers if we do not understand the nature of the soil they have grown in.

We are more likely to be immediately struck by the differences than the similarities between the work of these two poets. Awoonor's style is lyric while Soyinka's is dramatic. Awoonor is a master of the lament and his poems are often anguished songs of death. Soyinka is a master of the dramatic scene vividly rendered with brilliant and often incisive wit, though intensified with a lyricism that has grown out of his familiarity with Western poetic forms. He has a feeling for tight tetrameter lines boxed in three, four, or five line stanzas, where Awoonor works effectively in free verse with lines that move fluidly from a four stress Anglo-Saxon rhythm to the rhythm of the Ewe drum. *Night of My Blood* begins and ends with two poems of personal alienation, "My God of Songs was Ill" and "They Do Not Sound for Me," both generally pessimistic in tone, but concluding with a sense of renewed strength. The final movement of the poem "Idanre," just as the first poem of the collection, "Dawn," is set in the early morning hours and is an unqualifiedly joyous hymn to creation. Yet if we were to simply continue our examination along these lines, we would soon get tangled in a web of contradictions and exceptions.

Throughout Awoonor's poetry there is an evenly sustained concern with death which we find in the predominance of the dirge or dirge-like forms that he employs. On the other hand, Soyinka's hymns to dawn and to birth are more than offset by a seemingly morbid fascination with the process of death in its most violent forms: car accidents, political massacres, and a god's slaughter of his own men. For both poets death is confronted less in terms of sheer physical loss and separation than as a metaphysical beginning, a point of contact with the mythic reality that gives sustenance to mundane existence. As Soyinka writes in "Dedication," "Taste this soil for death and plumb her deep for life" (p. 24).

If we looked at Soyinka's short prayer, "Koko Oloro," outside the frame of *Idanre*, it would seem to have more in common with John Skelton's "Philip Sparrow" than with any of Awoonor's laments. The tumbling lines of Skeltonic verse and the very precise geometric progression of the refrain, which is repeated in the second, fourth, eighth, and sixteenth lines, might appear to belie what I have said about the common sensibility of these two West African poets, though here I am speaking only of form. The animated world of the child chanting the propitiation in "Koko Oloro" has little to do with the conventional world of Skelton's Jane Scroupe and much to do with the funereal rites of passage that are so integral a part of Awoonor's poetry as well as his prose.

"Koko Oloro" is the first of a group of poems in *Idanre* entitled "of birth and death." It is a monologue of a young child pleading to an ancestor to intercede with the gods on his behalf and have them aid him in crossing from one state to another, most likely from childhood through puberty to adulthood:

Dolorous Knot
plead for me
Farm or hill
Plead for me
Stream and wind
Take my voice
Home or road
Plead for me
On this shoot, I
Bind your leaves
Stalk and bud
Berries three
On the threshold
Cast my voice
Knot of bitters
Plead for me. (p. 23)

The child, who is between the two states ("On the threshold"), cannot proceed unless literally the entire universe is in accord, not merely that which is close to him (home), but that which is distant as well (farm). The three berries are symbols of those in the three areas of existence, as are the leaves (the living), the stalk (the dead) and the bud (the unborn). The shoot is the child himself, no longer a bud, but not yet a stalk. Only through the anguish of the initiatory experience ("Knot of bitters") can he successfully move from the one state to the other.

The situation portrayed in this poem is much like that at the end of *A Dance of the Forests* where the Half-Child is tossed about by the forest creatures and is on the threshold of an escape from a seemingly endless cycle of suffering. The escape is necessary not merely for the incomplete child, but for all mankind, whose suffering he sacrificially bears. Yet he may also prove to be an *enfant terrible* unleashing dangerous forces on those who would see him saved. The creatures who toss the child about feign catching him on the ends of their knives before quickly throwing him on as in a game of "hot potato." When Demoke finally rescues the child, Forest Head warns him of the risk he is taking.[8]

While this is going beyond what we have in "Koko Oloro," it is exactly the idea that Soyinka had taken up in "Abiku," his poem of the child who dies and returns to the mother only to die again. Because of high infant mortality, the child in West Africa has a very ambiguous status and is often not considered one who has fully entered the world of humans until he reaches puberty. If he dies before he has left this ambiguous status behind him, he is not even given the same burial accorded an adult.[9] On the one hand, as the child in "Koko Oloro," he is the shoot who can grow into another branch of the ancestral tree, or like the Abiku, he can stop the growth by refusing to be completely born. It has been argued that Soyinka's Abiku is presented as so alien a creature that he is beyond eliciting any pity or anger from us.[10] We see Abiku's actions from his own point of view in a semi-dramatic monologue that reveals him as a calculating, almost frighteningly chilling anti-life force. In the penultimate stanza this is brought to a powerful climax in the image of the coiled snake lying in wait to attack mothers, an apparent reversal of the common Yoruba symbol of regeneration, a snake coiled with its tail in its mouth.[11]

But it seems to me that the poem is more subtle than this. The final stanza partially steps outside Abiku's point of view, allowing us to penetrate the pathos of his situation:

> The ripest fruit was saddest;
> Where I crept, the warmth was cloying.
> In silence of webs, Abiku moans, shaping
> Mounds from the yolk. (p. 30)

We see him caught in a trap, not because of some demonic assertion of will, but because of a failure of will. In refusing to grow, Abiku has become a dangerous as well as pathetic figure who has short-circuited the life cycle to a simple alternation between "the yolk" and "mounds," the womb and the tomb, the one being no less "cloying" to him than the other. It is the kind of apostasy and withdrawal Soyinka would later look at again in *The Interpreters* in the character of Noah. With both there "is simply the refusal to be, the refusal to be a living being...."[12]

The important point here is that the power gained from having been outside the physical and psychological structures of society is seldom neutral. It may be used either to aid or to harm. As Awoonor writes, those who have been abroad may become "The smart professionals in three piece/ Sweating away their humanity in driblets." They see their own culture as an object for exploitation, "Our songs are dead and we sell them dead to the other side" (p. 28). But they may also become those who are "Caught between the anvil and the hammer/In the forging house of a new life,/ Transforming the pangs that delivered ... [them]/Into the joy of new songs" (p. 29). Neither Soyinka nor Awoonor is a prophet of doom, however much they reveal a sensitive awareness to the dangers a society must face. Most of their poetry, just as their novels, is ultimately concerned with the individual "Caught between the anvil and the hammer," namely the hero, his anguish, and the boon he brings to his society.

In a very broad sense we may look at the poetry of these writers in terms of a thematic progression from chaos to order, from insufficiency to fulfillment, and from alienation to incorporation. With Awoonor we must look beyond *Night of My Blood* to his poetic novel *This Earth, My Brother* for the journey in which this progression culminates, while we find a similar journey in Soyinka's poem, "Idanre." But looking at the poetry exclusive of these longer end pieces, we find less of a linear progression than a dynamic opposition between these binary relationships. Where in Awoonor we find the traditional ritual process of the funeral at the center of this opposition, in Soyinka it is the myth of Ogun. The mediating factors are, respectively, death and violence, two negations of societal order and thus processes that offer effective symbols of transformation.

The opening poems of *Night of My Blood* explore questions regarding the necessity, the difficulties and dangers of the exile's return to his home:

The return is tedious
And the exiled souls gather on the beach
Arguing and deciding their future
Should they return home
And face the fences the termites had eaten
And see the dunghill that has mounted on their birthplace? (p. 23)

The exile, like the mythic hero, or even Soyinka's Abiku, faces a critical moment where he either decides to make the second crossing and be completely reborn, or remain as the dead man who wakes up:

> And dies again
> The glow worm shows your way to the place of skulls
> And there you find yourself reclining in an arm-chair
> Supervising the ceremony of the lost
> Yes the ceremony of the bewildered
> The wanderers that lost their way homewards
> And chose the scented putrefaction of death. (p. 25)

The individual who can bear the pain of crossing the threshold will be the priest, one able to draw from the strength gained on his own journey and also from renewed contact with ancestral power:

> The cure god said I had violated my god
> "Take him to your father's gods"
> But before they opened the hut
> My god burst into songs, new strong songs
> That I am still singing with him. (p. 22)

These first twenty-three poems, leading up to "I Heard a Bird Cry," can be considered as a single unit in which the poet looks into the various aspects and ramifications of this exile motif. All but a few were published in Awoonor's first collection of poems, *Rediscovery*, and they establish a matrix in which the funeral metaphor operates. The final poems of this section, "Salvation," "The Purification," "The Gone Locusts," "Messages," and "The Journey Beyond," are transitional in that they syncretize the exile motif and the funeral metaphor. They are short dirge pieces which clearly establish the link between the dead individual and the exile, who are both in touch with powers outside the society that are potentially useful to those behind:

> When discoverers land on far off shores
> And the others who took the big boats return
> We shall find our salvation here on the shore. (p. 38)

Moreover, they must both undergo a purification ritual[13] to enable them to make the journey:

> We stood on the shore and watched you sail
> To the roar of the sea and the priest's bell.
> They didn't forget to place the sacrificial cow

On the bow of the storm experienced canoe.... (p. 39)

There is the necessity to send messages to those away so they will not forget those left behind and will return with their boon:

> I shall wish for the return
> Of the sowing season
> In which the farmer
> Will remember his harvest. (p. 40)

And finally there is the very central idea of the journey itself, the strongest of all links between the two:

> The howling cry through door posts
> carrying boiling pots
> ready for the feasters.
> Kutsiami the benevolent boatman;
> when I come to the river shore
> please ferry me across.... (p. 41)

"I Heard a Bird Cry" and "Night of My Blood," two long laments, are not only literally in the middle of the collection, but also at the thematic center. They bring together all the above ideas of death and exile and celebrate the movement from the anguish of the initiatory experience to the joy of reincorporation, from ritualized suffering to newfound individual and collective strength. Images of long painful journeys through deserts, as well as images of death, destruction and decay, circumscribe the rituals necessary to negate, or wash away as it were, the old order and enable a new one to be realized.

The dominant voice of "I Heard a Bird Cry" is the first person singular, the singer-priest telling of the agony and loneliness of death:

> There was a tree which dried in the desert
> Birds came and built their nests on it
> Funeral songs reached us on the village square
> and our eyes were filled with tears
> The singing voice which the gods gave me
> has become the desert wind. (p. 42)[14]

He explains the propitiatory rites he must perform to assuage the gods and remove the affliction from the land. The ultimate rite in this process is his own mortification and self-sacrifice:

> I am the bird on the dunghill
> The birds flew and left me behind.
> My wings have not broken
> But my joints are weak.
> I too shall carry the fetish bell
> and start towards the sacred hut.... (pp. 45-46)

The anguish he expresses, however, is not merely his own but also that of the dead individual and the community now seen as wandering in a wilderness. The rapid succession of images and shifts in point of view are only confusing if we fail to keep in mind that what is true of the part is true of the whole, the singer-priest, the dead individual and the community.

In an immediate sense death is something to be afraid of:

> There is war in the land of the dead
> And ghosts are doing a war dance
> Marching with drums towards the land of the living.
> If I had known, if only I had known
> I would have stayed at home. (pp. 47-48)

It is an enemy, a disease that strikes in the night:

> They say it is in the night
> When the monster terrorizes the people
> They say it is in the night
> When they give birth to the evil child
> And the smallpox god walked the village lanes. (p. 49)

The ordeal of life as well as death is so great a trial that no one could expect to make it on his own, and hence aid is forthcoming from the ancestors:

> The journey beyond is a long journey
> That is why not one alone can make it.
> The gone-befores will receive us
> And give us water to drink.... (p. 48)

The assertion is to serve as comfort to the bereaved community and the dead individual, who has doubts about his journey, "... I would not have followed/ The trancers to another land/Which cannot give me food to eat" (p. 49). As an ancestor he will be able to aid the community he has left, but now in his liminal state he poses a threat and thus needs encouragement:

> Where has it been heard before
> That a snake bit a child

In front of its own mother? (p. 51)

At the end of the journey is the final, perfect rest:

> Some day, by some rivers
> I shall sit down among the elephant grass
> And listen to the roar of the estuary
> Till the end of the world. (p. 52)

The danger having passed, a feast is to be shared by all, a celebration affirming the renewed bridging of the ontological gap between the living and the dead:[15]

> My heart, be at rest,
> For the vultures that came,
> Shaking the rafters of your house,
> Have flown away, flown far away ...

> And the feast is ready for us. (p. 52)

In "Night of My Blood" Awoonor further extends his metaphor of exile and death to give it an allegorical dimension. The "night" of the poet's "blood" is the long legendary migration of his ancestors from central Africa to what is now Eweland, a migration that still plays an important part in the stories and songs of the elders and is reported to have taken place roughly a thousand years ago.[16] Paralleling the experiences of the exile and the dead individual, the journey is seen in the context of an initiatory experience. According to the poem, then, the group was once collectively purified in a tribal rite of passage as it is continually re-purified by the individual re-enactment. Continuity with the past is established, the ritual process now encompassing the ancestors, the living community and the individual. Just as the group lives under the protection of the ancestors in addition to living for them, so it is with the individual in the "shadow" of the community who is called to bear its burdens:

> We sat in the shadow of our ancient trees
> While the waters of the land washed
> Washed against our hearts,
> Cleansing, cleansing.
> The purifier sat among us
> In sackcloth and ashes,
> Bearing on himself the burdens
> of these people ....

> We walked from the beginning
> towards the land of sunset ....
> The purifier walked in our shadow
> bearing the fly-wisk [sic] of his ancestors
> for his task is not finished. (p. 54)

Though the poem maintains legendary touchstones, referring to various stages in the migration, the vision is essentially the same apocalyptic one that we find in Awoonor's other dirges. Suffering, at times, is even seen in a syncretically African and Calvinistic sense as the agent through which the timeless, utopian world is reached:

> We are the sons of the land
> bearing the terror of this journey
> carrying the million crucifixes of time ...
> We opened wide our hearts
> washed by the desert wind
> for cleansing in the sacred river
> Our dreams were of a homeland
> forever;
> Of a happier world. (pp. 56-57)

In comparing his poetry with Christopher Okigbo's, Awoonor has noted that they arrived at a similar blend of form derived from English and traditional African poetry, though they came at this from different directions. Where Okigbo first wrote poetry closely modeled after Yeats, Pound, and Eliot, Awoonor wrote poetry very close to Ewe oral literature. Often he first wrote his poems in Ewe and then worked out English translations.[17] As he began to be influenced by English poetry he also asserted his own independence from traditional forms. This in no way entailed a complete break; on the contrary, the basis of much, if not most of his poetry is still in traditional lyrics. Rather it meant that instead of simply imitating these lyrics, he could comfortably draw from them, as well as English poetry, in writing verse that is simultaneously an expression of his own personal experience and his community's. While the poetry in *Night of My Blood* is not organized in a strictly chronological sequence based on when the poems were written, the sequence does reflect this growth.

Here we have yet another dimension of the ritual movement from insufficiency to fulfillment, the poet's own initiation into his art. "The Years Behind," one of the early poems in the unit that begins with "I Heard a Bird Cry" and culminates with "Hymn to My Dumb Earth," reflects the poet's new awareness in a singularly poignant lyric that accepts the passing of an early naiveté while invoking the ancestors for strength to bear this new sensibility. On the most obvious level, this is a poem about the modern African caught between Africa and the West and coming into an awareness of the power that is inherent in his liminal position; but beyond that, it is a poem about the poet in Africa, "the purifier" who has accepted the fly-whisk of his sacred office and is now aware of the paradoxical centrality of that office vis-à-vis his society and the concomitant alienation of the individual who fills it. It is, of course, because of the alienation, the liminality, that he has the power to be the harbinger of a new order. Socially, in other words, he is an exile, but in that exile he has learned that which puts him at the center of the societal structure, the center of his culture.

The poem begins with an echo of Shakespeare's Enobarbus describing Cleopatra:

> Age they say cannot wither the summer smiles
> nor will the trappings of our working clothes
> change into the glamour of high office. (p. 59)

The *persona* has turned from the material aspirations of his youth, aspirations perhaps sharpened at first by his being away. His attention is drawn towards the neglected ancestral altar of his home and he realizes he must return:

> The palm-oil on the stone gods has turned green
> and the gods look on concerned and forgotten ....
> My life's song falls low among alien peoples
> whose songs are mingled with mine.... (p. 59)

On going back he finds his new calling as a poet synthesizing the old with the new and preparing for a new order. Effectively, the lines slide from English to Ewe style, from a highly accentual alliterative verse to the freer repetitive rhythm of traditional poetry:

> ... the tuneful reverberate is reborn,
> reborn on the tabernacle of my father's temple.
> Sew the old days for me, my fathers,
> Sew them that I may wear them
> for the feast that is coming,
> the feast of the new season that is coming. (p. 59)

Several of the poems that follow are expressions of this rebirth and the ensuing sense of newly found power. In "Stop the Death-Cry" the poet-shaman talks of a willingness to be a sacrifice for his people, "... I stood at death's door/and knocked throughout the night./Have patience and I shall pay the debt" (p. 62). But the initiatory process is not yet complete, and he must leave to further prepare his gods. Only with a very thorough process of mortification can the shaman be ready, and "More Messages" deals with his perseverance and his hope:

> I can go placing maggots on those fires
> fanning the innerwards: I can sneak
> along like crawling beetles
> Seeking through dust and dirt
> the lonely miracle of redemption ...
>
> Will they let me go
> and pick the curing herbs behind fallen huts
> to make our cure, their cure? (pp. 65-66)

Then, "At the Gates" shows the poet fully prepared to enter his homeland bearing the boon he has brought from his exile:

> Open the gates, my mother's children,
> and let me enter.
> Our thunder initiates have run amok
> and we sleep in the desert land ...
>
> ... for all that I have done
> I bear the magic of the singer that has come.... (pp. 68-69)

Interspersed among these poems are a few seemingly incongruous lyrics celebrating sensuality ("The Dance") and brotherhood ("All Men My Brothers" and "The Noble Herd"). Yet in the three penultimate poems, "Lament of the Silent Sister," "This Earth, My Brother," and especially in "Hymn to My Dumb Earth," sensuality and brotherhood are clearly introduced as factors that transcend the sheer agony of lamentation, showing that beyond our immediate suffering there must be an ultimate joy, and that through our suffering we become linked with our fellow man in both a local and universal sense of community. The apocalyptic joy, as expressed in the sensual imagery, and the goal of a newly forged community become, in fact, one and the same thing. In "Lament of the Silent Sister," his poem for Christopher Okigbo, this is clearly seen in the apocalyptic turn the sensual imagery takes at the end of the poem:

> ... As he pierced my agony
> with his cry, my river burst into flood.
> My shores reeled and rolled

to the world's end, where they say
at the world's end the graves are green. (p. 77)

This vision, moreover, is reasserted at the end of "This Earth, My Brother":
"and my mountains reel and roll/to the world's end" (p. 81).

Without being destroyed, the vision is grounded in a strong corresponding sense of the reality of political unrest in Africa, unrest that has led to the
deaths of Okigbo and others and crushed earlier hopes of unity:

The dawn crack of sounds known
rending our air
shattering our temples toppling
raising earthwards our cathedrals of hope,
In demand of lives offered on those altars
for the cleansing that was done long ago. (p. 78)

The sense of reality leads to an ironic tone in "Hymn to My Dumb Earth"
that comes dangerously close to negating the vision the poet has established.
There is even at times an angry bitterness that runs through the poem, the
bitterness of a Moses returning from the mountain to find his people in
chaos:

Slow, slow rock not the boat
baa baa black sheep have you any wool was the theme song
of the cantata in which the patients fled

the hospital
for they said he operated every case including fever.
A man with hernia jumped over a six-foot wall
trekked eighty miles to his home town
to die ....

He wrote the anthem Uncle Philip
One day in his lagoon home at home
for the nation. There were yells, Ashanti yells.
The politicians removed them,
that all may be one.
United we stand.
Divided we stand.
Everything comes from God. (p. 82-83)

But the bitterness dissolves into the anguish of a lament for the land, anguish
which is again followed by hope for reunion that the dissolution enables:

Then my mother's only daughter died.
They wailed, beat their hands
over their mouths;
Ao, when you go, where you are going
tell them tell the ancestors
that the trees in the fences were eaten
by termites ...

I hear Thy welcome voice
I am coming Lord.
Dear one, hold on
for I come. (pp. 94-95)

Between the statements of bitterness and hope we are given flashes of the exile's experiences in England, Paris, New York and Moscow, all areas of preparation for his return. The three penultimate laments are sung, as it were, "at the gates," the point at which the novel, *This Earth, My Brother* begins. Amamu's journey within his country completes the sacrificial journey begun in exile. Yet the final poem here, "They Do Not Sound for Me," is of one who will not pass beyond the gates. Apparently contradicting the idea of fulfillment and complete return that we have come to expect, the poem actually affirms the poet's paradoxical position of marginality and centrality in his society. The main pulse and action of society is continuously distant from the poet:

Fetish drums sounding away
Many songs did the initiates begin
in Kleve. Where are they?

Where are they? Where did they pass
with these songs
and drums and songs and dance? (p. 96)

This is his fulfillment, for it is he who now also has the sensitivity to hear and the power to interpret those sounds for his society:

they sound in top voice hand beating
over mouth
revealing to me always
The messages of far away. (p. 96)

Writing of his own field work with traditional Ewe poets, Awoonor has said he "was immensely struck by the discovery that each poet within the oral tradition is a distinct individual, propelled by a deep sense of loneliness and an overwhelming ennui...."[18] He later goes on to add that "most poet-cantors are plagued by ... a deep feeling that they are not in the mainstream of the human family. They neither make great farmers nor great fishermen; and in a society where leaders are men of action and of measurable success, poet-cantors, even though they may be respected, are never among the aristocracy of leaders."[19] These feelings, along with a feeling of continuous proximity to death, make the dirge perhaps the most poignant of their poetry, and a stanza that he quotes from one of the dirge poets he studied clearly establishes the close ties this poetry has with his own:

Xexeame fe dzogoedzi nyea mele
Nye mele amewoamewo kasa o
Amesiwo mye aklamatowo wokpo dome no
Heno anyi de me nu
Wogblobe nudzi gee nyea meyi
Vinoko, mayi tsyie made nu di

I am on the world's extreme corner
I am not sitting in the row with the eminent
Those who are lucky sit in the middle
Sitting and leaning against a wall
They say I came to search,
I, Vinoko, can only go beyond and forget.[20]

There is the same feeling of solitude and alienation in the poetry of Wole Soyinka, and it grows out of a similar sense of continuous proximity to death. This is defined in terms of Ogun's violent and defiant relation to death as opposed to the calmer, more controlled acceptance of death implicit in Awoonor's laments. As I have already noted, where in Awoonor it is death that is the transforming factor in his poetic rite of passage, for Soyinka it is the violence that is particular to Ogun.

Here is precisely where their sensibilities converge, for it is in these rites of passage that they see their poetic steel being tempered. To switch to a linguistic metaphor, the surface structure of Awoonor's poetry is built around the rituals of death as expressed in his reinterpretation of the traditional dirge or lament, while Soyinka's poetry is built around the rituals of Ogun as expressed in his reinterpretation of the myths of Ogun. Nevertheless, though the forms are different, the substance — namely the deep structure — is the same. In each case the poetry is a symbolic expression of a rite of renewal coming out of the poet's solitary journey. Awoonor writes of the need to "Sew the old days" (p. 59), and Soyinka writes of "the ideal fusion — to preserve the original uniqueness and yet absorb another essence" (p. 86n). These are two expressions of the same vision.

I have shown how Awoonor's poetry has dealt with several layers of cyclic regeneration, the poet himself going into exile and returning, the past society in its long migration, and the present society in which the ritual process continues. Another critic has already shown that a similar layering is found in Soyinka's poem, "Idanre."[21] However, these poets are not dealing with a simple repetition of an unchanging process, but with continual reinterpretation of it. The process can even be seen as having an analogical relation to the poet as maintainer of tradition and instigator of change. Once again we face the paradox of marginality and centrality that we find in the poet's relation to his society. Analogically, the ritual process he expresses in his work is central to the society insofar as it is an expression of the society's unchanging spiritual needs. To the extent that it does this it serves to maintain the existant social order, but in addition, the process is a means by which change can be contemplated and is often effected. Thus too we have seen that Egbo, Amamu, and the man are all very typical of their societies in terms of the social positions they hold; it is simply their unwavering pursuit of a spirituality that also sets them apart.

On the back of the manuscript of "Idanre" in the British Museum, Bernth Lindfors found a note written by Soyinka in which Soyinka's typically cryptic manner puts this paradox into the perspective of his poetry:

> For a long time, I could not accept why Ogun, the Creative God should also be the agency of death. Interpretation of his domain, the Road, proved particularly depressing and symbolically uninspiring especially inasmuch as the road is so obviously part of this same cyclic order. I know of nothing more futile, more monotonous or boring than a circle.
>
> My contact with the "Mobius strip," a mathematical circle full of infinite configurations would of itself, have remained purposeless but for an awareness of Ogun's essence — a scientific as well as an artistic spirit. Then only was it possible to experience his passions in terms of a total human significance, embracing both continuity and equilibrium. It became possible to accept Death and creativity not on that revolting cyclic level, but as incidents within occupations, the most trivial of which far exceed the *knowledge* of Death and the accident of Birth.[22]

While the full import of this statement is difficult to ascertain, the general thrust is that he has found in the myths of Ogun a poetic archetype that holds the infinite series of binary opposites that express the paradoxical spirit of man, namely his "circle full of infinite configurations." The most general of these configurations (read binary opposites) is that of "continuity and equilibrium," other parallel ones being life/death, hot/cool, progress/stasis, creativity/stagnation, creation/destruction, etc. We have, in short, an expression of mysticism not unlike Blake's "The Marriage of Heaven and Hell." Ogun is both a master carver and a killer of men. It is through the bloody carnage of his own men that he comes to his great creative wisdom. As William Blake would have put it, "The road of excess leads to the palace of wisdom."

The first section of *Idanre*, "of the road," begins at dawn with an imagistic poem of a palm tree. Everything here is Ogun's: the place, the hour and the tree itself. Against the morning sky the tree even appears as an image of the god:

Blood-drops in the air, above
The even belt of tassels, above
Coarse leaf teasing on the waist, steals
The lone intruder, tearing wide

The chaste hide of the sky

O celebration of the rites of dawn
Night-spread in tatters and a god
Received, aflame with kernals. ("Dawn," p. 9)

The poem, in effect, is the poet's invocation to this primal artisan, who in his solitary, fierce and violent mien, is as creative as he is dangerous.

"Death in the Dawn" is the logical follow-up to the invocation. An early morning journey to Lagos becomes part of "the rites of dawn," a propitiatory ritual for Ogun in which the traveller hits a white cockerel with his car and then passes an accident and a dead man. Grim though the ritual is, it presages a passage that encompasses fulfillment as well as danger. The traveller can only hope that the passage will be a safe one, but there is no question of his having to make the journey nor of the results of a successful passage:

The right foot for joy, the left, dread
And the mother prayed, Child
May you never walk
When the road waits, famished.
Traveller you must set forth
At dawn
I promise marvels of the holy hour
Presages as the white cock's flapped.
Perverse impalement — as who would dare
The wrathful wings of man's progression.... (p. 11)

"Around Us, Dawning" and "Luo Plains" shift from the dread to the joy, from the agony to the fulfillment of Ogun's hour. The traveller finds himself filled with a new sense of power and energy, though there is a self-consciousness here that prevents the poems from being entirely convincing:

> The mountains range in spire on spire
> Lances at the bold carbuncle
> On the still night air. I am light honed
>
> To a still point in the incandescent
> Onrush, a fine ash in the beast's sudden
> Dessication when the sun explodes. ("Around Us, Dawning," p. 12)

The final poem of this section, "In Memory of Segun Awolowo," is a transitional one bridging the opening ritual of Ogun and the studies of liminality in the sections that precede "Idanre." Segun Awolowo was a son of Chief Obafemi Awolowo, the well-known Nigerian politician. A close friend of Soyinka's, he was killed in a car accident, and like Sekoni in *The Interpreters* he is seen as a victim of Ogun:

> Death the scrap-iron dealer
> Breeds a glut on trade. The fault
> Is His of seven paths whose whim
> Gave Death his agency. (p. 14)[23]

Yet Awolowo has now become a grey specter of the dawn, a being between life and death as liminal as Ogun himself. In bearing the anguish of this state he is like one of Awoonor's "lost souls ... at the gate":

> They make complaint
>
> Grey presences of head and hands
> Who wander still
> Adrift from understanding. (p. 15)

While only the first and last sections, "of the road" and "Idanre," deal overtly with the myth of Ogun, the entire collection can be seen as an exploration into facets of his personality, into the characteristics he bears as an archetypical liminal *persona*. Both the book and the title poem are divided into seven sections, the sacred number of Ogun, who is said to have seven personalities. The number itself would seem to be arbitrary,[24] since the archetype really embodies an infinite series of relationships, but the sections frame the most salient ones: "of the road" focuses on Ogun's violence, the primary characteristic of his creative essence; "lone figure" then turns to the alienation and the regenerative powers of the asocial and ahistorical figure, namely the mythic hero (in one sense there is no difference between freak and mythic hero — both are liminal *personae*); "of birth and death" plunges us deeper into the contradictions in liminality, into the almost overwhelming tensions of the life/death opposition; "for women" releases us from this tension, complementing the "hot," violent masculine side of Ogun with the "cool" contemplative feminine side;[25] "grey seasons" goes further into the "cool" and looks at the result, the harvest that follows the violent assertion (Ogun's rage) and the creative release (rain); "october '66," a section presaging war, returns to Ogun's violence, but in the larger perspective of the relation of the liminal figure to society, his ability to face dissolution and thus forestall the collapse of society (the scapegoat ritual); and in "Idanre" Soyinka pulls these disparate elements together, both the "hot" and the "cool" of Ogun, into a unified experience of the poet's journey into the night and his return at dawn. In other words, all seven sections function paradigmatically as discrete units which explore the structure of liminality, while the first section, and to a greater extent the seventh section additionally function syntagmatically, for they not only define Ogun as an archetypal unified sensibility but also examine the ritual process that the liminal figure (poet as well as Ogun) is engaged in.

The absence of Ogun per se in the five central sections can thus be explained by the metaphorical intensity of the pattern. My argument becomes somewhat tautological here, but the existence of such a pattern explains as metaphor what otherwise remains a collection of brilliant, though apparently unrelated poems. "The Dreamer" and "The Hunchback of Dugbe," both from the section "lone figure," deal with individuals as disparate as Christ and a freak in an Ibadan market. Having little obvious relation to one another, they would seem to have even less to Ogun. Yet there is an area of contiguity in their liminality. They bear the anguish of being different and separate from society, of having to live on "the fourth stage" of existence. In writing of these other "lone figures" in addition to Ogun, Soyinka is expanding Ogun into an archetype via the shared characteristics. The lines "Higher than trees a cryptic crown/Lord of the rebel three" are an obvious reference to Christ, but if we see them in terms of Soyinka's interpretation of Yoruba mythology, the reference is also, though less directly, to Ogun. In the poem "Idanre" Soyinka brings in two rebels of Yoruba mythology in apposition to Ogun, who nevertheless is clearly above them in the Yoruba pantheon. Of Ajantala we are told that he is the "archetype of the rebel child, iconoclast, anarchic, anti-clan, anti-matriarch, virile essence in opposition to womb-domination" (p. 87*n*). The other, Atọ́da, was "slave to first deity. Either from pique or revolutionary ideas he rolled a rock down onto his unsuspecting master, smashing him to bits and creating the multiple godhead" (p. 87n). While the reference to myrrh and nails relates to Christ, the central image of the poem regarding the fruit born out of suffering fits Ogun no less than it does Christ:

> The fruit will fall to searchers
> Cleansed of mould
> Chronicles of gold
> Mourn a fruit in prime.
>
> The burden bowed the boughs to earth ...
> And bitter pods gave voices birth.... (p. 17)

Looking at "The Hunchback of Dugbe" in terms of Yoruba mythology I am reminded of Orishanla who purposely makes all freaks and keeps them sacred to him that they may worship him.[26] Nevertheless, this "calmest nudist/Of the roadside lunatics" is also a reflection of another aspect of Ogun, the quiet, lonely Ogun after the slaughter of his men. It is an image of one whose experience has not only put him beyond the realm of men, but also beyond words, beyond the possibility of any expression of the experience:

> Not in disdain, but in truth immune
> From song or terror, taxi turns
> And sale fuss of the mad, beyond
> Ugliness or beauty, whom thought-sealing
> Solemnly transfigures — the world
> Spins on his spine, in still illusion. (pp. 18-19)

The poems "of birth and death" take us to the center of this "thought-sealed" area, *contra mundum*, the mythic world where the mundane oppositions are harmonized. The tumbling meter of the chant "Koko Oloro" breaks down any rational response to the paradoxical monition to "Taste this soil for death and plumb her deep for life" ("Dedication," p. 24), the celebration of "A First Deathday," the actions of the Abiku, or the hymns to old age and death ("To My First White Hairs" and "Post Mortem"). The paradoxical nature of these poems is highlighted by the fact that formally they are among the most derived of Soyinka's poems, owing much to T.S. Eliot, Gerard Manley Hopkins, Dylan Thomas, John Skelton, and perhaps W.H. Auden and others. Imagistically and symbolically, however, they are among the most inaccessible to a Western reader.

Having earlier looked at two poems from this section, we might consider the final one, "Post Mortem." Modeled somewhat after "Pied Beauty," the poem is seemingly a negation of Hopkins's praise of God, life and the mottled colors of nature:

> there are more functions to a freezing plant
> than stocking beer; cold biers of mortuaries
> submit their dues, harnessed — glory be! ...
>
> let us love all things of grey; grey slabs
> grey scalpel, one grey sleep and form,
> grey images. (p. 31)

However, the praise of "all things of grey," namely of death, is in effect praise of the process of transformation for which death stands. Death, the final rite of passage in life, is but the first in another area of existence. It is a process of bridging, which from the opening poems has become associated with Ogun. The grey of this poem is thus a link with the "Grey presences" of the earlier poems and those of the fifth section, "grey seasons." The color is progressively more evocative as we move from the shock of violent confrontation with death into the heart of the paradox of death and through the rebirth that the process affords. We have here the metaphor writ large, the paradigm of separation, initiation and return that Soyinka explores syntagmatically in "Idanre."

The poems in "for women" and "grey seasons" are the "coolest" poems of the collection for they are at the still center of the ritual process following the "hot" poems of return. That is, between the very personal confrontation with the violence "of the road" and the confrontation with violence in the community in "october '66," we have poems that deal with the transformation of anguish into love and into a larger understanding of life. Here is forged the boon that enables the *persona* of "Civilian and Soldier" to face the soldier's gun:

> I hope some day
> Intent upon my trade of living, to be checked
> In stride by your *apparition* in a trench,
> Signalling, I am a soldier. No hesitation then
> But I shall shoot you clean and fair
> With meat and bread, a gourd of wine
> A bunch of breasts from either arm, and that
> Lone question — do you friend, even now, know
> What it is all about? (p. 53)

The dominant image in these poems is water, which as we saw in the preceding chapter is a symbol among the Yoruba of "coolness." Moreover, "coolness" according to Thompson is virtually synonymous with love.[27] The first poems of "for women" establish a contrast between pain and water, anguish and love in simple nursery-rhyme stanzas:

> Deserted markets
> Runnels of rain
>
> Seeds fill your gutters
> And a long night of pain. ("Song: Deserted Markets," p. 33)
>
> moist the quickening consciousness
> sealed in warm mis-shapenness
>
> ivory granaries are filled
> a prize of pain will be fulfilled. ("Psalm," p. 34)

In "Bringer of Peace" this rain/pain contrast is clearly expanded as a contrast between the "hot" and the "cool":

> You come as light rain not to quench
> But question out the pride of fire.... (p. 37)

And the "cool" is further seen as the means by which one can cope with "the anguish of severance":

> You come as light rain, swift to soothe
> The rent in earth with deft intrusion
> To test your peace on a hiss of ashes
> Your sky of lakes on thirsts of embers
>
> ... your rain, a tacit lie of stillness
> A smile to test the python's throes, a touch
> To bring the bowstring's nerve to rest. (p. 37)

Then in the poem, "In Paths of Rain," Soyinka refers to "the chronicle of severance" (p. 40), an allusion to his own interpretation of Yoruba mythology as later developed in "The Fourth Stage." The contextual meaning of the line is not very clear, but it would seem to also refer to what he is "telling" in *Idanre*, though the verb used in apposition to the above phrase is "till." The words are, of course, close enough for this to be a misprint. The final poem in this section, "By Little Loving," supports this reading. For the chronicle he is telling is of the primal separation between man and man as well as that between man and gods. This once again is the gap Ogun dared to bridge:

> The paradox of crowds set a marble wall
> Where I fled for keeping. Loneliness feeds
> On open faces — once by little seeing, fell
> To the still centre, off the ruptured wheel
>
> Of blood. And this, the accident of flesh I hailed
> Man's eternal lesson — by little yearning to unwind
> Cords of closeness. (p. 41)

The rainy season, the fertile period of growth, along with the harvest that follows, belongs to Ogun. The epitome of dynamic energy, he is not one who can rest for long. Growth and fulfillment require that one does not stay at "the still centre" or fail to make the return. The *persona* of "grey seasons" sees himself as a prisoner trapped in walls of ennui: "sadness/Closed him, rootless, lacking cause" ("Prisoner," p. 44). The rain and "coolness" that has healed the rents of violence is now something from which he must escape:

> Queen of night torments, you strain
> Sutures of song to bear imposition of the rites
> Of living and of death. You
>
> Pluck strange dirges from the storm
> Sift rare stones from ashes of the moon, and ride
> Night errands to the throne of anguish ...
>
> Too much pain, oh midwife at the cry
> Of severance ...
>
> I would be free of your tyranny.... (p. 47).

The return, however, is not the harvest that was hoped for in "Season," but a bloody perversion of the ritual, a confrontation with violence that threatens dissolution of the community:

> Unbidden offering on the lie of altars
> A crop of wrath when hands retract and reason falters
>
> No feast but the eternal retch of human surfeit
> No drink but dregs at reckoning of loss and profit.... ("Ikeja, Friday, Four O'Clock," p. 49)

The poem on the death of Fajuyi, a young idealistic Yoruba military officer who was killed late in 1966 as a result of his attempts to heal the rents of political severance that were occurring in Nigeria, is both a lament for what has happened to the land and reaffirmation of what the strength of Ogun means beyond the sheer terror of his violence. As in "Civilian and Soldier" the *persona* moves beyond the shock of what he has encountered on his return:

> ... journeys must end.
> Home, forgotten is the bridge ...
>
> Weeds triumph. What goals for pilgrim feet
> But to a dearth of wills ...
>
> Who seeks breath of him
> Tread the span of bridges, look not down to gravestones. (p. 54)

In "Idanre" the timeless, mythical pattern that Ogun represents is imposed upon a real physical journey of the poet. Soyinka's own words make this clear in his preface to the poem: "'Idanre' is the record of that walk through wet woods on the outskirts of Molete, a pilgrimage to Idanre in company of presences such as dilate the head and erase known worlds" (p. 57). The poem is in effect a fugue which plays variations of the theme established in the preceding six sections. Where the earlier poems simply cut across time, this poem also goes through time, harmoniously fusing the diachronic reality of the mundane world with the synchronic reality of myth. The *persona* sees Sango in the thunder storm, sees him hurling his thunderbolts to the ground and sees Ogun in the giant towers that hold the high tension wires among the Idanre hills and catch Sango's electricity during the storm. The walk becomes, as it were, an initiatory experience in which the poet becomes a priest of Ogun.

Little else about "Idanre" need be said here since a fairly solid explication has been written along the lines I have been discussing.[28] There is, however, one very important point I touched on earlier that needs further elaboration. Taken separately, the first six sections of the book *Idanre* can be seen as a cycle of poems beginning and ending with the carnage of Ogun. It forms a pessimistic view of man locked in the recurrent cycle of his own stupidity. "Idanre" is a similar cycle of poems, but it ends with a twist, an optimistic note. In fact, "Idanre" should probably be seen as the seventh section, the section which makes the entire collection a non-cycle to the extent that it breaks the cycle with its implicit apocalyptic vision.[29] I spoke of the first six sections being metaphorical in that they represent the recurrent pattern of creation/destruction that Ogun embodies. "Idanre" repeats this pattern in its first five sections, but the sixth and seventh break out of it. The Mobius strip there becomes a symbol of the poet's reinterpretation of the myth of Ogun — in fact a metonym for the god, replacing the traditional symbol of the self-devouring snake which, for Soyinka, stands for an endless process of repetition. The point was important enough to Soyinka that aside from the manuscript notes I referred to, he had a detailed explanation of his use of the Mobius strip printed with the poem:

> A symbol of optimism ... as it gives the illusion of a "kink" in the circle and a possible centrifugal escape from the eternal cycle of karmas that has become the evil history of man. Only an illusion but a poetic one, for the Mobius strip is a very simple figure of aesthetic and scientific truths and contradictions. In this sense, it is the symbol of Ogun in particular, an evolution from the tail-devouring snake which he sometimes hangs around his neck and symbolizes the doom of repetition. (pp. 87-88*n*)

Lacking the vague, strained quality of the earlier positive assertions regarding dawn in "Around Us, Dawning" and "Luo Plains," the closing stanzas of "Idanre" are the clear, self-confident statements of a prophet possessed of a newly received vision of "A dawn of bright procession." Here is the obverse of his statement in "Post Mortem," and not surprisingly he turns once again to the rhythms of Hopkins to frame his vision of abundance. Nor is Ogun any less at the center of this vision for "the first fruits," his favorite foods, corn and palm wine,[30] are set aside for him:

> ... corn sheaves rose over the hill
> Long before the bearers, domes of eggs and flesh
> Of palm fruit, red, oil black, froth flew in sun bubbles
> Burst over throngs of golden gourds.... (p. 85)

Awoonor and Soyinka are indeed poets who stand astride two worlds, but neither of these worlds would be entirely strange to the traditional poets who preceded them. For Awoonor the conflict between Africa and the West that the modern African experiences provides a metaphor for the eternal ontological gap between men everywhere. For Soyinka the West provides new poetic forms within which he can express his reinterpretation of Yoruba mythology. There is a dynamic tension between his forms and the myths he expresses, but this only serves to highlight the tensions, the paradoxes that the myths themselves incorporate. To read these poets is to experience "the fragmenting process ... the deep black whirlpool of mythopoeic forces," to understand the nature of the experience, and to "emerge wiser, powerful from the draught of cosmic secrets."[31] Their concern is thus with the nature of liminality and their imagery, overwhelmingly of death and rebirth, focuses on the process of transformation, the process of bridging the ontological interstices that all of us face.

The Mythic Dimension of Soyinka's *The Trials of Brother Jero*: The Writer as Fantasist

Wole Soyinka undoubtedly enjoys his role as iconoclastic social and literary critic. First he attacked the Francophone writers in his famous négritude-tigritude remark in Kampala, and then in Stockholm he also turned on the Anglophone writers who seemed to be overly concerned with an ethical consciousness, their didactic realism. Later he wrote a scathing exposé of the Nigerian military government of the late sixties in *The Man Died*,[1] an account of his detention during the Nigerian-Biafran War. Certainly his plays are no less polemical. He will, as in *The Dance of the Forests*, attack any attempt to foolishly glorify the past; or he will unleash his satiric barbs at those who, as Lakunle in *The Lion and the Jewel*, would seek only to praise the merits of technology at the expense of traditional society.

Even where he appears to be most contradictory and inconsistent in what he writes, Soyinka has one major concern that lends unity to all his work. He is always angered at the misuse of power and office whether by a poet or a politician. In his creative writing this is usually translated into a theme dealing either with the perversion or revitalization of myth and ritual. I have just shown that *Idanre* deals with the latter while *The Interpreters* shows a group of young intellectuals struggling with the social and political forces that threaten to pervert the ritual basis of their society. Repeatedly, Soyinka has made the point that this basis is so real, so integral a part of the society it cannot be avoided or ignored, but only used or abused. Thus Sagoe in *The Interpreters* notes that the corruption that had been a part of Sir Derinola's life extends even into the ceremony of his death. What is supposed to be a ritual that bridges differences serves only to accentuate them. Observing Derinola's gaudy funeral procession, and thinking of the feast to follow, Sagoe wryly comments that one could spend his life living off funerals. Then he also sardonically notes the imposition on the poor as Derinola's cortège holds up the humbler funeral led by Lazarus.[2]

The Swamp Dwellers, The Trials of Brother Jero and *The Strong Breed*, three of his earliest and shortest plays, are all seminal with respect to the way Soyinka has developed as an artist. With the notable exception of *Jero* they are dramatically weak, lacking the complexity of character and sophistication of technique in all of his longer works. Yet it is because of this simplicity that we have rather direct access to the relationship that Soyinka sees between office, ritual and myth. What he later wove into one play, *The Road*, can be seen here as three separate strands. The Professor, that incredible enigma, a paradoxical admixture of buffoon, man of words and scapegoat, is already visible in part in the unctuous Kadiye, the protean Jero and the tragic Eman. More importantly, almost all his longer plays are an intricate melding of the melodramatic, comic, and tragic forms that these three plays respectively represent.

Seen collectively and in relation to his other work, these plays reflect the fundamental interest of the mythic consciousness, the relation between life and death, and comic and the tragic. On the one hand there are characters like Jero, Sagoe, the old Bale, the Professor, Oba Danlola and Bero's father who can invert the corrupted order, create chaos and through their comic disruption revitalize society; on the other hand there are the victimizers like the Kadiye, Jaguna, Derinola, and Adenebi, who bleed society for their own ends. However, it is not only the comic figure who is able to revitalize the group, but also the sacrifice, the individual like Eman, Sekoni, Demoke, or even Ogun. The sacrifice must be a willing one, a point Soyinka stresses in *The Strong Breed*, for in the victim's willing acceptance of his role lies his commonality with the comic figure, a willful stepping out of the bounds of society. In the former case this takes the form of the sacrifice's facing annihilation, and in the latter case it is the introduction of chaos into society. The tragic figure's carrying evil out of society and the comic figure's introduction of new life are effectively two sides of the same coin, for both aid society through their contact with the numinous.

A folklorist has argued that the continual mixture and juxtapositioning of the serious and the ludic is *the* hallmark of ritual.[3] Where in everyday interaction we have distinct bounds within which those two modes of behavior tend to operate separately, much in the same way as work and play, in ritual performance these distinctions break down entirely. For the outsider who happens upon a ritual performance it all must appear like a traffic intersection where there are two policemen simultaneously directing traffic, but each in his own way. The result seems to be pure cacophony, the very antithesis of harmony and order. To an extent, this is exactly what is happening, an inversion and parody of what we would expect to find at an ordinary intersection. What is difficult for us to perceive is that if one of the policemen is creating confusion, another one is in the process of reordering the flow of traffic. Likewise, we might on first reading *The Interpreters* see only the confusion and none of the order, the havoc of Eshu and Sagoe, but not the serenity of Obatala and Bandele.

In other words, if we wish to go deeper into the mythic and ritual implications of Soyinka's work than is usually possible for an outsider, we should take into account the fact that Soyinka assumes two authorial voices, the prophetic and the fantastic, often within the same piece. What the latter heats up, the former cools down with the result that a dynamic balance is maintained between the two. This is no less true of his plays than it is of his novel. Even in *The Lion and the Jewel*, generally thought to be one of Soyinka's lightest plays, there is an undercurrent of this prophetic tone. To be sure, the play is a situational comedy drawing its humor from a reversal of audience expectations regarding the choice a young girl will make between a modern young man and an old traditional chief. Each of the three acts, however, contains a mime scene which not only corresponds to the action of the play and intensifies the comedy, but also functions antiphonally as a very serious argument for traditional life.[4] For the more complex plays, such as *A Dance of the Forests, Kongi's Harvest, The Road, Madmen and Specialists*, and *Death and the King's Horseman*, the categories of comedy and tragedy are not even appropriate, for these plays all have the tragic-comic mixture that is common to ritual.[5]

As in his collection of poems, *Idanre*, the authorial presence in *The Swamp Dwellers* and *The Strong Breed* is clearly prophetic. Both plays, however, are rather straightforward, interesting in the evolution of Soyinka's dramatic talent, but lacking the force that the prophetic voice carries in the poetry. The origins of Soyinka's genius lie in Yoruba ritual and myth and none of these early plays demonstrates this so fully as *The Trials of Brother Jero*. More than anything else, Soyinka failed to impart the other two short plays with a sense of life, and above all Jero, that archetypal fantasist, is such an overwhelming success on stage because he is so entirely alive. To find the origins then is not enough, we must also see Soyinka's particular genius at work. He never again returned to the forms he experimented with in the three short plays, but he apparently learned that his forte is comedy. Though his interest is in "serious" writing, he must have found that his prophetic voice in drama was too sharp and brittle, that only by mellowing this voice with the fantastic could he achieve a roundness and suppleness in his plays.

Relatively little critical attention has been given to *Brother Jero* despite the fact that much of the action is generally considered quite successful as comedy. The play is usually dismissed as a rather conventional farce, saved somewhat by the effective interplay of Pidgin and conventional speech, but ruined by a weak ending.[6]

Nevertheless, with the theater public, both in Nigeria and abroad, the play has proven to be one of the most popular Soyinka has written and possibly the most frequently produced.[7] As an audience we become active participants in Jero's trials. The play opens with Jero speaking directly to us, telling us about himself. We learn that he is "a prophet by birth and by inclination" and has worked his way up against a lot of competition from others in his field as well as the modern diversions which keep his "wealthier patrons at home." In short, he tells us that he views his work as a profession that happens to be his chosen one by virtue of his extraordinary ability to gain money and power through his practice of it. Three of the five scenes in the play begin in a similar fashion with Jero addressing us and confiding in us secrets of his business. Since Brother Jero has told us much more than he would dare tell any of his usual patrons, this does more than merely set the point of view from which we are going to view the rest of the action. We are conned into letting him lead us through a day in his life and even into conspiring with him as he moves his other pawns around.

This relationship of Jero to us is central to any analysis of the comedy, for the humor is the result of Soyinka's having woven at least three things into this pattern of which we are so integral a part. Jero is a trickster whose verbal skills and clever machinations foster satire which is political, social, and personal (authorial self-parody). Though much of the play is very topical, the timeless, mythic dimension of Jero takes us beyond the three-dimensional bounds of a good situational comedy.

Trickster stories are extremely common throughout all of West Africa. In fact, the trickster may be seen as a popular hero whose triumphs are due more to "shrewdness and cunning ... than ... steadiness and industriousness, as in European tales."[8] In West Africa he usually has the attributes which Melville J. and Francis S. Herskovits ascribe to Legba, the Dahomean trickster. Legba is a major deity in the Dahomean pantheon and was chosen by his mother, the creator, to be the linguist of the gods. The Herskovits explain "that while he dupes others, he is rarely duped himself. His activity, again, is calculated, highly conscious. His acts are rarely impulsive, but for the most are directed toward the achievement of a well-defined end. He knows socially accepted values even when he behaves contrary to them; he is in no wise the source of them."[9]

The relation of this figure to Jero becomes quite clear when we compare Jero with the Yoruba counterpart to Legba, Eshu-Elegba. The prophet Jero, like Eshu, is something of a mediator between men and god(s); they are independent spirits, subservient to no one. The similarity of these two can be noticed from the moment the curtain rises, for Jero's dress bespeaks a veritable personification of Eshu. His hair is described as "thick and high" and his appearance "suave."[10] Soon we learn of his general attraction to women and of their attraction to him. Eshu is also always depicted as having long hair. In fact, in sculpture his hair is often shaped as a phallus indicative of his association with libidinous energy. Moreover, Jero's divine rod can be seen as corresponding to the club that Eshu carries, an object which is also symbolic of general, as well as sexual, power and aggression.[11]

Susan Yankowitz sees Jero's control of his flock as paralleling Amope's domination of Chume. Her conclusion is that Soyinka shows "religion itself is an emasculating force that supports man's impulse to escape the responsibility of his manhood."[12] While this element of false religion is satirized in the play, it should be understood in terms of the significance of the trickster figure in Yoruba society. Joan Wescott's comments on Eshu are particularly illuminating here:

> ... he is the principle of chance and uncertainty.... By postulating Eshu-Elegba, the Yoruba compensate for the rigidity of their social system on the one hand, and externalize responsibility for any disruption that might occur on the other .... Thus the autonomous Eshu, a creature of instinct and of great energy and power, serves a dual role: as a rule-breaker he is, as it were, the spanner in the social works, and beyond this he is a generating symbol who promotes change by offering opportunities for exploring what possibilities lie beyond the *status quo*. He is also a satirist who dramatizes the dangers which face men and the follies to which they are prone....[13]

In light of this we can see that Jero is not simply a rogue to be scorned, but a figure to be admired. Our relationship to him is thus as paradoxical as his dual role. At the end of the play Chume cries out: "O God, wetin a do for you wey you go spoil my life so? Wetin make you vex for me so? I offend you?" (p. 75). The implicit answer to his question is simply, "Nothing." The element of chance has been at work in the form of Jero, and with Chume's life it has unfortunately played havoc. In this there is no question of right or wrong action, for chance is clearly amoral.

I would undoubtedly be very hard-pressed to find any specific trickster tales that Soyinka has drawn on for this play, but that is beside the point. What is important is that he has created Jero out of a relatively large oral tradition in which such figures play a major role. Such a tradition quite obviously establishes which comic patterns work well and which figures are most successful in a story. Stories which are not very good are soon forgotten.

Jero lives by outwitting others. There are moments when his tricks get him into trouble, but in the end he is in control of things. He almost gets caught by Amope at the beginning, but manages to slip away. Later Chume catches on to his tricks and almost gets back at him, but Jero's mind as well as his feet are too fast for his opponents, and we see in the end that Chume will be carried off to the lunatic asylum. Much of our attachment to Jero can be accounted for in this archetypal pattern. Quite simply, we enjoy seeing someone manipulate others with his wits.

It is no accident that Jero is the most articulate character in the play. Nor, for that matter, is it merely coincidental that Legba is the linguist of the gods. Both these tricksters use their linguistic talents to exercise power and gain control over people. Note, for example, how Jero handles the politician in the last scene. The man at first has no time for Jero, but Jero has observed him closely and discerned his weakness. Furthermore, he knows just what to say to convince the politician that he controls his political future:

> Indeed the matter is quite plain. You are not of the Lord. And yet such is the mystery of God's ways that his favour has lighted upon you ... Minister ... Minister by the grace of God ...

> [*The Member stops dead.*]
> Yes, brother, we have met. I saw this country plunged into strife. I saw the mustering of men, gathered in the name of peace through strength. And at a desk, in a large gilt room, great men of the land awaited your decision. Emissaries of foreign nations hung on your word, and on the door leading into your office, I read the words, Minister for War.... (p. 74).

In short, Jero says exactly what the politician wants to hear. The choice and rhythm of the words serve as devastatingly effective rhetoric, yet Jero removes any doubts the politician might have about this through his flair for dramatic exits and entrances. The play closes with the politician lying prostrate before him, fully convinced that Jero is indeed a prophet.

The action of the play mainly centers around Jero's scheming to get out of paying Amope for the white velvet cape she sold him. To do this he figures it is worth relinquishing the power he exerts over Chume through not letting him beat his wife. In the end he must go further and quite literally sacrifice Chume himself, but in the process he also gains power over a more important person, the politician.

Now this is where our active participation in his scheming is important. For despite Jero's very strong archetypal appeal we could quite simply react against him when we see him destroying Chume. Naturally we feel Amope deserves everything she gets, but Chume is simply a helpless fool. A look at the asides in the scene we have just been discussing shows that our sympathy is controlled. Jero opens the scene by commenting on the politician. Through Jero's eyes he too appears as something of a fool. Jero dares us to doubt that he can draw him into his flock. The result is that we rather anxiously await seeing the rascal at work again. Later he brags to us of his success: "By tomorrow, the whole town will have heard of the miraculous disappearance of Brother Jeroboam. Testified to and witnessed by no less than one of the elected Rulers of the country ..." (p. 76). The childlike quality of this bragging reduces the act to merely a prank at which we can laugh. Moreover, we are prepared for his final aside to us: "... It is a pity about Chume. But he has given me a fright, and no prophet likes to be frightened. With the influence of that nincompoop I should succeed in getting him certified with ease. A year in the lunatic asylum would do him good anyway" (p. 77).[14] A rather harsh judgment for Chume, but since we are seeing this all through Jero's eyes we are almost inclined to accept this amorality.

The fact that we do qualify our acceptance of Jero's behavior is important. As amusing as this scene is, we are left with a rather uncomfortable feeling concerning the way in which we have been amused. Jero, after all, has not completely controlled the point of view throughout the play. Had he done so, we would have had a very simple comic play, very closely patterned after the trickster tales but lacking much of the dramatic irony and political satire that we find here.

Scenes II and IV are almost totally dominated by Chume and Amope. The one time in these scenes that we do see Jero he is in the position of making a somewhat humiliating escape from Amope. The absence of Jero's guidance at the beginning of these scenes enables us to develop a more personal perspective of the couple. We come to feel real empathy for Chume in his plight as a henpecked husband, however comic it is, for there are no redeeming qualities in his shrewish wife. By the time he leaves in Scene II we feel we would like nothing better than to see him thrash her. What is of interest to us here is the light this sheds on Jero's personality.

Jero, as we discover in Scene III, is really the cause of Chume's emasculation. Our knowledge of this, along with the view we have just had of Chume, give rise to the humor in one of the most comical dialogues in the play. Here we actually see Jero control Chume's desire to beat his wife. It is at this point that the political satire becomes rather evident. Jero's actions are a travesty of the behavior expected of a politician. Instead of ministering to Chume's need, he utilizes it to control him. Through his aside to us we learn that the same situation is true of everyone in his congregation: the man who wants to become chief, the couple that wants to live to an old age, the lady who wants children, and so on. As Jero explains to us earlier in this scene, knowing how to keep people dissatisfied is the key to power. Once people realize that they do not need you, you lose control over them.

The political machinations of Jero are exactly what we would expect of a trickster, though the opposite of what we would wish for in a politician. Like Eshu, Jero is extremely interested in money[15] as demonstrated by the fact that he sacrifices Chume for the one pound, eight shillings and ninepence he owes Amope. But money is only a means to the power that Jero enjoys, the manipulation of people. Now we expect a politician to manipulate people, but for social rather than personal ends. Eshu and Jero are completely asocial, and their actions serve only their own vanity.[16]

According to Gerald Moore, *Brother Jero* is one of Soyinka's earliest plays and was written just prior to Nigerian independence in 1960.[17] This being the case, the play is an interesting foreshadowing of the political events which followed independence. As we hear of the competition Jero has had in gaining control of his section of the beach, we think of the great political scramble wherein many tried, in the phrase then popular, to "get a piece of the cake." Two Nigerian novels of the sixties, Cyprian Ekwensi's *Jagua Nana* and Chinua Achebe's *A Man of the People*, appear to be rather accurate reflectors of the political milieu. As we can see in these novels, the attempts by the prophets to gain their beaches through the use of "women penitents to shake their bosoms in spiritual ecstasy" (p. 45) varies only slightly in style from the tactics employed by the politicians to get their "cake." This thrust at the avariciousness of the politicians is very obviously echoed in later comments on the "penitent" who believes he will be the Prime Minister of the yet to be created "Mid-North-East State" and the member of the Federal House who sees in Jero his chance to become Minister for War.

Jero, then, is a perfect parody of a politician. This trickster realizes that style is everything. Thus, he set out to create a spectacular image of himself as witnessed by his white velvet cape and the name he chose: Immaculate Jero, Articulate Hero of Christ's Crusade. Compare this name with the one which Nanga took in *A Man of the People*: Chief the Honourable Dr. M.A. Nanga, M.P., LL.D. Such empty titles were, by the way, not at all uncommon. Soyinka's implied comment is, with the addition of irony, much like the journalist's in Achebe's book. "Na waa! Nothing fit passam."[18] The goal of the politician would seem to be some type of political security comparable to Jero's artificial apotheosis at the end of the play.

In line with this image, Jero is aware that how you say something is often more important than what you say. I have already looked at Jero's talent as a rhetorician, but one further comment is noteworthy. Towards the middle of Scene III Chume is in a situation where Jero has left him alone with the congregation. One of the women falls into a religious paroxysm. After stumbling blindly for a few moments, Chume slips into the appropriate rhetoric and gains control of the congregation:

CHUME: Forgive 'am, Father.

CONGREGATION: Amen.

CHUME: Forgive us all.

CONGREGATION: Amen.

CHUME: Forgive us all.

[*And then, punctuated regularly with Amens ...*]

Yes, Father, make you forgive us all. Make you save us from palaver. Save us from trouble at home. Tell our wives not to give us trouble ...

[*The penitent has become placid. She is stretched out flat on the ground.*]

Tell our wives not to give us trouble. And give us money to have a happy home. Give us money to satisfy our daily necessities. Make you no forget those of us who dey struggle daily. Those who be clerk today, make them Chief Clerk tomorrow. Those who are Messenger today, make them Senior Service tomorrow. Yes Father, those who are Messenger today, make them Senior Service tomorrow.

[*The Amens grow more and more ecstatic.*]

Those who are petty trader today, make them big contractor tomorrow. Those who dey sweep street today, give them their own big office tomorrow. If we dey walka today, give us our own bicycle tomorrow. I say those who dey walka today, give them their own bicycle tomorrow. Those who have bicycle today, they will ride their own car tomorrow.

[*The enthusiasm of the response, becomes, at this point, quite overpowering.*]

I say those who dey push bicycle, give them big car tomorrow. Give them big car tomorrow. Give them big car tomorrow, give them big car tomorrow. (pp. 63-64)

It is obvious that the humor in this scene stems in part from Chume's unconscious parody of Jero. But in doing this Chume is also burlesquing popular political rhetoric of a chicken in every pot.

The social satire parallels the political satire and is of some interest, though it is not nearly so integral to the comedy. Part of the problem here is that it is not so evident to one unfamiliar with the rather rampant sectarianism in Nigeria.

After the missionaries had established a strong footing, Nigeria went through a situation similar to the great revival waves in America in the 18th and 19th centuries. Many people got caught up in the new religion. Rivalries broke out within, as well as between sects. The result was that by the 1960s almost every town in southern Nigeria had at least one sect which had formed from people who had broken away from the Baptists, the Anglicans, or any of the other larger sects. Then, as in America, Elmer Gantrys and Brother Jeros began soon to create even more sects. One sect, the Aladura, was especially common along the beaches. Some insight into all this can be gained from *The Interpreters* where another prophet, Lazarus, elicits several comments from Sagoe about how religion is good business.[19] Sagoe's cynicism in respect to such religion is not at all uncommon among Nigerian intellectuals.

Brother Jero, then, is the comedy of a religious fraud, the humor coming from the discrepancy between what he is and what he professes. He ministers to no one but himself, but since he is such an effective trickster and politician, we greet Brother Jero's escapades with laughter. Look at the situation in Scene IV where Amope is trying to flee from Chume's wrath. She pounds on Jero's door yelling, "Let me in or God will punish you!" Jero replies, "[sticking his fingers in his ears] Blasphemy!" (p. 69). No one in the play could be less sincere in saying this, but it is not Amope to whom this is said. She does not even hear him. It is to us — the fact that he has already told us that he is a fraud only serves to heighten the humor. We laugh because of our conspiracy with him.

The fraudulent nature of Jero the beach prophet leads us also to suspect that for Soyinka there was more than a little element of self-parody in Jero's character. While this is not perhaps so immediately important to our appreciation of the play as performed drama, it does give us further insight into the play as a literary work. If in Yoruba mythology Eshu is the leveller of gods and kings, who but Eshu can keep perspective on his own relative importance? The writer also is a trickster, a divine linguist like Eshu, and if his prophetic sensibility becomes distorted, he must always be in a position to pull back and laugh at himself.

In a sense, Jero's message was for Soyinka himself and his fellow writers, but its subtlety was apparently lost on the latter. Hence seven years later in his address at Stockholm[20] Soyinka made very explicit what he felt about the artist's misuse of his position and power in society. In particular he felt that society would always be threatened by any courtship or marriage between the artist and the politician. What he said in *Brother Jero* and in that address is that the writer who takes himself seriously as "Immaculate Jero, Articulate Hero of Christ's Crusade" is one who is concerned with phony mythologies and not with his culture. The net result of such seriousness will be the devitalization of his society, the type of emasculation and ultimate "insanity" we witnessed in Chume. Yet the artist and trickster know that style *is* everything, and to the extent they can laugh at what they are doing, they maintain the power to invert old orders and revitalize their society. In short, the argument is that the artist, like the trickster, must be a type of culture hero.

Outwardly, Jero is quite different from the heroes in Armah and Awoonor's novels. He is verbal, outgoing, consciously manipulative, and comic; they are all quiet, withdrawn, very consciously non-political, and tragic. However, they all maintain a marginal, hence problematical relation to society, sharing the experience of liminality, that "realm of pure possibility whence novel configurations of ideas and relations may arise."[21]

The question remains, how serious is Jero? Because he is such a perfect chameleon it is difficult to say, but therein also lies our answer. He shifts from one role to another with ease, and as he does so we laugh with him. Nevertheless, there is more ambiguity here than just his role shifting. There are glimpses of Jero being absolutely serious in his desire to control the politician at the end of the play. In using a trickster figure as the central character in the play, Soyinka introduced a mechanism for controlling the temperature of the satire. Throughout, the satire stays at a mild level, never getting so hot that we are unable to laugh at the folly that we ourselves have become involved in. Yet it is, after all, this folly that has resulted in Chume's being led off to an insane asylum, and despite our intimate association with Jero, we see too much of ourselves in Chume to rest comfortably in our laughter.

Ethical Consciousness and Ghanaian Popular Fiction:
A Rhetoric and Sociology of a Literature

The riddler, however playful his motivation, puts himself into an aggressive rhetorical stance vis-à-vis his audience. The riddler throws out a challenge when he asks his question and exercises power so long as he withholds the answer. If he is a clever riddler, he may employ a riddle that has more than one answer. Even if the audience guesses a correct answer, he can deny it as being *the* answer and thus maintain his power and his aggressive stance. If he is a good riddler, he may also move through a series of riddles; thus, even if the audience guesses or he tells the answer, he immediately poses a new riddle, a new challenge. The riddler, of course, can only play his aggressive game with the tacit approval of his audience. His game must be their game. Hence, there are clearly marked off times for riddling sessions. An individual who would persist in riddling in ordinary discourse without regard to sanctioned time might well be judged a madman or a fool. Conversely, the proverb user tries to minimize conflict, to conspire with his audience to find a solution to a problem through a clear and direct appeal to tradition.

To the extent that we can see works arising out of a mythic consciousness to be riddles writ large and those arising out of an ethical consciousness to be proverbs writ large, we might be able to account for rather different kinds of audience response. There have been disagreements among critics over Achebe regarding points of interpretation, but there has been little disagreement regarding the value of his work. In contrast, there have been numerous critical debates over the value of Tutuloa's and even Soyinka's work. For the most part, we can see the most controversial West African writers, especially in the West African social and cultural context, have been those I have been discussing in terms of a mythic consciousness. In their relentness questioning, their playing with and transgressing boundaries, these writers have often taxed and even alienated their audience. They have won a following, but have lost many who have become impatient with, and even angered by, their constant riddling.

While Achebe is a more uniformly popular writer than Soyinka, it is easy for the critic to lose sight of the fact that the actual audience for either an Achebe or a Soyinka is very small relative to the actual population in West Africa. This is not anything particular to West Africa as the audience for an elite literature is always relatively small. The following for such literature will always be restricted to a small percentage of individuals who have gone through a fairly high level of formal education. If we are to use the term "popular" to cover literature that truly has a mass audience, we must turn to a literature different than that written by Achebe and Soyinka. There is a popular literature in West Africa, and it is different than the elite literature, but the difference has mainly to do with formal considerations. From any kind of formal analysis the literature is simpler, less complex. From a rhetorical perspective, it can be just as complex as the elite literature. What we will also see is that the popular writers are essentially making proverbs writ large; there are no riddlers among them. To the extent that it addresses, simplifies, clarifies, and reduces the tension involved in current social problems, the popular text becomes "popular." And it always does so with reference to the accepted norms of the mass audience. Escapism may be a factor, but the mass audience longs for answers. We will be looking, then, at another dimension of the ethical consciousness, and we will do this by examining the production as well as the consumption of a popular literature.

In Ghana there are a number of popular writers who have enjoyed a large audience. Their audience abroad is nonexistent, but at home their work is accessible to the average reader. Until the severe economic problems hit Ghana in the mid seventies, the material was also inexpensive enough for the average reader to buy. It is understandable that scholars have preferred to mine the chapbook literature from the prolific writers of Onitsha, but regretable that Ghanaian popular literature has been so completely ignored. Approximately four to five times as many pamphlets have come out of Onitsha as have come out of Accra, but this is deceptive if we consider the relative populations of Nigeria and Ghana. There is, moreover, another body of popular literature in Ghana that has more sociological significance, and perhaps even more literary significance than the pamphlets: the creative writing that has been published in newspapers and magazines. The short story and the comic strip were the most common forms, but poetry and even serialized novels were published in the popular press.

My thesis here is that material factors have shaped production, form, and content of a rich body of popular literature, and by extension, an elite literature as well. I have found that a consideration of the economic, social, and political factors that have influenced both production and consumption of popular literature make it exciting to study that literature in and of itself, in addition to what the study reveals about elite literature. In both literatures I see the influence and the reflection of life.[1]

I am stating the obvious, but the obvious has been overlooked in studies such as the *Area Handbook for Ghana*,[2] a work which dismisses all written Ghanaian literature in two short paragraphs. The quality of literature produced in Ghana can be easily verified, and any evaluation of the quality must first proceed from an understanding of the context in which it was produced — not from an externally generated value judgment regarding the "critical standing." Actually, evaluation and judgment should not even be an issue; the more important question is whether or not our understanding of a literature is furthered.

In three sections I will look at a single text, at the production of popular literature, and at the historical development of the literature. More specifically, I will start with a summary and analysis of E.K. Micksen's *Woman Is Poison* to lay a base for an understanding of the rhetorical relationship between the fictional situation and the real social situation (in this case, the political situation).[3] Secondly, I will examine the way in which the literature was produced and marketed and thus explore the economic factors that influenced the literature. Finally, I will look rather closely at the factors that gave rise to a particular important period of popular writing between 1966 and 1971, and I will survey the popular literature produced in Ghana in the early seventies, showing areas of continuity with earlier written and oral literature and indicating ways in which the literature changed in order to adjust to the political and economic changes of the late sixties and early seventies.

Clearly, here is another literature which reflects an ethical consciousness. The literature is essentially realistic (certainly in terms of what it reflects of the community ethos, though at times the literature seems quite "romantic") and very didactic. Additionally, there is a relationship between the material and the culture that points to ways in which the textually more complex elite literature, both ethical and mythic, can be seen in relation to society.

E.K. Mickson's *Woman Is Poison* is a novelette published in Accra in 1968. It is the story of a woman, Janet, who is the mistress of a wealthy Ghanaian businessman and later his third wife. When she falls in love with an employee of her husband, she poisons the husband and takes his money from his Swiss bank accounts. The story opens after the murder and moves toward justice being done, with Janet captured, tried, and sent to prison. As in most Ghanaian novelettes, there is little attempt at creating any suspense. We are told at the outset what has been done and what lesson we are to learn from the events. Immediately following the title page is part of a letter that tells the story in as explicit a manner as we find in the rest of the novelette:

Sweet Alex,

... To prove to you that I am in earnest about this, I am today confiding in you alone that it was I who killed, poisoned, or murdered Mr. Tuffuor. And I did that because of love; because of the burning love I had, and still have for you, and because I wanted to marry you, which I knew was practically impossible as long as Mr. Tuffuor was alive.... It is very rare for a woman to propose marriage to a man. But when that does happen, then you must realize that the kind of love which that woman has for the man of her heart is also very rare indeed.

And so, please, don't let me down.

Janet

In case we miss the point about what the theme will be, we are given a quotation which follows the table of contents, a quotation that also concludes the story itself: "... Truly, woman is poison. And the moment you begin to move with a woman, you must know you are moving with poison." Minus "the sordid details," the rest is simply an elaboration and amplification of what we have already been given.

The elaboration and amplification, however, come close to making explicit a connection between political hygiene and the mortification of the flesh. We learn that after they are married, Janet and Mr. Tuffuor live the good life, making frequent visits to the Hotel Continental in Accra, Abidjan in the Ivory Coast, Switzerland, Paris and Niagara Falls. Then follows the bizarre note that they even fly to Dallas when Kennedy is assassinated just to see where he was shot. In the next paragraph we are informed that Kumasi and all of Ghana is shocked three years later to learn of Tuffuor's death. Perhaps it is only coincidence that this was also the time of Nkrumah's ouster, an event not even mentioned in the story. Yet despite, and perhaps even because of, this absence, it is not hard to see a connection between Mr. Tuffuor and Nkrumah when in the following paragraphs we are told:

When popular "O.T." was alive, many were those who held that it would be terrible and that the earth would literally stand still the day he would die.
But he did die.
And what happened?
To the ordinary man — and there are, by far, more ordinary men than extraordinary men in this world — it was only surprising and shocking. Apart from that, his death was like any other ordinary death; the usual end of the cycle of man — birth, life, death — no matter one is buried in a diamond coffin or buried without coffin. And it would by all means be the usual six feet.
"O.T." was dead, but everything was going on as usual. The shops opened, the buses and taxis ran, the markets were crowded by housewives, hawkers went about with their wares, people crowded the chop bars, there were dances in the evenings, and every other aspect of life went on as usual — no change — and the sun too shone brightly; and unconcerned people in houses near the place of the funeral were beating their fufu and eating all right.

Someone observed all this and remarked: "Such is the end of man; a great lesson."

Even, to people closely connected with, or who lived in, the business world of Mr. Osei Tuffuor, the earth did not stand still. All his workers, direct or indirect, throughout the country, had laid down their tools and were wailing — mourning him for three days. But all the same, they ate as usual when they should eat and slept when they felt like sleeping even when "O.T.'s" body lay in state.

His was a grand funeral never before witnessed in Kumasi; and riches were displayed when he was laid in state — gold, diamond, silver — all pure.

But he had, by all means, to be buried. Not with riches, though; and alone, too.

That was the end of the scheming, indomitable, energetic, and super-rich Mr. Osei Tuffuor, popularly called "O.T." (pp. 29-30)

I hardly need to note that death is the ultimate symbol of change. Whether it was consciously intended or not, we have a statement here that in its own way is as elegant a commentary on politics and life as any we find in Ayi Kwei Armah's *The Beautyful Ones Are Not Yet Born*.

Alex, Mr. Tuffuor's employee, is at first thought to be the murderer. Near the beginning of the novelette we see him on an airplane on the day of "O.T.'s" death about to fly to Nigeria. The plane, however, is brought back to the airport where "two top police officers from the C.I.D. headquarters" board the plane and arrest Alex. We are given a description of activity at the airport that by implication may be seen as the smoothly running polis itself as yet unaware of the deed that has threatened its well-being:

It was a bright Friday afternoon, at about four o'clock, and at the Accra International Airport. The place was crowded as was the case on very rare occasions, and agog with activity. A Head of State from a sister African country was arriving in about an hour's time to begin a three-day official visit to Ghana, and there was drumming and dancing by several groups, ready to accord him the usual traditional Ghanaian hospitable welcome. The citizens of that sister African state resident in Ghana, were also at the airport in their hundreds to give their Head of State a befitting welcome. On top of this, some seventy Ghanaian students who had been awarded various scholarships by two foreign governments, were also leaving that day, and their respective parents, relatives and friends were at the airport to see them off. Some were also there to welcome their dear ones whom they were expecting back home. (p. 9)

Alex is tried and acquitted, but not before there is a change in venue from Kumasi to Accra because of the angry crowds that are upset about the murder of their leading citizen, crowds that threaten Alex's life and make a fair trial impossible. Even though he is found innocent of the charge, Alex finds he must leave for Nigeria as his life is no longer safe in Ghana. Two years later, he receives the letter quoted earlier and immediately hands it over to the Nigerian police who, in cooperation with Alex and the Ghanaian C.I.D., trap and arrest Janet.

Through it all Alex is shown as a Mr. Clean who can always make the right moral choices. What is of particular interest here is the connection that we see between Alex's ability to control his desires and his readiness to aid the state. In a passage that comes about as close as the work ever comes to being a potboiler, we see as much contorted sublimation and repression as one could ever find in a piece of writing. We learn that the reason Alex was leaving Ghana on the day of the murder was that he had known of Janet's interest in him and wanted to save his boss from an embarrassing situation:

> At one stage, Alex was determined to report the matter to Mr. Tuffuor. But he thought of what the repercussions could be — a possible forthright dissolution of their marriage. And since he did not want to wreck anybody's marriage, he refrained from telling him.
>
> But the temptation continued, with Janet writing love letters to him in Accra whenever he had not been to Kumasi for say a week. And since the spirit is always willing but the body is weak, Alex's body, naturally, gave way and began to have some sympathic feelings for Janet which later developed into latent love. But he never made it manifest to Janet though it was there and growing steadily, fanned and nursed by Janet's constant temptations and secret proposals. (p. 62)

I am not trying to argue for an allegorical interpretation of a work that aside from rhetorical considerations remains rather simple, but we can, in the context of post-Nkrumah Ghana, see Alex as an everyman figure in much the same way that we see "the man" in *The Beautyful Ones*. Though the average citizen may be concerned about questions of political morality, they are not of the same immediate importance as questions of personal morality, and it is through the latter that the former can be understood. Later in this chapter I will return to this point and show that the creation and even the reading of popular literature between 1966 and 1971 was connected with the people's response to a political situation, a response that was not simply an escape from political realities.

It is easy to think of popular literature in terms of stereotypes. All popular literature seems to draw from a common pool of worn-out experiences, characters, and situations. The destructive female of *Woman Is Poison* is a type common not only to a large number of Ghanaian novelettes, but also to Onitsha chapbooks. Stereotyping, however, even in its less invidious forms, only takes surface phenomena into consideration; it always discards individuating elements. All Orientals do not look alike, nor is all popular literature the same. The text-context relationship just examined distinguishes one particular piece of Ghanaian popular literature, but there are some more general characteristics of the literature that are apparent when we examine the way it was produced: that is, when we look at who wrote it and the manner in which it was marketed.

While the term "chapbook" is descriptively accurate of the type of booklets Mickson and other Ghanaians have produced, it has only limited value in discussing Ghanaian popular literature. First of all, in the criticism of African literature the term has come to be associated with Onitsha literature, pamphlets of rougher literary quality and printing than what we find in Ghana. Many of the Ghanaian works are also much longer than the Onitsha chapbooks. Hence, I will use the terms "booklet," "pamphlet," and, as most of this chapter is concerned with fiction, "novelette."

In Onitsha there are a large number of independent printers and publishers who buy manuscripts outright from local writers and then take care of publication, distributorship, and sales of the pamphlets.[4] The economic risk is entirely in the hands of the publishers, but so are most of the profits. Few of the Onitsha pamphleteers have succeeded in circumventing the tight control the printers have over publishing there. In Accra an entirely different system existed. The potential audience for any pamphlet was smaller and the risk greater, so most publishers did not even want to look at the manuscript of a pamphlet. The margin of profit was so small that in most cases the writers had no choice but to serve as their own publisher and distributor. One writer, J. Benibengor Blay, was quite successful and produced over twenty pamphlets in a twenty-year period. Most writers, however, gave up after producing one or two pamphlets finding the effort to be more than expected and the profit less than expected.

While it is obvious that publishing, like any business, is clearly affected by changes in local and international economics, even the slightest negative change in economic conditions can stop all but the most essential publishing in a country like Ghana. Throughout the sixties, but especially in the second half of the decade, a substantial number of booklets were published. Ghana was, of course, severely affected by major changes in the world cocoa market and internally by two changes in government. Yet these changes came at a time when the country was achieving its highest literacy rates ever, a result of Kwame Nkrumah's massive efforts in the late fifties to expand primary and adult education. Despite economic conditions, a market had been created, and one writer-publisher, Samuel Asare Konadu, took advantage of the situation to amass a small fortune in publishing. The margin of profit was small, but you could do well if you sold large editions of a book or pamphlet. Under these conditions more than half a dozen writers did well enough to write and publish their own work until even the small profit margin was virtually wiped out by the world paper shortages and general inflation of the early seventies.

The average literate worker in the early seventies made 40 cedis a month. He probably read a daily newspaper which cost him 5 pesewas.[5] If he bought the paper five times a week, he had already committed 1 cedi a month, or two and a half percent of a subsistence income to reading material! We can understand that he would balk at paying out a cedi for additional material, but it is surprising that he would even consider spending 50 pesewas for a pamphlet or magazine! We must consider, though, that this was not thought of simply as money spent on entertainment, but rather as money spent on education and social status. However questionable it might be in fact, the buyer saw in the pamphlet the possibility of expanding his own general knowledge of the world as well as the possibility of improving his reading skills. He might also carry the pamphlet or newspaper as he would wear a watch — as a visible symbol of achievement, a means of impressing others with his affluence and abilities.

Regardless of the potential interest a pamphlet might generate, the public was willing to pay more than 50 pesewas only for rare exceptions. Ghana has a very fine government-owned publishing house, the Ghana Publishing Corporation. They have the best printing equipment and the best editors available in Ghana, but even they could not afford to print very much material aimed at the general public. By the early seventies they were printing more popular material than ever before; still, only on very large editions could they print anything to sell at less than 1 cedi, twice what much of the public was generally willing to pay.

Unlike Onitsha, where the chapbook industry is still flourishing, the popular booklet in Ghana is dying. Nigeria's oil-rich economy can support the increasing expense of imported paper and printing material, but Ghana cannot, with the result that the public's demand for reading material must be met in a cheaper way, generally through newspapers, and, to a lesser extent, magazines.

To succeed, even in the best of times, Ghanaian popular writers had to be as wise in business matters as they were skilled in their art. In fact, business acumen was probably more important than artistic talent. True, in a few cases booklets were published by business people who fancied they could sell anything they could write; while it is difficult to get exact sales figures, some of these pamphlets are so unreadable it is doubtful they have ever sold more than a few copies. For the most part, however, the business-people/writers seemed to know exactly what they were doing, even in cases in which they might have harbored some illusion about their art.

Undoubtedly the best-known popular writer in Ghana has been J. Benibengor Blay. He was in his sixties, when he died a few years ago, but he had been writing and publishing for over thirty-seven years. Starting with *Immortal Deeds: A Book of Verse*, which he published in London in 1940, he published twenty-eight booklets. He began his career as a writer in the early thirties doing freelance work for a Gold Coast newspaper. In 1944 he decided he could make a living in journalism, free-lancing for the Gold Coast newspapers, and in 1949 he went to England, where he studied journalism for two years. Then, in the early fifties, he worked for a few years on a paper founded by Kwame Nkrumah, the *Kumasi Evening News*, and in 1958, following independence, was elected to the National Assembly of Ghana. He served as a member of the Assembly until the coup in 1965, holding office as a deputy minister of education and later as minister of arts and culture. He said shortly before his death that he was at the time supporting himself exclusively through his booklets, but he saw himself more as a politician than as a writer or journalist.

He tried almost every genre: novelette, short story, poetry, biography, essay, and history. He said he loved poetry the most, but it was mainly his fiction that gained him a popular reputation in Ghana. Younger writers respect him, but see his Victorian-style romances mainly as material for young school children. It would appear that he has probably lost his appeal with the reading public, his material now being seen as old-fashioned.

He does, however, offer us some insight into the current problem in publishing. One 37-page love story, *Alomo*, he originally published as a booklet in 1969 in an edition of 7,500. He brought out another edition in 1974, also of 7,500, and explained his expenses as follows:

> *Alomo* ... left the press at 17 pesewas and I'm selling it at 40 pesewas ... About 200 copies go out as complimentary copies. Those who hawk the book on the street get 25% of the selling price and those who buy the book in bulk, such as bookstores, take 33% of the selling price. Now I should multiply the 17 pesewas by 3, but 50 pesewas is too much for this book in this market. The total over-head is around 34 pesewas per book, so I must bite into my own profit and make only under 5-6 pesewas per copy.[6]

Blay went on to argue that the two biggest problems of the publisher are the cost of printing and distribution. Newsprint, which in the late sixties went for 5 cedis a ream, went up to 18 to 20 cedis a ream by 1974. The cost of ink, plates, and parts for presses had not risen quite so dramatically, but the jumps were large. He explained that a work he planned to sell at 80 pesewas went up to over a cedi before the printing was completed, simply because of a sudden rise in printing costs. When he was younger, he used to do most of the selling himself and at one time could sell 2,000 copies of a booklet just in Accra. He would then go to Takoradi and other cities, selling a proportionate number of copies and doing this simply in a door-to-door manner, mainly stopping at schools and offices. In the early seventies he got young boys to sell some of his books in this manner, but he mainly distributed them to large department stores like Kingsway, the university bookstores, the various church bookstores, and smaller booksellers. Once he distributed the books on a "sales or return" basis, but he found it more practical to simply sell them outright to the retailers. His distribution in the seventies was also limited more to Accra as gasoline increases made transportation costs almost prohibitive. Those books he sold outside of Accra were sold mainly in a few other large cities and were shipped there by government transport.

Blay did most of the editorial work himself, but had four or five secretaries working for him part-time. Like most of the writers I talked with, he would have had his own press if he could have afforded it, believing this to be the only way he could expand his business. He explained that he had had no trouble in finding manuscripts from other writers and had about twenty-five sent to him, but he could only afford to publish his own works. If, for example, he had had to pay a royalty on *Alomo*, it would have been ten percent of the sales price or 4 pesewas, leaving him virtually no profit.

One of the most interesting figures involved with popular writing in Ghana is an expatriate, James Moxon. Probably very few others in Ghana have worked so hard at publishing popular material, and certainly fewer still have so thorough an understanding of virtually all aspects of the mass media there. At the beginning of World War II, in 1941, Moxon arrived in Ghana as a district commissioner at the age of 21. From the outset of his tour there he was involved in the mass media and was placed in charge of local broadcast news bulletins. In 1948 when the first series of political disturbances occurred following Nkrumah's return, Moxon was made district commissioner of Accra. A commission of inquiry had criticized the government severely for its lack of public relations, and Moxon was given the job as D.C. in part because he was in close contact with the newspaper editors and had had earlier experience in broadcasting. After independence, between 1957 and 1960, he worked and traveled with Nkrumah as a press secretary; between 1960 and 1967 he served under him, as well as the government that followed the coup, as an advisor on information. By the time he retired, he had worked with the Ghana News Agency, founded the School of Journalism in Accra, and worked in filmmaking and publishing. He then went into private publishing combined with importing and selling books and has been doing that since. It has not, however, been a business in which he could make a living. For that he depends on a restaurant he owns in Accra and a farm he owns outside the city.

The economic situation in Ghana has made it difficult — in Moxon's words, "almost impossible" — to import books. The little store, The Atlas Bookshop, that he operated for many years across from the Ambassador Hotel, was by 1974 mainly carrying some magazines and a few old, very dusty books. In 1970 he published two novelettes by a young writer, Cofie Quaye. They were, and in fact still are, quite different from most of the popular writing you find in Ghana, or even Nigeria. *Sammy Slams the Gang* and *Murder in Kumasi* are both detective stories about a West African James Bond. Figuring they would sell, Moxon brought them out in editions he considered large for Ghana, 10,000 each. Moxon discussed his publishing in much more conservative terms than many of the publishers I spoke with and explained that even very popular books moved very slowly in Ghana. He said he had about 2,500 copies of each work that were still unsold. Most of his sales had been in Ghana, and mainly in Accra, but about 2,000 copies were ordered by overseas booksellers, most of these orders coming from Nigeria.

The booklets, each about 100 pages in length, cost 15 pesewas to print and were sold at 40 pesewas. They were distributed mainly to department stores and bookstores that sold them on a sale or return basis, keeping twenty-five percent of the sales for themselves. For each work Moxon gave Quaye the unusually high advance of 250 cedis. Figuring this in and allowing at least five percent for additional overhead, Moxon made at the most 875 cedis on the two novels. Corroborating Blay's point about printing costs, Moxon explained it would cost him in 1974 three times what it had cost him in 1970 to print were he to run another edition of either novel. In short, printing costs would be 5 pesewas per copy over what he was selling the remaining stock for. It had become impossible for him to continue with book publishing, as the market would not bear the necessary markup. Moxon thought of keeping the sales price down, as Blay had done, by including four or five advertisements with each book, but was not able to find the advertisers to support him.

In a short piece on Asare Konadu that appeared in *Africa Report* in 1972, "Publisher for the Many," Stephen H. Grant has considered a third individual's case.[7] Despite some obvious errors (Konadu, for example, was not the first to publish works in Ghana), the article made the fascinating claim that Konadu at 39 was running a publishing house, Anowuno Educational Publications, that was publishing popular material and bringing in $500,000 a year in sales. This alone would have made him one of Ghana's most successful businessmen — but the publishing house was only one of a number of enterprises he was engaged in. Educated as a journalist, he worked for a while at the Ghana News Agency. While there he started writing popular novels and had his first one, *The Wizard of Asamang*, published by a Presbyterian publishing firm (Waterville Publishing House) in 1964. Two years later he set up his own publishing house, which in 1967 actually grossed around half a million dollars in sales, but only for that one year — and this mainly because his firm had a government contract to print 534,000 copies (at 35 pesewas per copy) of a booklet that was distributed to every Ghanaian school child.[8] The booklet was *Courtesy for Boys and Girls*, a booklet Konadu had adapted for use in Ghana from one written in Ireland by a priest.

In a paper on Ghanaian popular fiction presented at a conference in Ife in 1968, Ime Ikiddeh said that for six of Konadu's publications, press runs ranged from 8,000 for one work to 30,000 for another.[9] Six years later, in an interview with Konadu, I found that he had gone into four printings of that last work, his own novel, *Come Back Dora!*, and that they totaled 100,000 copies. To my knowledge no other piece of popular literature has done so well in Ghana. Yet here again we need to be careful in drawing any conclusion. First of all, the figures may not be entirely accurate. There are some notable discrepancies between my figures and Ikiddeh's (and Ikiddeh does not give his source). The work Ikiddeh reports as coming out in one printing of 8,000 (another novel by Konadu, *Night Watchers of Korlebu*) Konadu told me came out in one printing of 25,000. Secondly, more research needs to be done on the extent to which Konadu used his influence in government to have his other books used in Ghanaian schools. He was firmly straightforward about this in relation to the *Courtesy* book, but hedged when questioned about his fiction. Moxon, among others, however, indicated to me that government influence did, in part, account for Konadu's high sales. Still, he was a shrewd businessman and when I asked him about the distribution of his books he explained that he would send an agent into a town to locate a person in a position of authority who could handle the sales of his books. "In many cases, the postmaster can always be located or the headmaster of a school, or perhaps the librarian in a secondary school who will always be there. Where we find out it's going to be [someone from] a government department, perhaps the accounts clerk who pays people at the end of the month (we can easily collect whatever is owed). So, when you are sending books, and the chap refuses to pay, they have the access to deduct the money."

Altogether, Konadu published about twenty-two titles, mostly fiction and school textbooks. It is interesting that given the scale of his business, he ran it the same as the person who only publishes one or two works. That is, his publishing house was essentially a one-man operation — he could not have operated with much of a profit had it been otherwise. He did not do his own printing, sending it out to the state press at Tema when he wanted fairly high quality work done, or to one of the smaller presses in Accra when he was operating on a tighter budget. Moreover, most of the works he published were ones he had written himself, though his wife did a cookbook and two other writers wrote novels he published. In those two cases he paid royalties of five percent immediately following the printing (and not on a basis of sales) and seven and one-half percent on any additional printings.

All of this is now history. Since 1971 Konadu has published some reprints of works that had sold out but has published nothing new. There are at least three reasons for this. When he started his press in 1966 he had about ten manuscripts of his own material. Several were manuscripts of novels that had been rejected by foreign publishers, though one, *Come Back, Dora!*, was later picked up by Heinemann for their African Writers Series and published under the title *Ordained by the Oracle*. By 1971 he had made enough in publishing that he was also able to expand into a number of other business enterprises: a sawmill, textiles, real estate, and the importation and distribution of books from foreign publishers. He had, for example, the distribution rights in Ghana for Scott, Foresman and Houghton Mifflin. He even purchased an offset printing machine to reprint some of their texts for use in Ghana. He had, then, little time to do any more writing. Secondly, the rise of printing costs prevented him from expanding with the works of other Ghanaian writers as he had originally planned — like Blay and Moxon, he could not pay a royalty and still make a profit. Finally, one can see that Konadu's rise as a publisher roughly corresponded with the end of one political regime, and his cessation of publishing activity with the fall of another. This may be coincidence, but I think not. It is clear that with at least one publication Konadu made significant profits from his publishing house because of government connections.

Konadu's situation is especially interesting in that the six-year period of his major publishing activity corresponds with the period in which the greatest number of literary works by Ghanaians was produced. It would be rash to call this a golden age of Ghanaian letters, but certainly Ghana did experience a literary renaissance similar to the one in Nigeria roughly a decade earlier. Kofi Awoonor, Joe de Graft, Ama Ata Aidoo, Ayi Kwei Armah, and Joseph Abruquah published their most important works to date in this period. About fifty percent of all the booklets written in English that I collected, or could find reference to, were published in this period. This percentage does not even include the large number of reprints Blay published from his earlier works. What is more important, the editions of any ten of the booklets published in this period (even excluding Konadu's works) would probably constitute a greater number of copies than all the editions of all the popular booklets published prior to 1966. For example, when Blay started publishing his works in the forties and fifties he would come out with editions of a few thousand copies — 5,000 at the very most.

E.K. Mickson, who has published five novelettes, all in the "renaissance" period,[10] brought out editions of 10,000 or more, some works going into four printings. Several of these printings sold out in less than a month.[11]

There were a number of factors converging to stimulate this renaissance. I have mentioned the increased literacy, and discussed the economics of publishing, but there were political factors as well. According to the Area *Handbook for Ghana*, "From 1961 through 1966 public policy was concentrated on the creation of savings and investment, particularly government investment. Private consumption and investment were curbed, and taxation and public indebtedness were increased" (p. 293). Obviously a publisher like Konadu would have had trouble getting started during the Nkrumah years. Nkrumah brought in the presses at Tema, aiding in the establishment of the Ghana Publishing Corporation. But there are no signs he did anything to encourage private publishing houses. Like other businesses, publishing must have been affected by government pressure to curb investment. And, in fact, during the Nkrumah era there was relatively little publication of popular literature, even by the small writer-publisher operations. There were a few writers, like Blay, who continued to get materials on the market, and some Onitsha literature found its way into Ghana, but there was simply little opportunity either to produce or import chapbooks.

It is unlikely that the production of popular literature was very much affected by censorship during the Nkrumah period, as most Ghanaian popular literature is, on the surface at least, apolitical. However, there are a few exceptions that are worth noting. Jim Bailey, an English South African who founded *Drum* magazine, started a Ghanaian edition in 1956, about the time Nkrumah came into power. Bailey put Henry Ofori, a Ghanaian journalist, in charge of the picture magazine, which ran news stories and political commentary, but also had a fair amount of creative writing in it. Nkrumah did not like some of the things Ofori was putting in the magazine, so in 1960 he shut it down. Several years later Ofori made arrangements with Waterville Publishing House in Accra to have them publish a collection of his writings: mostly essays, some short stories, and a short play. Though the writings are all light satire, there is nothing overtly political about the book. In fact, about the strongest political statement he makes is a reference to the P.W.D. (Public Works Department) as The Palm Wine Drinkers. The work, *Young Tigers vs. Venomous Vipers and Other Stories*, was to be published under Ofori's pen name, Carl Mutt. Ofori maintains that Waterville had the book printed up before the coup, but that they were afraid to release it. At any rate, they released it immediately following the coup and it sold quite well. In eight years it went through three printings totaling 50,000 copies.

It almost goes without saying that the Nkrumah era had a profound effect on the Ghanaian people. Aside from leading his people to independence, Nkrumah ruled for over a decade with a great political vision for Africa, however shortsighted he might have been in relation to the more immediate needs of his people. After he fell from power, many commentators noted that his "overthrow had been greeted with almost universal jubilation throughout the country."[12] Ghanaians are a pragmatic people and they had felt the immediate pinch of Nkrumah's economic policies. But it is also a shortsighted evaluation — one need only see the stature Nkrumah now has as a hero of the populace. Again, there is a pragmatic base to this. For example, looking just at tangible results in the area of education, we can see that the opportunities he provided produced over a million elementary school graduates and over twenty thousand college level graduates in a decade.[13] My point is that even in 1966 there must have been ambivalence regarding Nkrumah's fall. Granted, there may have been "universal jubilation," but there was probably a great deal of inner disquietude as well. (All violent political shocks produce consternation.) I would maintain that this ambivalence can be seen in the literature produced in Ghana in the six years following the coup and that those feelings of ambivalence were instrumental in the production, if not the consumption, of literature in that period. This is not the type of argument one can ultimately prove, but a strong case can be made with respect to both popular and elite literature of the time. *Woman Is Poison*, then, can be seen in many respects as being representative of this period.

Leaving aside questions of literary quality, we can look at the popular and elite literature and wonder how they came out of the same social setting. With regard to content alone these literatures as different as night and day. Ayi Kwei Armah's *The Beautyful Ones Are Not Yet Born* and Kofi Awoonor's *This Earth, My Brother*, perhaps the two best-known Ghanaian novels, were written in this period. Both are informed with a deep sense of *gravitas*, a concern about the political and moral well-being of the state. On the popular level, however, we find numerous novelettes that are concerned with love and romance. Such a contrast is not all that startling, as it is one we could readily find elsewhere — one we might even expect to find between popular and elite literature almost anywhere (and do find in Nigeria, for example), but there is ultimately less of a contrast than we might at first think.

The titles of many of the novelettes sound like they belong either to potboilers or sexual comedies: *Woman Is Poison, Now I Know, The Tears of a Jealous Husband, The Tears of a Jealous Wife, The Tears of a Prostitute, The Forbidden Taste.* Yet the titles of the three works in the "Tears" trilogy point more directly to the serious moral nature of all these works, to the fact that they are comments on the consequence of deviating from a strict sexual morality. In the foreword to Blay's *Alomo*, a writer (Blay himself?) comments:

> The author has asked me to write a foreword to this book and, to gratify his wish, I solemnly venture to give his readers a brief summary of the interesting story which blots its pages.
> The ancient philosophy of the "Eternal Triangle" whose angles must needs to be two men with one woman or two women with one man, is becoming more and more complicated in modern times.
> Today, romance, in this accelerated tempo of human existence, is fraught with conflicting episodes and men and women are cutting awkward figures with many angles. Consequently, we now see the first-created dual nature of love, developing into heptagons, octagons, and nonagons., This blot on human behavior baffles the understanding of many a moral philosopher.

To the outsider and to the academic this may appear simply as a humorous statement, but there is every reason to believe it was written with the intention of making a serious point. The jargon here is almost reminiscent of the language of Onitsha literature, though we might keep in mind that more care is generally taken in the production of Ghanaian popular literature. Aside from the printing, which is generally of higher quality, more care is taken in proofreading and editing material. Even writers like Henry Ofori, who is intentionally humorous, take their work seriously. It would be very easy to document that the above quotation serves not only as a summary of *Alomo*, but also as a summary of a very large proportion of the popular literature. Moving into the difficult area of intention, I see a serious and very conservative statement about the moral health of society. Blay, E.K. Mickson, Willie Donkor, and several other popular writers of this period are explicitly saying that the good life is contingent on one's adherence to certain rules of conduct. Mickson builds his Lucy stories (*When the Heart Decides*, *Who Killed Lucy?* and *Now I Know*) around a motto he puts in quotation marks and capitals for emphasis: "LOVE EITHER MAKES OR MARS A LIFE." The point cannot be missed; it is repeated on nearly every page, only to be spelled out once again at the end of *Who Killed Lucy?*. Lucy and her "sweetie," Frank, are both dead, and between their graves an unknown person places a tombstone with the inscription (again, given with quotation marks and in capitals): "HEREIN LIE THE REMAINS OF A WORTHWHILE LESSON."

In times of national stress, or political or economic turmoil, it is not uncommon for people to respond conservatively and look in themselves (or at their immediate neighbors) for the causes of the problems. A colleague of mine, a Renaissance scholar, once made the comment about Petrarch that you could always find commentary on the body politic in the poetry concerned with the body Petrarch.[14] More immediate than Petrarch was the concern among middle-class Americans during the Nixon years with the "problem" of pornography. There was extensive corruption in the government, but until the reality of that corruption became absolutely unavoidable, public concern was directed more at the existence of adult movie houses and pornographic bookstores than at government break-ins and payoffs.

The connection between public and private morality is implicitly made in a comparison in the preface to *Tears of a Jealous Wife*, a novelette by Skot (a pseudonym for Seth Osae):

> Yaa Mente was happily married to Kwasi Asempa a peace-loving and faithful husband, who, as a welfare officer, had contacts with people in all walks of life. His contact with all people, as his duties demanded, did not mean he had illicit dealings with some of the female clients who flocked his office and home to lay their problems before him; and that view was shared by Yaa Mente also.
>
> A bad counsellor can ruin a nation, and it was a pity that Yaa Mente, a well-educated and cultured lady, should fall a victim to an envious inmate's bad counsel and received as her prizes — deformity and misfortune.

In other words, to have a good, well-ordered life one must lead a morally clean life. In *Woman Is Poison* Alex realizes this and, in controlling his own desires, is able to aid the state.

Private morality, then, has to do with the physical body and ultimately with bodily functions. In the writings of Awoonor and Armah the physical body/political body connection is simultaneously more direct and more complex. (Consider the catharsis at the end of *Why Are We So Blest?* which I discussed in Ch. II, p. 46) Both writers seem to comment rather directly on the unfulfilled hope Nkrumah gave the people and the state of anomie that followed his fall. In *The Beautyful Ones* Armah writes of a change in government that brought no change to the people and of a nameless man in search of moral stability in the midst of corruption. In *This Earth* Awoonor makes the state of anomie palpable through the insanity of his hero, Amamu, who, as we have seen, is sane in comparison to the world through which he moves. The complexity of such writing lies in the art the writer brings to the work, and, as I have argued earlier, in the mythic dimension of both these novels. The protagonists are engaged in circular journeys, the action is complexly symbolic, and the places, despite the specificity, must be discounted as fictional. The Ghanas of both works are states of mind as much as, or even more than, they are real places.

Now we can see where the elite and popular literatures touch. Maybe with less consciousness, certainly with less art, popular writers also inform their work with symbolic action. I would like again to refer to Kenneth Burke's *Language as Symbolic Action*, specifically to a chapter entitled "The Thinking of the Body: Comments on the Imagery of Catharsis in Literature." Starting with the point that the very idea of catharsis, or purgation, has in it the idea of bodily excretion, Burke argues that even though we generally associate catharsis with literature written in "the grand style," we can find it, often very concealed, in other works as well (he uses as one of his examples *Alice in Wonderland*). In other words, catharsis is a mode of experience not limited to "such sacrifices and victimage as attain their fulfillment in the ritualistic use of the 'scapegoat' for poetic purposes."[15] We can identify with Awoonor's Amamu and experience catharsis in the ritual suicide he commits, but even though we may not experience catharsis in relation to Mickson's Lucy or the Onitsha *Mabel, The Sweet Honey That Poured Away*, is not the idea of purgation present in these works? Lucy, her child, her mother, and her lover, Frank, all die as a result of Lucy's actions. In his introduction, Mickson tells us that one of his purposes in writing the story was so that it would "serve as a reprimand and perhaps a 'purgative' to those our ladies who, flattered by their beauty, popularity or position in life, make not only folly but also donkeys of themselves by remaining rolling stones in the hands of men — changing from man to man." Mabel's end is in a lavatory, where the seventeen-year-old girl bleeds to death, having tried to give herself an abortion.

A lot has been said about the scatological imagery in Armah and Awoonor, much of it based on a misunderstanding of language, symbolism, and fiction, namely that the name and the thing named are not the same, and are especially not to be confused in fiction where inversion and irony are often present. Ama Ata Aidoo, as I mentioned in Chapter IV, interprets the novel in a very literal manner.[16] The open sewers and excrement are simply seen by her as real objects and not as symbols — symbols, in fact, that are used ironically. Burke says, "As I write these words I am living on a Florida key, where I have to walk among the whole and broken shells (skeletons and parts of skeletons) that the waves toss up on the beach. Never for a moment do I cease to think of these things as the detritus of *death*, aspects of life's offal. I live with the thought that digestion and fertilization involve the life-giving properties of corruption, that life grows out of rot."[17] Thus we can understand why Awoonor himself has been so insistent that Amamu's death be seen in positive terms,[18] but we need look no further than his novel. The point can be sharpened with a Burkian-style pun — offal imagery is good imagery.

The common people have little time for complexity in their literature; in fact, when they look to literature they try to find resolution for the complexities of life. Thus the world of the popular novelette is often an unambiguous world where good is rewarded and evil punished. In the Ghanaian novelette we tend to find a world where individuals are punished for giving vent to their lust and desire. A recurrent phrase in several works and the title of one book is "paid in his own coin." As in Awoonor and Armah, negation occurs, but it is much less ambiguous. Again, Burke can carry us further with a point he makes about the negative: "All told, though the principle of the negative is often embodied in 'No-no' kinds of imagery, it is itself neither 'life-affirming' nor 'life-denying.' It is a marvel of language, perhaps *the marvel* of language — and though 'Don't' can constrain us (thus, to an extent, 'mortifying' our desires) it can also save us (when inducing us to guard against a real danger)."[19] The fictional danger in the novelette may be the physical body — but the real danger is in the body politic.

In both the popular and elite literatures primary motivation for the action of characters is that something is rotten in the state. The elite literature of the mythic type transcends the reality through symbolic inversion; the popular literature avoids reality through sublimation. The former offers a positive vision; the latter simply reflects real concerns. In effect, I am saying the literatures are complementary, affording in different terms mirror images of the same social condition. In the works of Armah and Awoonor we see a disordered world, peopled with corrupt individuals and challenged by the positive vision of a good man. It is no accident that Armah's hero is simply called "the man" — he is the one person who sees possibility in the midst of corruption, the possibility of people acting in a humane manner. In the popular literature we are shown the obverse. Into a healthy, well-ordered world steps the individual who threatens the order with his or her (usually her) immoral actions. Despite the actions of the fallen individual, which are always described in rather puritanical language, this is a world of almost perfect cleanliness — to state the essence of what Mark Twain once said about James Fenimore Cooper, no one's hair is messed and no one farts. Yet in terms of the rhetorical motivation in the popular works, we see an escape from an unhealthy world. As Burke reminds us, only through excretion can the body remain in a healthy state; stopping the process can only be associated with death. In both the popular and the elite literatures, then, we can see a process in which the good is transmuted into the bad and the bad into the good.

The problem is that due to the elite artist's conscious artistic will, we can more easily grant such transmutation to elite literature than to popular literature. We can ascribe complexity more readily where we see the possibility of conscious artistic complexity. But in dealing with rhetorical motivation we are dealing not just with the work itself, but with the whole social situation out of which the work has come — and this relationship between the work (any work) and the social situation is always complex. In short, there is a problematical relationship in both literatures — one that is defined in terms of a symbolic relationship between bodily functions and political functions.

We find a great amount of scatological imagery in the writings of the Nigerian, Wole Soyinka. In *The Interpreters* Sagoe discusses the need to establish a national project in which the excrement of Lagos could be transported to fertilize the fields in the north. Elsewhere Sagoe discusses the virtues of a flatulent aunt and his own philosophy of voidancy. As in the writings of Jonathan Swift the humor, and hence the irony, is clear from the context. Even in parts of *This Earth*, Awoonor draws back from the pathos of the situation in which his protagonist is caught, making clear the ironic thrust of the heavy scatological imagery — hence the recurrent phrase ironically echoing T.S. Eliot, "fear death by shit trucks."

I have been discussing three modes of symbolic commentary on the social context: Soyinka employs irony and humor (open scatological imagery); Armah employs irony and pathos (open scatological imagery); the Ghanaian popular writers employ realism and pathos (disguised scatological imagery). The first two modes are very similar (the mythic consciousness), but in the third mode we see a complete inversion of the manner in which the social context is presented.[20] The popular Ghanaian works under consideration are filled with violence, theft, murder, and other antisocial acts, all of which are causally linked with acts of infidelity. We can also see that the antisocial acts are ultimately linked with the sex act itself. In fact, the one may be seen as implying the others, or in Burke's terms, as "ambiguously standing for the others" (p. 341). Neither the sex act nor the other antisocial acts are explicitly shown, as we might expect in a Western potboiler or detective story. The flesh, then, is to be mortified, not aroused. Anything that is sensual, and we can see violence as a kind of perverted sensuality, is disguised in such a manner that we are to see the pathos and the moral lesson more clearly than the specific antisocial acts.

I would never maintain that all popular literature in Ghana in the late sixties can be interpreted in terms of the political situation. The cultural and social influences of the West obviously can be seen in the production of popular literature in Ghana as well as in Onitsha and elsewhere in Africa. In part, however, it would seem we can account for an explosion in the production and consumption of popular literature in that period by the shared political experience of author and audience that found expression in fictionalized situations that were concerned with difficult relationships between men and women.

My larger point, going beyond the boundaries of Ghana, is that the literature I call ethical, including works by elite writers such as Achebe, present a realistic and didactic view of society, a view that might only be complex when viewed in terms of the rhetorical relationship between the work and the society. On the other hand, in the works I call mythic, the complexity — symbolic inversion, problematic elements, etc. — is all self-contained in the work itself. Because of the clear-cut morality and the manner in which reality is portrayed, ethical works seem to be simpler than the mythic. Popular literature is, in this regard, the simplest expression of the ethical consciousness. It is no accident, then, that Achebe is, in the general sense of the term "popular," both a very popular writer and one who is often praised for his simple style. Simple, of course, is not to be confused with "simplistic." Moreover, it is possible for a work to be simple in some ways and very complex in others. Ethical literature, whether popular or elite, is stylistically simple, but rhetorically complex.

Most of the few pieces of longer fiction (novelettes) that have appeared in Ghana since the early seventies have been published by the Ghana Publishing Corporation (G.P.C.). Founded by Nkrumah in 1965 when he set up presses at Tema, the G.P.C. has mainly published textbooks and government documents.[21] Elite writers brought their works there reluctantly, as they could expect less financial remuneration, poorer editing, less care in the printing, and less prestige than they might hope to find in a European publishing house. Moreover, they could expect to wait up to four years to see their work in print once it was accepted. Not only were there the ordinary delays in printing, but also delays brought about by the major uses of the publishing facilities. In short, a government document would always take precedence over a novel. Looking mainly for quality material, however, the G.P.C. received many more manuscripts than they could, or even cared to, publish. Then, in the early seventies, they began to publish fiction, as well as children's literature, aimed at a popular audience. One of their more successful works has been Obeng's *Eighteenpence*, a reprint of a novel first published in the Gold Coast in 1941 about a Ghanaian Horatio Alger who achieves success through thriftiness, honesty, and hard work. Another, W.K. Ansah's *Denizens of the Street*, deals with street gangs in Accra. Such works differ less in content from the other novelettes than in the quality of production. Only their cost kept them from reaching a wider audience, yet the G.P.C. was still able to sell editions of 5,000 and over, due to the fact that these works were cheaper than most works that could be imported. I would suspect, though I was unable to corroborate this, that the G.P.C. does not publish fiction at a profit. Whatever losses they incur, however, are probably covered by a steady income from textbook sales.

In the private sector, there were in the mid-seventies only two outlets for the popular writer: magazines and newspapers. In 1973, as it became increasingly more difficult for him to publish books, Moxon started a monthly magazine, *Pleisure*. Though the magazine was an expansion and continuation of an earlier magazine, *When and Where?*, which he had published for five years, the new magazine signaled a shift in emphasis in his publishing. The reason for the shift to a larger magazine was clear enough; even when production costs go up you can keep the sales price down, providing you can find support in advertisers. The magazine was produced with good-quality paper and a slick cover so the sales price of 40 pesewas would not even cover cost of production. However, it was a forty-page magazine with about eighteen pages of advertisements, each page bringing in around 200 cedis per month (less a twenty-percent discount for those advertisers running ads on a twelve-month contract). Keeping up a circulation of 5,000 copies enabled Moxon to run the magazine at a profit, but by the middle of 1974 he was doubling issues and by the end of the year he had to cease publication, as the advertising and sales could no longer cover costs.

As long as it ran, *Pleisure* had a rather broad popular appeal. The format appeared to be a cross between *The New Yorker*, *Reader's Digest*, and *The Ladies' Home Journal*. There were essays, short stories, poems, an occasional play, cartoons, a humor page, recipes, a "Pen Pals" section, book reviews, and other articles of cultural interest. The printing of humorous blurbs at the expense of local newspapers is particularly reminiscent of the fillers one finds in *The New Yorker* or the *Reader's Digest*. Under a heading containing a rather sophisticated pun, "Fundamental," followed the quotation, "Amongst the visitors to last week's Agricultural Show was the distinguished international cocoa scientist, Dr. Podd, elegantly dressed in a dove-gray suit with a red rose in his bottom-hole." Then followed a blurb regarding an accident: "When the accident occurred the two farmers were cycling behind each other on the way to market...."

Some of Ghana's best-known local writers wrote regularly for the magazine. Henry Ofori had a column under the pseudonym "Carl Mutt" in which he wrote short sketches satirizing local concerns. Bill Marshall, who has published some popular works with the Ghana Publishing Corporation, had an ongoing serialized story called "Bukom." Ali Yemoh, a Ghanaian soldier moonlighting as a cartoonist, did the covers and ran a comic-strip series about two private investigators, Oko and Ebo. Cofie Quaye, who served as the general editor of the magazine, wrote mystery stories that were sometimes serialized.

A number of magazines were started, but rarely did they last beyond one or two issues. The publishers of *Drum* tried to get a license to resurrect the Ghanaian edition, but were unsuccessful for reasons known only to the government.[22] Only one magazine continued to appear very much on a regular basis. Since it first appeared in August 1971, *Ideal Woman* (subtitled with the Akan equivalent, Ɔbaa Sima) has had a steady circulation of around 15,000 copies per month. In 1974 it sold for 30 pesewas, but by 1981 the cost had risen to 4 cedis, an increase of more than 1,000 percent. Published and edited by a Ghanaian businesswoman, Kate Abbam, the magazine has a format directed mainly, though not exclusively, at a female audience. The magazine is approximately the same size as *Pleisure* (fewer but larger pages) having a slick color cover, but using less expensive news print for the inside. Having a large circulation meant Abbam could almost cover publishing expenses with a sales price less than that of *Pleisure*. Moreover, she could charge more for her advertisements, 290 cedis for a full page and 455 cedis for the inside front and back covers (1974 figures), thus making a fairly handsome profit.[23]

There are at least three reasons we can isolate as accounting for the success of *Ideal Woman* in a market where no other magazine publisher has been able to last very long. First of all, Abbam's feature articles mainly deal with personal, family, and household subjects from the "everything-you-wanted-to-know" orientation. Thus, a registered nurse runs a column where questions are answered about medical problems, a lawyer has a column about legal problems, and numerous features discuss topics from how to save money to how to care for your wig to everything you ever wanted to know about deodorants. Whether the subject is medicine or food, "experts" are brought in for the topic. Occasionally Abbam will run a series on a semi-controversial subject like abortion, but the magazine is anything but a handbook for the liberated woman. The Ideal Woman, in fact, is something like the Total Woman in the West. The Ideal Woman's concern, however, is not with how to "stand by her man," but with gaining security in being a modern, middle-class woman. The magazine, then, addresses itself to the insecurities of a growing section of the Ghanaian populace.

Secondly, the magazine fills the lacunae left by the disappearance of the romantic novelette from the Ghanaian market. Every month there is a short story and a serialized novelette. Occasionally one of the two is a mystery story, but generally they are tragic romances with such alluring titles as *Sweet Deceit* or *My Sordid Past*.

Finally, the magazine does not generally draw on writers as well known or as established as those who wrote for *Pleisure*. This does not have much effect on how much Abbam has to pay for material, since the fees do not vary much in relation to the experience of the author. Ironically, however, her writers help the magazine in a subtle way, since the more established writers aim for a "sophistication" that limits rather than broadens their popular appeal. This may have been a problem faced by *Pleisure*. Abbam herself has written a few novelettes under the pseudonym Awura Ekuwa Badoe, and she continues to publish stories in her magazine under that name. Her own writings are all simple romances and she looks for young writers who produce similar material.

In the mid-seventies, the most important medium for popular literature in Ghana was the newspaper. There were two papers published in Ghana with circulations of over 100,000, the *Daily Graphic* and the *Ghanaian Times*. Both papers had a weekly that carried fiction and, occasionally, poetry. The weekly *Spectator*, connected with the *Ghanaian Times*, had a circulation of 137,000, and the *Mirror*, connected with the *Daily Graphic*, had a circulation of 110,000.[24] There was, additionally, a small independent weekly, *The Echo*, which had some creative writing. It had a circulation of 30,000 and was also published in Accra.

These papers paid between 5 and 20 cedis for a short story and 3 to 5 cedis for a poem, depending on the paper and the name of the author.[25] The most popular stories appeared to be ghost stories, crime stories, and mysteries, with love stories only appearing on occasion.[26] Longer stories were serialized, though very rarely was anything as long as a novelette published. Once, however, in the spring of 1974, the *Graphic* attempted to serialize Ayi Kwei Armah's *Two Thousand Seasons*, but the earthy quality of certain passages offended someone in the military government, with the result that the serialization ceased very abruptly after running only a couple of weeks.

Three of the more experienced authors who wrote regularly for the papers are Bill Marshall, Frank Parkes, and Kwesi Woode. Bill Marshall, who works for an advertising firm in Accra, used a pseudonym, Tuli Blanko (a name similar to the one he used for *Pleisure*), and wrote humorous sketches of family life in *The Echo* in a column called "Blanko's Diary." Parkes, who has a reputation outside Ghana mainly as a poet, runs the Ghana Film Corporation. He also had a regular feature in the *Mirror* entitled "Kwesi Dompo on the Hunt." It was light satire and fantasy set in the fictional town of Dompokrom. Woode, the youngest of the three, is an essayist who did a regular column in the *Spectator* on the various arts in Ghana.

Combining the verbal and the visual, an extremely popular genre in the newspapers was the comic strip. Some strips were imported from Europe, but there were at least three artists whose work appeared regularly in the Ghanaian papers, John Minnah, Frank Odoi, and Yaw Boakye Ghanatta. John Minnah is a self-taught artist who did topical/satirical cartoons for the *Graphic*. Frank Odoi, a former student of Ghanatta, did two comic strips about African Superman figures, "Gakan" in the *Graphic* and "Kwame" in the *Mirror*. By far the most popular comic strip artist was Ghanatta, who was also the pioneer in the field. His work appeared regularly in Ghanaian papers from 1957 until the mid-seventies when his three strips completely ceased to appear. The 5 cedis he received for each strip was only a small part of his income, for he had founded an art school in Accra and like Konadu had spread his investments into other areas. In 1967 he came out with what was probably the first Ghanaian comic book, *Abankaba*, which sold 85,000 copies at 23 pesewas a copy and netted him a profit of 11 pesewas a copy. He illustrated books for a number of Ghanaian authors and even tried publishing a magazine in 1972, *The New Age Magazine*, but the publication only came out once.

Odoi very clearly modeled both his strips after two of Ghanatta's. "Kwame," a mystery/adventure strip, was rather similar to Ghanatta's "Kofi Blowman," a strip that ran for over fifteen years and was published in the *Spectator* (both, incidentally, were similar to a British strip, "Garth," that was syndicated throughout Africa); Gakan, a fantasy/adventure strip had a hero who in many ways was like the hero of Ghanatta's "Kong," a strip that was published in the *Times*.

Perhaps the most interesting comic strip in Ghana, and certainly the one that most clearly showed Ghanatta's skill and imagination as an illustrator, was "Ananse," a strip that appeared for several years in the *Spectator*. Ghanatta had, in effect, taken Ananse, the old folk hero, and adapted him for an urban audience. Essentially, however, the characters and the tales came straight out of oral tradition. When asked about his interest in the tales, he told me:

> I learned them as a child. I came from the Akan area of Ghana, and I am Akim (an area in the East). Elders — uncles, aunts, as well as my mother — told these tales in the evening. I was always ready to hear them. After dinner we would gather around the fire in the compound, and the elders would take turns telling these tales. It was always a very dramatic event. They would get up and animate the story with their hands, and sometimes they would even dance around .... There were other characters [other than Ananse] — especially ghouls and *mmotia* [dwarfs] ... I have sharp images of these characters in my mind — the way they sing and talk.

He bemoaned the fact that the young are no longer interested in learning the skills to tell such stories, but when asked why his comic strip is so popular, he said:

> I think this is because I've adapted it to the times. The real Ananse is a spider — literally a "man-spider." I still keep his basic characteristics — especially his cunning, his ability to trick people — but I need to change him physically to

catch and hold the imagination of my readers. I make him more of a human-like figure, but give him a large head to indicate he is a man of great wisdom.

Even the changes he has made in Ananse, especially the large head, would seem to be changes made within the framework of a traditional aesthetic.[27]

Though we can probably trace the origins of popular writing in Ghana back to the booklets Blay wrote in the forties and had privately printed in England, the rise of a true literature for the masses probably goes back only to the sixties and is mainly an indigenous phenomenon. In a little over twenty-five years there have been dramatic changes in the types, quantity, and production of literature created in Ghana. They are changes that bear out the premise of Marx and Engels that life determines consciousness, that material circumstances determine awareness and, ultimately, action. Thus, increased literacy not only made popular literature possible, but also created a demand for it. Other social, economic, and political changes have directly influenced what has been produced, in what form, and with what content. The woman aspiring to middle-class status assured the success of *Ideal Woman*; the paper shortage and printing costs led to the demise of the novelette in chapbook form; and the special appeal of tragic romances in the late sixties can be linked to the political turmoil of Ghana in that period.

No elite literature, ethical or mythic, could be so fully tied to the economic and social realities of Africa as the Ghanaian popular literature. In troubled economic times the elite writer might still publish abroad, assured of an audience, albeit a foreign one. The economic situation in Ghana now (1986) is so critical, it is almost impossible to find any literature in the bookstores, even in the universities. Writers such as Awoonor and Armah do, however, continue to sell in other African countries and in the West. Still, the economic situation in Ghana is so bad that it is not conducive to even the writing, let alone the production, of creative writing. Paper and printing supplies, or rather the lack of them, are only a few of the many problems facing the future of writing in Ghana.

Conclusion

One hopes the time has arrived when it is possible to smile at the early
Western reviews of Chinua Achebe's novels that found his work too filled
with anthropological data and wanting any literary merit, and at the early
African reviews of Amos Tutuola's writings that found his seemingly crude
style a source of embarrassment to his country's international reputation.[1]
Yet academically, African literature written in English now holds a very
tenuous position in relation to the larger body of English literature over
which British and American literature maintains almost monolithic
hegemony. There are, of course, those who would still see American
literature simply as a subdivision of British literature, but little serious
debate continues as to whether or not American literature is a distinct area of
English literature comprising a field that has academic integrity. The
obvious analogy here is that African literature is in very much the same position that American literature was in fifty years ago, a point worth noting
for it clearly reveals why it is untenable for us to see English literature exclusively in relation to England and the United States.

Perhaps it is only in terms of the medium of expression and British
literary tradition that we could hope to find elements of commonality that
bring together all those who have chosen to write in English. However, the
basic terms we turn to in trying to understand an author should always be
those we find in his own culture. How else can we confront a writer like
Amos Tutuola? A critic cannot approach his works solely in terms of the
language and the tradition of Shakespeare, although, as I have shown
elsewhere, that influence is there.[2] Even where in other writers such
influence is more clearly recognizable, it can all too easily lead us away
from acknowledging native genius. This, in fact, is what happened with
critical appraisal of American literature for quite a long time after Emerson.

For over two thousand years mainstream Western humanism has
fostered the belief that we are all basically alike. We re-confirm this belief

165

every time we recognize "universals" in a great work of literature. Ultimately, there may be something to this, but to the extent that we have a unified/unifying concept of what man is, we run the risk of simply looking for mirror images of ourselves. In literature as in life, when we fail to find the mirror image, we think we have an abberation. We have been slow in learning two relatively simple lessons that anthropologists such as Claude Lévi-Strauss, Edmund Leach and Mary Douglas have set before us. First, that any culture, judged by the standards of another very different culture, can always be seen as "inferior," where "strange" or "different" become equated with "inferior." Secondly, that no culture can be found to be either qualitatively better or more complex than any other culture whenever each aspect of a given culture is examined in relation to the underlying rules that govern the dynamics of the entire social structure.

If we accept these perceptions as being true, and more humanistic than the search for mirror images, we should consider their ramifications in the study of literature. The New Critics' distinction between intrinsic and extrinsic factors in the analysis of a literary work ceases to have very much validity as a work cannot be studied outside the context of a specific culture. It is not as if we are dealing with a picture that has a removable frame, but rather a picture in which the frame is a substantive part.

I would qualify this assertion in view of the fact that some art, plastic as well as verbal, can be partially comprehended outside of its cultural frame. Specifically, art which strives toward naturalistic representation, that is toward the objectification of reality, is, in part, accessible to anyone, whether or not he is of the culture or even knows anything about it. One can, for example, enjoy the great beauty of an Ife bronze even though one's experience will undoubtedly differ qualitatively from that of an individual who lived in that culture. Yet looking at a pair of ibeji carvings for the first time, a person might see beauty or ugliness, depending on the way his individual imagination is predisposed. Only after one has found out about the facial markings, the hair styles, the exaggerated limbs, in short, the convention of these figures, can one really make a more educated and less impressionistic judgment about the work. But we must be cautious. Achebe seems to give us enough information within the situations he creates so that it rarely appears to be necessary to look outside his novels to understand what he has done. No writer, however, can in one novel convey all the details of the world view of his people. He may wish to teach in a clear and simple manner, but he must count on certain shared cultural knowledge. Even the simple proverb which is used to instruct and clarify will be a riddle to one who does not understand the particular context in which the proverb is used. It is understandable, then, that earlier Western reviewers did not like Achebe's "anthropological detail." They were, in short, confused by it.

The simpler and less detailed the expression of the ethical consciousness (i.e., the less contextual information that is given), the more confused the outsider may be in any attempt he makes to understand it. A proverb will often make little or no sense, a popular novelette will at best amuse,[3] and even a sophisticated novel like *Things Fall Apart* will only be partially clear to someone with no understanding of Ibo life. Any expression of the mythical consciousness is going to be a problem for an outsider and may be no less of a problem for someone within the culture as the expression is far more esoteric. The insider's knowledge may aid him in puzzling through a riddle, but he is still faced with a problem. Tutuola may entertain the outsider with his virtuosity in using hyperbole and conjuring up wild creatures, but the outsider will be lost without detailed understanding of Yoruba traditional literature and culture.

In his study of the literary representation of reality in European culture, Erich Auerbach has described what he calls the two basic styles of European literature, Homeric realism and Old Testament expressionism: "on the one hand fully externalized description, uniform illumination, uninterrupted connection, free expression, all events in the foreground, displaying unmistakable meanings ... on the other hand, certain parts brought into high relief, others left obscure, abruptness, suggestive influence of the unexpressed, 'background' quality, multiplicity of meanings and the need for interpretation ... preoccupation with the problematic."[4] Leaving aside Auerbach's labels of "Homeric" and "Old Testament," and avoiding his more detailed examination of the two styles, we probably have a distinction that is valid for any literature.

What has concerned me here, however, is that while these two styles are clearly recognizable in Anglophone West African literature, any perceptions this gives us about African literature must come from a firm grasp of the particularly African qualities the literature has and not just from studying the influence of European literature or seeking out universal patterns. The two styles, then, needed to be differentiated within the context of African culture, the second being given special attention as it makes the greatest demands of cultural awareness. Approaching this question from the perspective of the writer's consciousness, I have tried to show that the realistic and expressionistic styles are the respective products of two opposite, yet complementary sensibilities, the ethical and the mythic.

The deepest and most complex cultural symbols are to be found in myth and ritual, and those writers who draw most heavily on these symbols are extremely susceptible to being misunderstood, especially by an audience that is unfamiliar with the basic counters that the writers employ. It is not at all surprising that there is more critical controversy surrounding Soyinka's first novel than there is around all the novels of Achebe. The exception here proves the rule, for *Arrow of God* has been subjected to a number of very different critical analyses and evaluations, and it is the one work of Achebe's that comes very close to the mythic. The hero, Ezeulu, is presented to us as an individual who is half man and half god — the resultant ambiguities of his role cannot be easily accomodated within the realistic parameters of the novel.

Just as Achebe has worked from an ethical consciousness and touched on the mythic, so have Soyinka, Awoonor, and Armah shown, in the sense I am employing the term, very definite signs of the ethical in their work. Armah, especially, would seem to be closer to the ethical than the mythic in light of the consistent position he takes regarding the colonial and post-colonial political situation in Africa. Nevertheless, even if we are aware of the extent to which Fanon has influenced the ethical dimension of Armah's work, our understanding will be rather clouded if we ignore the mythic basis of Armah's style, his motifs, and above all, his characters. The very problematic, open-ended structure of his novels and the liminality of his heroes, moreover, can be seen almost as paradigmatic of the works of Awoonor and Soyinka.

My underlying assumption has been that much of what has been found to be obscure in these writers need not be attributed to their creating private mythologies, but rather to their re-creation of the mythologies in their societies. To that end I have had to draw on aid from anthropologists, folklorists, musicologists, and even from the authors themselves for whatever light they could shed on the culturally defined aesthetics of the works. For Armah and Awoonor I have had to turn to an analysis of the shamanistic role of the artist, and in particular to the artist's special relation to the mythical Mammy Water, a source of creative energy. Expanding my analysis of the potential power maintained by the mythic hero, namely the liminal *persona*, I examined this role in relation to the dirge structure and funereal elements in Awoonor's work and "the aesthetic of the cool" which is so clearly operative in Soyinka's writing.

Much like Egbo in *The Interpreters*, the mythic consciousness is drawn inevitably toward things of death, an impulse we can only misinterpret if we approach the mythic in the same way we approach the ethical. In effect, we must discount the literal implications of this impulse and see behind it a metaphor of an essentially revolutionary move. Death is taken ultimately as the basic symbol of that which breaks continuity and insures change. Hence, in their characters as well as in their imagery, we see a tendency toward the inversion of normal order, toward ambiguity rather than definition. Death, decay, and insanity are presented as processes that insure rather than deny the vitality of society.

One could point out that this is also true of Achebe, for Okonkwo's death and Ezeulu's insanity are phenomena that confirm the fact that society must adapt and survive. However, we observe these as objective events, whereas through the mythic consciousness we would experience them as subjective processes. I am only dealing in comparisons here, but relatively speaking, Achebe handles death and insanity as having distinct, concrete consequences for society. What we know of the specific consequences of Amamu, Sekoni, or Baako's dementia, or even of Modin or the professor's death is virtually nothing. Nor do we find any clear resolution or answers to the problems these individuals have confronted, beyond the integrity of their search and perhaps the revitalizing shock their experience of liminality will have on those who are close to them.

An attempt to understand these characters through this experience will take us much further than any analysis that tries to see them in terms of alienation and existential thought. We can hardly see Brother Jero as an alienated individual, and even where we do find alienation, it is more the anguish of an African going through his special *rite de passage* than it is the angst of everyman in the modern world. The *personae* of Soyinka and Awoonor's poetry are often priest-like men, poet-cantors, bearers of the flywhisk whose anguish is attendant to their office. In fact, Awoonor has said of his hero in *This Earth, My Brother*: "Amamu is not everyman. He is not everyman, I insist upon that. He is a more sensitive, a more aware, and a more spiritual person. I might say in the religious sense he is more of the priest...."[5]

My intention has not been one of drawing light away from Achebe or the popular writers, but of shedding more light on both. Ultimately my hypothesis rests on the assumption that reality is given confirmation by the mythic just as life is given confirmation by death. The way in which we perceive and render objective reality is always preconditioned by the very subjective cultural and personal values we hold. Anything we have gained regarding a better understanding of the mythic consciousness should thus, if it is worth anything, be useful in expanding our appreciation of the ethical consciousness.

In any society a number of different literatures may flourish simultaneously. They may be "different" not simply in terms of form, but also in the manner of transmission and the relation of the literature to the audience. Thus, folk or oral literature, popular literature, and elite literature do co-exist in West Africa, but in some ways more independently than scholars would like. (It would be easier to talk about the development of a literature if the influences were less complicated.) Granted, any lines we draw between these literatures will be somewhat arbitrary and academic. There are, obviously, differences in form between a folktale and a short story, but there are also ways in which they are similar. Folk literature is transmitted orally, but traditional performances, such as the concert party, can now be seen on television. Gross distinctions between audiences might be made, but those individuals who read novels have not necessarily cut themselves off entirely from oral performances in their home villages.

In West Africa, where written literature is a relatively recent phenomenon, it is all too easy for scholars to look for a line of development from folk literature through popular literature to elite literature. I have done this myself. In a major portion of this book I have, in fact, shown how elite writers have used traditional material in their works. The influences are there, so I must speak of the independent existence of these literatures with some qualification. I mainly wish to stress the point that a scholar would find it extremely difficult to show any evolutionary development from one literature to the other. I take it as axiomatic that all artists work out of a tradition, but to the extent that the scholar chases after influences, he may all too easily overlook the fact that these literatures co-exist in time, and do not just develop through time. Another, more obvious way of looking at what I am saying is to see, for example, that folk stories about Eshu Elegba did not cease to exist once Wole Soyinka, the elite writer, drew on those stories in his own work.

Where the influence of one literature on another is perhaps more clearly seen, is the influence of folk literature on elite literature — and studies in this area, especially in the case of writers like Wole Soyinka and Amos Tutuola, are most important. These writers have drawn extensively on stylistic features as well as the content of oral tradition. However important these one-way influences might be, we cannot forget that the biggest influence is the common culture — and culture is manifested in many more ways than just through literature. The literatures are not at all independent of these broader influences; moreover, the influences are multiple and simultaneous.

Though I have been focusing mainly on elite literature, I have tried to do so in terms of two types of consciousness that I believe extend beyond that literature to include both folk and popular literature. In the chapter on Achebe I discussed the way in which his novels might be seen as "proverbs writ large." His novels are ethically and rhetorically structured in a manner analogous to the proverb. In their directness, his novels and the proverb express a "rhythm of continuity," the basis of the ethical consciousness. This is no less true of folktales which end with clear moral tags, as well as all popular writing, which is also very clearly and directly didactic. One line of relationships among folk, popular and elite literatures in West Africa might be represented as follows:

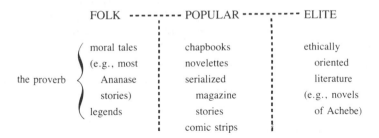

The proverb is followed by an arrow as it is the prototypical example of the ethical consciousness. The relationships among these forms, however, is analogical rather than developmental. All these forms display a clearly functional and didactic relationship with society.

The riddle, then, as I started to indicate in the chapter on Tutuola, is the prototypical example of the mythical consciousness. The relationships among forms reflecting this awareness might be indicated in this manner:

FOLK --------	POPULAR -------------	ELITE
the riddle { dilemma tales, myths		mythically oriented literature (e.g., poetry of Soyinka)

Again the relationships among the forms is analogical. The riddler, be he an actual riddler, a teller of dilemma tales, or a poet such as Soyinka, confronts society in an essentially antagonistic manner. Questions are raised, but answers are withheld. The challenge is to the audience to provide the answers. Where the proverb user displays and shows something that can be clearly apprehended, the riddler asserts something that will confuse.

There is a lacuna in the second diagram. In the sense that I have been employing the term "myth," it does not appear to be possible to have a popular literature which is mythic. As I mentioned in the last chapter, the public wants literature which simplifies and clarifies the problems of daily life. Their lives are problematic enough and their time is limited; hence they have no patience with any literature which deals with the problematic. A given situation might be problematic, but not the moral resolution. Thus, an Achebe might be read by the general public, but not a Soyinka. This in part explains the rather anomolous position of a writer like Amos Tutuola. His language is essentially vernacular and his delineation of character and

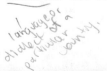

Tutuola

situation is rather simple; he might appear to be a writer who would appeal to a popular audience. This has not been the case. His readers are the same as Soyinka's — a relatively small body of people who have had extensive formal education. Regardless of that which is simple in Tutuola, he has most clearly in *The Palm-Wine Drinkard*, avoided moral resolution and closure.

In northern Ghana the Lo Dagaa have a secret society, Bagre, with which two very long narratives are associated. The first of these, "The White Bagre," appears to be a fairly straightforward narrative in which the Bagre ritual and explanation of the ritual are set forth. We learn of the medical reasons for joining the Bagre, of the ordeals of the neophytes and the duties of members; by my criteria the piece would seem to be ethical. The second narrative, "The Black Bagre," would in contrast seem to be mythic. From the opening lines we can see the problematical nature of this piece:

> In the beginning was god,
> the god of the initiates,
> and their gods,
> the god who comes,
> the god with the mark between the eyes,
> the god with white and black stripes,
> the god with the white arse,
> the thieving god,
> the lying god,
> the troubling god.[6]

Five thousand lines later we are given an explanation of who these gods are, no simple feat in a piece of oral literature of this length. Yet for the Western sensibility it is difficult to account for the apparent "blasphemy" of the invocation. A god should be revered and not slandered. However, we find, for example, that "the lying god" is a trickster who attempted to deceive man into thinking he could banish death if he learned to perform Bagre. In a very immediate way, this trick has taught man, as the neophyte is continually taught, a very skeptical approach to one's sensory apprehension of reality:

> I had this sense [of banishing death]
> but it changed
> into a treacherous sense.
> I had this sense
> but it changed
> into an untruthful sense.
> Too much sense
> is the thing that ruins a man's head.
> Too much foolishness

is also what
ruins a man's head,
though not as readily.[7]

In an ultimate way, "the lying god" is no liar, for although man cannot efface the physical reality of death, his "foolishness" will enable him to transcend that reality, to overcome his sensory perception of death as absolute extinction. If man has too much "sense," he will only perceive myth as a deceptive attempt to make something out of nothing.

Notes

I.   Myth and the African Writer

1.   Publication 71-92 (Waltham, Mass.: African Studies Association, 1971). Reprinted in *Pan-African Journal*, 5 (1972), 253-61.

2.   Snyder, p. 7.

3.   2nd ed. (London: Oxford University Press, 1966), p. 57.

4.   "Amos Tutuola: Debts and Assets," *Cahiers D'études Africaines*, 10, No. 38 (1970), 333.

5.   *Anatomy of Criticism: Four Essays*, 2nd ed. (New York: Atheneum, 1967), p. 136.

6.   "From a Common Back Cloth," *The American Scholar*, 32, No.4 (1963), 392.

7.   Ibid., pp. 392, 394.

8.   "Amos Tutuola on Stage," *Ibadan*, 16 (1962), 24.

9.   Wole Soyinka, "The Writer in a Modern African State," in *The Writer in Modern Africa*, ed. Per Wästberg (New York: Africana, 1969), p. 21.

10.   See Sunday O. Anozie, "Structure and Utopia in Tutuola's *Palm-Wine Drinkard*," *The Conch*, 2, No. 2 (1970), 80-88.

11.   Bernth Lindfors, Ian Munro, Richard Priebe, and Reinhard Sander, eds., *Palaver: Interviews with Five African Writers in Texas*, Occasional Publication No. 3 (Austin, Texas: African and Afro-American Research Institute, 1972), pp. 60-61.

12.   Snyder, p. 8.

13.   Soyinka, "From a Common Back Cloth," p. 390.

14.   Lindfors, Munro, et al., p. 55.

15.   "The Fourth Stage," *The Morality of Art*, ed. D.W. Jefferson (London: Routledge and Kegan Paul, 1969), p. 122.

16.   *Aspects of the Novel*, 2nd ed. (Harmondsworth: Pelican, 1962), pp. 125-26. Chinua Achebe and others have responded to Armah in a similar manner. Consider his remark in *Morning Yet on Creation Day*: "It is a well-written book.... But it is a sick book." (London: Heinemann, 1975), p. 25.

17.   2nd ed. (Harmondsworth: Pelican, 1970).

18.   *The Politics of Experience* (New York: Ballantine, 1967), p. 115.

19.   Soyinka, "From a Common Back Cloth," p. 392.

20.   (New York: Doubleday, 1969), p. 261.

21.   (New York: Doubleday, 1971), pp. 17-19.

22.   See Donald Ackley, "*The Interpreters,*" *Black Orpheus*, 2, Nos. 5 and 6 (1972), 50-55, and Charles Larson, "Time, Space, and Description: The Tutuolan World," *The*

Emergence of African Literature (Bloomington, Ind.: Indiana University Press, 1972), pp. 93-112.

23. Forster, pp. 111-50.

II. A Man Betwixt and Between

1. *The Hero with a Thousand Faces*, 2nd ed. (Princeton: Princeton University Press, 1972), p. 50.

2. *The Ritual Process: Structure and Anti-Structure* (Chicago: Aldine, 1969), p. 167.

3. *The Forest of Symbols: Aspects of Ndembu Ritual* (Ithaca, New York: Cornell University Press, 1970), p. 95.

4. *Purity and Danger: An Analysis of Concepts of Pollution and Taboo*, 2nd ed. (Harmondsworth: Pelican, 1970), p. 136.

5. See Max Gluckman, *Custom and Conflict in Africa* (Glencoe, Illinois: Free Press, 1955).

6. *The Ritual Process*, p. 106.

7. (London: Oxford University Press, 1965), p. 45.

8. *The Ritual Process*, pp. 106-07.

9. (New York: Collier, 1969), p. 1. Subsequent references are to this edition and to the following editions of Armah's other works: *Fragments* (New York: Collier, 1971); *Why Are We So Blest?* (New York: Doubleday, 1972).

10. It is interesting to note, however, that with Koomson the symbolism of the conductor's smelling the money has come full circle. The source of power that the conductor has inhaled, Koomson must now exhale. One of the first things the man notices about Koomson after the coup is the fact that "His mouth had the rich stench of rotten menstrual blood" (p. 161).

11. "Anthropological Aspects of Language: Animal Categories and Verbal Abuse," in *New Directions in the Study of Language*, ed. Eric H. Lenneberg (Cambridge, Mass.: M.I.T. Press, 1969), pp. 37-38.

12. *The Politics of Experience* (New York: Ballantine, 1969), pp. 118-19.

13. "The Ironic Imagery of Armah's *The Beautyful Ones Are Not Yet Born*: The Putrescent Vision," *World Literature Written in English*, No. 20 (1971), pp. 37-50.

14. *Language as Symbolic Action* (Berkeley: University of California Press, 1968), p. 469.

15. Note the oxymoron, "creation of chaos." Even chaos is not thought of in strictly negative terms. See Joan Wescott, "The Sculpture and Myth of Eshu-Elegba, the Yoruba Trickster," *Africa*, 32, No. 4, 336-54. Eshu is an important figure in the works of Wole Soyinka, and I will discuss the way he uses Eshu in chapters VI and VIII.

16. Burke, p. 462.

17. Later we learn that Koomson has also accepted because he plans to use the man and his family as a front for his fishing business.

18. See *Forest of Symbols*, pp. 97-98.

19. "Structure and Image in Kwei Armah's *The Beautyful Ones Are Not Yet Born*," *Studies in Black Literature*, 2, No. 2 (1971), 4.

20. From a "universal" perspective she may also correspond to what Campbell has called "the Queen Goddess of the World." See *The Hero*, pp. 109-20.

21. An example of this alienation is to be seen in the case of Unoko, the father of Okonkwo in Achebe's *Things Fall Apart*. His poetic sensibility continually kept him at odds with his society.

22. "The Writer and the Cargo Cult," in *Common Wealth*, ed. Anna Rutherford (Aarhus, Denmark: Akademisk Boghandel, 1972), p. 73.

23. Campbell, pp. 196-97.

24. See J.H. Nketia, *Funeral Dirges of the Akan People* (Achimota, Ghana, 1955), p. 84.

25. Ibid., p. 120.

26. A ceremony in which a child, approximately one week old is taken out of the house for the first time and is given its name. Relatives and friends come, suggest names and bring gifts of money for the child.

27. Moore, p. 78.

28. See *Beautyful Ones*, p. 91 and *Fragments*, pp. 52-55.

29. See "Structure and Image," also "The Language of Disillusion in the African Novel," in *Common Wealth*, pp. 62-72.

30. See David Caute, *Frantz Fanon* (1970), p. 52. It is interesting to note that *Why Are We So Blest?* ends with such an image of transformation in the desert and *Two Thousand Seasons* begins with such an image.

31. Trans. Constance Farrington (New York: Grove Press, 1963), p. 37.

32. Burke, pp. 472-73.

33. See Turner, *The Forest of Symbols*: "... much of the grotesqueness and monstrosity of liminal *sacra* may be seen to be aimed not so much at terrorizing or bemusing the neophytes into submission or out of their wits as at making them vividly and rapidly aware of what may be called the 'factors' of their culture" (p. 105). Translated in terms of *Why Are We So Blest?* this means an awareness of neo-colonial mystification. For a further elaboration of this process see Kenneth Burke on the "Dialectic of the Scapegoat," in *A Grammar of Rhetoric* (Berkeley: University of California Press, 1969), pp. 406-08.

III. The Proverb, Realism and Achebe

1. Kenneth Burke, *The Philosophy of Literary Form* (New York: Vintage, 1961), p. 256.

2. Ibid., p. 255. Proverbs are often structured around a metaphor, but if the proverb is to function when used in a social context, the analogue to the real situation must be readily apprehended by those to whom the proverb is directed.

3. (London: Cambridge University Press, 1959).

4. (London: Heinemann, 1962), p. 25. Subsequent references are to this edition.

5. Meyer Fortes, pp. 70-71.

6. This is borne out in the other two Theban plays of Sophocles and also in Achebe's *No Longer at Ease* .

7. Meyer Fortes, p. 71.

8. "The Palm Oil with Which Achebe's Words are Eaten," *African Literature Today*, 1 (1968), 8.

9. Meyer Fortes, pp. 17-18.

10. Though the Tale and the Ibo are two very distinct cultural groups, the level of generalization is high enough that I can avoid the problems that can come from examining cultures that are both similar and distinct.

11. Meyer Fortes, p. 53.

12. Ibid., p. 54.

13. See Claude Lévi-Strauss, *Structural Anthropology*, trans. Claire Jacobson and Brooke Grundfest Schoepf, 2nd ed. (New York: Anchor, 1967), p. 211.

14. Meyer Fortes, p. 74.

15. Ibid., p. 59.

IV. The Riddle, Myth and Tutuola

1. Bernth Lindfors, "Amos Tutuola: Debts and Assets," *Cahiers D'études Africaines*, 10, No. 38 (1970), 333.

2. *The Palm-Wine Drinkard* (New York: Grove Press, 1953), p. 27, and *My Life in the Bush of Ghosts* (New York: Grove Press, 1954), p. 156. Page references in parentheses will refer to these editions.

3. Trans. S.H. Butcher, ed. Milton C. Nahn (New York: Library of Liberal Arts, 1956), p. 29. For a further discussion of this see Robert A. Georges and Alan Dundes, "Toward a Structural Definition of the Riddle," *Journal of American Folklore*, 76 (1963), 111-18.

4. Roger D. Abrahams, "The Literary Study of the Riddle," *Texas Studies in Literature and Language*, 14, No. 1 (1972), 191.

5. This figure is somewhat arbitrary as one might see a few of these adventures as constituting more than one distinct adventure.

6. Achebe's realism establishes a universe that is fully comprehensible, even to a non-African, just within the literary work itself. However, as we shall see in subsequent chapters, the universe created by the writer employing the rhetoric of myth, is not a universe we can fully relate to unless we know something about the social reality he is re-structuring.

7. "African Dilemma Tales: An Introduction," in *African Folklore*, ed. Richard M. Dorson (New York: Anchor Books, 1972), p. 155.

8. (New York: Fawcett, 1969), pp. 52-53.

9. For a discussion of Achebe's symbolic use of this tale see Donald Weinstock and Cathy Ramada, "Symbolic Structure in *Things Fall Apart*," *Critique: Studies in Modern Fiction*, 2 (1969), 22-41.

10. Michael Linn, "Degrees of Grammaticalness in Amos Tutuola's *The Palm-Wine Drinkard*," presented at the Annual Meeting of the African Studies Association, Chicago, October 1974.

V. *This Earth, My Brother*

1. Bernth Lindfors, Ian Munro, Richard Priebe, and Reinhard Sander, eds., *Palaver: Interviews with Five African Writers in Texas*, Occasional Publication No. 3 (Austin: African and Afro-American Research Institute, 1972), p. 54.

2. Ibid., p. 52.

3. Personal communication, April 1973.

4. *Funeral Dirges of the Akan People* (Achimota, Ghana, 1955).

5. Confirmed by Kofi Awoonor (personal communication, April 1972).

6. *Aspects of the Novel* (Harmondsworth: Pelican, 1962), pp. 48-49.

7. In *The Morality of Art*, ed. D.W. Jefferson (London: Routledge and Kegan Paul, 1969), p. 122.

8. Lindfors, Munro, et al., p. 61.

9. Kofi Awoonor, *This Earth, My Brother* (New York: Doubleday, 1971), p. 8. Subsequent references to this edition.

10. See Janheinz Jahn, *Muntu: An Outline of Neo-African Culture*, trans. Marjorie Grene (New York: Grove Press, 1961).

11. In the interview referred to above, Awoonor was asked whether he felt the writer should be committed to some sort of social change. His response is worth noting here:

... the writer ... by the very commitment he imposes upon himself to tell the story of our woes, sorrows and joys is a committed writer. Achebe once said,

"What is the point of suffering if it is to go on forever." If suffering is not productive, it is no good .... The little man in the corner who goes through the grinding sorrow ... will perhaps one day be able to reach a little respite. (Lindfors, Munro, et al., p. 56)

12. John Goldblatt, interviewer, No. 41 (1972), p. 44.

13. *A Rhetoric of Motives* (Berkeley: University of California Press, 1969), p. 203.

14. Personal communication with Kofi Awoonor, November 1972.

15. See Christopher Marlowe, "Dr. Faustus" (Act V, scene i, ll. 54-55): "Where art thou, Faustus? Wretch, what hast thou done?/Damned art thou, Faustus, damned! Despair and die." An old man has been trying to talk Faustus into repenting, but Faustus, aware of his impossible situation, utters these lines, more to himself than to either the old man or Mephistophilis, who is also present. Like Faustus, Amamu feels he is beyond salvation. His anguish, however, is not just personal — he also feels despair because of the hopeless situation his land is caught in.

16. Probably a reference to Nkrumah Circle in Accra. After Nkrumah was overthrown it was renamed National Liberation Circle. Now, incidentally, it is again Nkrumah Circle.

17. Roger Abrahams has explored the relation between the ludic/serious opposition and ritual in "Ritual for Fun and Profit, or the Ends and Outs of Celebration," an unpublished manuscript.

18. Cf. Awoonor's poem, "The Journey Beyond," in *Night of My Blood* (New York: Doubleday, 1971): "Kutsiami the benevolent boatman;/when I come to the river shore/please ferry me across ..." (p. 41). The ferryman and the river are from Ewe mythology and are similar to the ferryman, Charon, and the rivers Cocytus and Acheron which the dead must cross in Roman mythology.

19. See Lindfors, Munro, et al., p. 60.

20. *The Morality of Art*, p. 123.

21. Ibid., p. 124.

22. See Janheinz Jahn.

23. Nketia, pp. 13-14.

24. See Nketia, p. 19.

25. *Aspects of the Novel*, p. 140.

VI. Yoruba Cosmology

1. "The Writer in a Modern African State," in *The Writer in Modern Africa*, ed. Per Wästberg (New York: Africana, 1969), p. 21.

2. There would seem to be sound support for the latter idea. Both Eshu and Oro are spirits who have status marginal to the domains of man and the *oriṣa*. Though Eshu is messenger and trickster, and Oro is an agent of revenge, it would be a reasonable move to combine their mediating powers. See Peter Morton-Williams, "An Outline of the Cosmology and Cult Organization of the Oyo Yoruba," *Africa*, 34, No. 1 (1964), 247-49.

3. (New York: Collier, 1970), p. 193. All subsequent references are to this edition.

4. Personal communication, February 1973.

5. Morton-Williams in discussing the individuating traits of the *oriṣa*, such as the impatience and arrogance of Ogun, states that "it is noteworthy that definite personalities or dispositions are believed to characterize members of their various cults ... and there seems to be good empirical support for this — worshippers' characteristics being either remarkably like those of the gods or else clearly complementary to them" (p. 246).

6.　In *The Morality of Art*, ed. D.W. Jefferson (London: Routledge and Kegan Paul, 1969), pp. 119-34.

7.　Ibid., p. 125.

8.　Ibid., p. 130.

9.　Ibid., p. 125.

10.　Cf. ibid., p. 127; *The Interpreters*, pp. 244 and 247; and Wole Soyinka, *Idanre* (New York: Hill and Wang, 1968), p. 87n.

11.　"The Fourth Stage," p. 125.

12.　See Soyinka, "The Writer in a Modern African State," p. 19.

13.　p. 86n.

14.　Soyinka also informs us in his notes to "Idanre" that Ogun annually "re-creates his deed of shame" (p. 87n).

15.　Cf. the following passage in "Idanre": "Yet had he fled when his primal task was done/Fugitive from man and god, ever seeking hills/And rock bounds" (p. 72).

16.　*The Hero with a Thousand Faces*, 2nd ed. (Princeton: Princeton University Press, 1972), p. 109.

17.　Ibid., pp. 120-21.

18.　Literally, queen of the sea, daughter of Yemoja. Soyinka also uses an interesting English equivalent in referring to her as "the Queen Bee." (See pp. 53 and 55.)

19.　"Anthropological Aspects of Language: Animal Categories and Verbal Abuse," in *New Directions in the Study of Language*, ed. Eric H. Lenneberg (Cambridge, Mass.: M.I.T. Press, 1964), p. 29.

20.　Leach, pp. 38-39.

21.　"An Outline," pp. 243-61.

22.　Ibid., p. 243; also see E. Bọlaji Idowu, *Olódùmarè: God in Yoruba Belief* (London: Longmans, 1962), pp.48-49.

23.　"The Fourth Stage," p. 127.

24.　Joan Wescott, "The Sculpture and Myths of Eshu-Elegba, the Yoruba Trickster," *Africa*, 32, No. 4 (1962), 336-53.

25.　Robert Farris Thompson, *Black Gods and Kings: Yoruba Art at UCLA*, Occasional Papers of the Museum and Laboratories of Ethnic Arts and Technology, University of California, No. 2 (Los Angeles, 1971), sig. CH/1.

26.　*The Yoruba of Southwestern Nigeria* (New York: Holt, Rinehart and Winston, 1969), p. 81.

27.　In discussing African music and dance Thompson has noted that they "seem joint bearers of a dynamic sensibility; both seem to fuse energy and decorum in a manner that confounds the either/or categories of Western thinking." "An Aesthetic of the Cool: West African Dance," *African Forum*, 2, No. 2 (1966), p. 87. Cf. with the following comment by Odili in Chinua Achebe's *A Man of the People* (New York: Doubleday, 1967), p. 48:

[The critic] committed a crime in my view because he transferred to an alien culture the same meanings and interpretation that his own people attach to certain gestures and facial expression. This critic, a Frenchman writing in a glossy magazine on African art said of a famous religious mask from this country: "Note the half-closed eyes, sharply drawn and tense eyebrow, the ecstatic and passionate mouth ..."

It was simply scandalous. All that the mask said, all that is felt for mankind was a certain superb, divine detachment and disdain. If I met a woman in the street and she looked at me with the face of that mask that would be its meaning.

28. See Thompson, *Black Gods and Kings*, sig. CH2/1-2.

29. "An Aesthetic of the Cool," p. 86.

30. Kofi Awoonor has explained that it is a common practice in West Africa to close all apertures of the dead with cotton wool (personal communication). See Soyinka's poem "Post Mortem" in *Idanre*, p. 31: "in the cold hand of death .../his mouth was cotton filled ..."

31. It may be of interest to note that Idowu (p. 35) has recorded a Yoruba myth that is similar to the Biblical myth of the rainbow as the sign of a covenant between heaven and earth. Moreover he corroborates the contention that the rainbow deity fills that gap (heaven/earth) with "tabooed ambiguity":

> The Yoruba believe, generally, that the rainbow is produced by a very large boa: the reptile discharges from its inside the sulphureous matter which sets all its surroundings aglow and causes a reflection, which is the rainbow (*Oṣùmarè*), in the sky. The matter which is so discharged is known as *Imi Oṣùmarè* ("rainbow-excrement") and is considered very valuable for making people wealthy and prosperous.... It is, however, very rarely obtained ... one reason being that anyone who approached the spot at the moment it is on the ground would be consumed forthwith.... (pp. 34-35)

32. Thompson, *Black Gods and Kings*, sig. CH2/2.

33. Thompson, "An Aesthetic of the Cool," p. 99.

34. See Thompson, *Black Gods and Kings*, sig. P/5 and CH3/1.

35. Like Tutuola, Soyinka is clearly a riddler. Even when he uses proverbs, he employs them to confuse, not clarify. Consider, for example, the abundance of proverbs in *Death and the Kings Horseman* (New York: Norton, 1975). He employs proverbs there to heighten the sense of the ineffable.

36. Wole Soyinka, *A Dance of the Forests* (London: Oxford University Press, 1963), p. 82.

VII. Liminality in Awoonor and Soyinka

1. Bernth Lindfors, Ian Munro, Richard Priebe, and Reinhard Sander, eds., *Palaver: Interviews with Five African Writers in Texas*, Occasional publication No. 3 (Austin: African and Afro-American Research Institute, 1972), pp. 58-60.

2. Wole Soyinka, *Idanre and Other Poems* (New York: Hill and Wang, 1969) and Kofi Awoonor, *Night of My Blood* (New York: Doubleday, 1971). All subsequent references are to these editions.

3. According to Awoonor there was a typographical error in the printing of this poem. (Personal communication, February 1973.) Cf. version in *Rediscovery* (Ibadan, Nigeria: Mbari, 1964), p. 11.

4. Personal communication, February 1973.

5. *Purity and Danger: An Analysis of Concepts of Pollution and Taboo* (Harmondsworth: Pelican, 1970), p. 190.

6. Ibid., pp. 190-91.

7. Ibid., p. 193.

8. (London: Oxford University Press, 1963), p. 82.

9. Meyer Fortes, *Oedipus and Job in West African Religion* (London: Cambridge University Press, 1959), pp. 35-36.

10. Gerald Moore, *Wole Soyinka* (New York: Africana, 1971), pp. 92-93.

11. There is a complexity in this image that will be more clearly apparent at the end of this chapter. Soyinka himself does not see this Yoruba symbol as a symbol of regeneration, but rather as a symbol of "the doom of repetition" (*Idanre*, p. 86n). Abiku is thus the antithesis of Atǫǫ́da, the archetypal revolutionary with the will to break the cycle. See pp. 119 and 125 of this volume.

12. (New York: Collier, 1970), p. 252.

13. Awoonor has said that among his people, the Ewe, the isolation, cleansing and subsequent celebration for the individual who has returned after a long journey is extremely similar to the ritual surrounding a death (personal communication, March 1970).

14. The images in this poem are those employed in a traditional Ewe dirge: the tree is the departed individual, the orphan is the mourner, the desert is life, and the fallen walls are a correlative to the loss the community has experienced in the death (personal communication with Awoonor, February 1973).

15. In *The Breast of the Earth: A Survey of the History, Culture and Literature of Africa South of the Sahara*, Awoonor has written that "the communal feast is still an active aspect of Ewe religious rites. It affirms and renews the bond that unites men, families, and clansmen; it eliminates ill-will and bad blood; emphasizes the unity between the living and the dead in its open communication with the dead through accompanying propitiatory rites; it, above all, affirms the living force of the community ..." (New York: Doubleday, 1975), p. 70.

16. The history of migrations into West Africa is almost entirely conjecture. See Donald L. Wiedner, *A History of Africa South of the Sahara* (New York: Vintage, 1962), pp. 39-43.

17. Personal communication with Awoonor, February 1973.

18. *Guardians of the Sacred Word: Ewe Poetry* (New York: Nok, 1974), p. 2.

19. Ibid., p. 19.

20. Ibid., pp. 19-20.

21. Christopher Scott, "Some Aspects of the Structural Unity of 'Idanre,'" *World Literature Written in English*, No. 20 (1971), pp. 11-14.

22. p. 19 (Add. MS. 53785).

23. According to William Bascom, "Ogun ... is the God of Iron and the patron of all those who use iron tools. He is a patron of hunters and warriors and thus a God of War, a patron of blacksmiths, of woodcarvers and leatherworkers, of barbers, of those who perform circumcision and cicitrization, and in recent times a patron of locomotive and automobile drivers. For this reason it is said there are seven kinds of Ogun ... but there are more than seven classes of people who are indebted to him because they use iron implements." *The Yoruba of Southwestern Nigeria* (New York: Holt, Rinehart and Winston, 1969), p. 82.

24. See preceding note.

25. I am again using Robert Farris Thompson's hot/cool opposition. See above, p. 94.

26. See Bascom, p. 81.

27. "An Aesthetic of the Cool: West African Dance," *African Forum*, 2, No. 2 (1966), 86.

28. Scott, "The Structural Unity of 'Idanre.'"

29. The argument that Soyinka later presented in Stockholm is a clear reflection of this vision. See "The Writer in a Modern African State," in *The Writer in Modern Africa*, ed. Per Wästberg (New York: Africana, 1969), pp. 19-20.

30. Bascom, p. 83.

31. Wole Soyinka, "The Fourth Stage," in *The Morality of Art*, ed. D. W. Jefferson (London: Routledge and Kegan Paul, 1969), p. 129.

VIII. *Brother Jero*'s Mythic Dimension

1. (London: Rex Collings, 1972).

2. (New York: Collier, 1970), pp. 118-20.

3. Roger Abrahams, "Ritual for Fun and Profit, or the Ends and Outs of Celebration," unpublished MS.

4. See Bill Walker, "Mime in *The Lion and the Jewel*," *World Literature Written in English*, 12, No. 1 (1973), 37-44.

5. Though my immediate concern is not with these later plays I might note that Soyinka himself has indicated his use of traditional ritual in *The Road* in his prefatory statement, "For the Producer," (London: Oxford University Press, 1965). Oyin Ogunba has written on ritual and festival in Soyinka's plays in "The Traditional Content of the Plays of Wole Soyinka," *African Literature Today*, No. 4, pp. 2-18 and No. 5, pp. 106-15.

6. See Susan Yankowitz, "The Plays of Wole Soyinka," *African Forum*, 1, No. 4 (1966), 132-33. Also see Margaret Laurence, *Long Drums and Cannons* (London: Macmillan, 1968), p. 22, and Gerald Moore, *Wole Soyinka* (New York: Africana, 1971), p. 22.

7. See Gerald Moore, p. 20.

8. William Bascom, "Folklore and Literature," in *The African World*, ed. Robert A. Lystad (New York: Praeger, 1965), p. 482.

9. *Dahomean Narrative* (Evanston, Ill.: Northwestern University Press, 1958), p. 101.

10. (London: Oxford University Press, 1969), p. 45. All subsequent references are to this edition.

11. Joan Wescott, "Sculpture and Myths of Eshu-Elegba," *Africa*, 32, No. 4 (1962), 348.

12. Yankowitz, p. 132.

13. Wescott, p. 345.

14. It is worth noting that the rhetorical skill of Jero seems to have no limits. In the second Jero play, *Jero's Metamorphosis*, Chume returns from the asylum only to be duped again by the prophet.

15. Joan Wescott points out (p. 345) that the Yoruba have a saying that "Elegba hides behind cowries." Eshu sculptures are always covered by strings of cowries (an old form of money) which attest to the belief that Eshu has something to do with all transactions of money.

16. It is interesting to note here that Eshu sculptures are almost always found with a small mirror strung around the neck. The mirror, of course, symbolizes vanity (Wescott, p. 346). While Jero does not have such a mirror on his body, the stage directions at the beginning of Scene III call for a mirror among the few objects on stage (p. 54).

17. See Gerald Moore, p. 15.

18. Chinua Achebe, *A Man of the People* (New York: Anchor Books, 1967), p. 18.

19. *The Interpreters*, pp. 175 and 193.

20. "The Writer in a Modern African State." in *The Writer in Modern Africa*, ed. Per Wästberg (New York: Africana, 1969), pp. 14-21.

21. Victor Turner, *The Forest of Symbols: Aspects of Ndembu Ritual* (Ithaca, New York: Cornell University Press, 1970), p. 95.

IX. Ethical Consciousness and Popular Fiction

1. An assumption in this paper is that popular literature is normative; it reflects the current values of a society. Elite literature, on the other hand, is progressive; it may reflect values, but it also anticipates change.

2. Irving Kaplan et al., *Area Handbook for Ghana* (Washington, D.C.: U.S. Government Printing Office, 1971), p. 184.

3. For bibliographical details regarding this piece and other Ghanaian popular literature see my bibliography in *Research in African Literatures*, 9, 3 (1978), 425-32.

4. Don Dodson, "The Role of the Publisher in Onitsha Market Literature," *Research in African Literatures*, 4 (1973), 180.

5. In 1974, when I did my research for this chapter, a cedi was worth approximately one U.S. dollar. (There are 100 pesewas in a cedi.) Due to an inflation which has averaged over one hundred percent per year since then, my figures do not apply to Ghana today. Throughout this chapter the costs I quote are those which existed in the mid-seventies.

6. This and other statements from writers and publishers quoted in this paper are from interviews I conducted in Ghana in May and June 1974.

7. *Africa Report*, 7, I (1972), 26-27.

8. He also printed and sold an additional 100,000 copies of this booklet.

9. "The Character of Popular Fiction in Ghana," *Perspectives on African Literature*, ed. Christopher Heywood (New York: Africana Publishing Corporation, 1971) p. 115.

10. Mickson's first novelette, *When the Heart Decides*, does not have a publication date in the text. Ikiddeh gives 1965 as the publication date (see Ikiddeh, "The Character of Popular Fiction," p. 116) and Janheinz Jahn and Claus Dressler say it was 1966, see *Bibliography of Creative African Writing* (Millwood, N.Y.: Kraus-Thompson, 1973), p. 156. I take the later date as probably being correct since it is also reported in Margaret D. Patten, *Ghanaian Imaginative Writing in English*, 1950-1969 (Legon, Ghana: Department of Library Studies, 1971), p. 42.

11. See Ikiddeh, "The Character of Popular Fiction," p. 115.

12. *Area Handbook*, p. 245.

13. Ibid., p. 249.

14. My colleague, Boyd Berry, has also been extremely helpful in my working out of the rhetorical relationship between physical body and political body in Ghanaian literature.

15. *Language as Symbolic Action* (Berkeley: University of California Press, 1966), p. 308.

16. See p. 66.

17. Burke, *Language*, pp. 341-42.

18. See *Palaver: Interviews with Five African Writers in Texas*, ed. Bernth Lindfors et al., Occasional Publication No. 3 (Austin: The African and Afro-American Research Institute, 1972), p. 60.

19. Burke, *Language*, p. 342.

20. The following quote from Burke might help to explain the distinctions between the first two modes and the third mode:

Motivationally, we might put the terministic problem thus: When several ideas integrally imply one another, we may take any one as ambiguously standing for the others ....

Except in works of frankly Rabelaisian, Aristophanic, or Swiftian cast, aesthetic ideals are such that any tendencies toward bathos will, if possible, be so transmuted that they bear the guise of pathos. However, as regards our exegesis, we are *not* reducing the whole set to the genius of the "problematical" member. Rather, we are trying simply to show that the problematical elements remain, however disguised by euphemism. (*Language*, p. 341)

21. For a history and an examination of the accomplishments of the G.P.C., see A.K. Brown, "State Publishing in Ghana: Has it Benefited Ghana?" *Publishing in Africa in the Seventies*, ed. Edwina Oluwasanmi, et al. (Ile-Ife, Nigeria: University of Ife Press, 1975), pp. 113-27.

22. It is interesting to note here that no magazine has ever had the popularity *Drum* had in Ghana. Ofori informed me that in 1961 the magazine reached a peak circulation of 65,000. At the time Ofori left, the publishers were trying to reach the circulation of 90,000 that the Nigeria edition of *Drum* had.

23. Less a discount of ten to fifteen percent for ads running more than five months.

24. Figures are from *Ghana Press Guide*, a pamphlet published by Information Services Department, Accra, 1973.

25. Poetry is only rarely published in the newspapers. Also, it is interesting that the *Spectator* pays less than the *Mirror* despite the fact that it has a larger circulation. They may do this because the daily with which the *Spectator* is associated (the *Times*) has a much smaller circulation than the daily with which the *Mirror* is associated (the *Graphic*).

26. Observations are based on an eight-week sample, mid-April through mid-June 1974.

27. The "Ananse" comic strip is one of the few cases in Ghanaian popular literature where we can see the direct influence of oral literature. In a paper delivered at the Annual Meeting of the African Studies Association at Syracuse in 1973, Cyprian Lamar Rowe argued that the popular novelettes are structured much like traditional stories ("Structural Continuity from Ghanaian Oral Narratives to Ghanaian Popular Fiction"). His argument is not at all convincing, but the study of the possible influences of folk literature on popular literature is an area worthy of further research.

Conclusion

1. See Bernth Lindfors, "The Folktale as Paradigm in Chinua Achebe's *Arrow of God*," *Studies in Black Literature*, 1, No. 1 (1970), 1-2, and "Amos Tutuola: Debts and Assets," *Cahiers D'études Africaines*, 10, No. 38 (1970), 330-32.

2. "Tutuola, Fagunwa, and Shakespeare," *The Journal of Commonwealth Literature*, 8, No. 1 (June 1973), 110-11.

3. I think a good analogy here is the way Americans and Europeans are often amused by headlines in African newspapers. Recently, in one Ghanaian paper was the headline "Lomé goes Gay." To any Ghanaian this simply meant that Lomé was having a big celebration. To Americans it was funny since "gay" has the implication of homosexuality.

4. *Mimesis: The Representation of Reality in Western Literature*, trans. Willard Trask, 2nd Ed. (New York: Anchor, 1957), p. 19.

5. Bernth Lindfors, Ian Munro, Richard Priebe, and Reinhard Sander, eds., *Palaver: Interviews with Five African Writers in Texas*, Occasional Publication No. 3 (Austin: African and Afro-American Research Institute,1972), p. 56.

6. Jack Goody, *The Myth of the Bagre* (London: Oxford University Press, 1972), p. 224.

7. Ibid., pp. 290-91.

Bibliography

Creative Writing

Achebe, Chinua. *Arrow of God*. New York: Doubleday, 1969.

—. *A Man of the People*. New York: Doubleday, 1967.

—. *Things Fall Apart*. New York: Fawcett, 1969.

Armah, Ayi Kwei. *The Beautyful Ones Are Not Yet Born*. New York: Collier, 1969.

—. *Fragments*. New York: Collier, 1971.

—. *The Healers*. Nairobi: East African Publishing House, 1978.

—. *Two Thousand Seasons*. Nairobi: East African Publishing House, 1973.

—. *Why Are We So Blest?* New York: Doubleday, 1972.

Awoonor, Kofi. *This Earth, My Brother*. New York: Doubleday, 1971.

—. *Night of My Blood*. New York: Doubleday, 1971.

—. *Rediscovery*. Ibadan, Nigeria: Mbari, 1964.

Ekwensi, Cyprian. *Jagua Nana*. New York: Fawcett, 1969.

Ogunmọla, Elijah Kọlawọle. *The Palm-wine Drinkard*. Trans. R.G. Armstrong, Robert L. Owujọọla and Val Olayẹmi. Occasional Papers of The Institute of African Studies, University of Ibadan, No. 12, Ibadan, Nigeria, 1968.
Soyinka, Wole. *A Dance of the Forests*. London: Oxford University Press, 1963.

—. *Collected Plays 1*. London: Oxford University Press, 1973.

—. *Collected Plays 2*. London: Oxford University Press, 1974.

—. *Death and the King's Horseman*. New York: Norton, 1975.

—. *Idanre and Other Poems*. New York: Hill and Wang, 1969.

—. "Idanre." British Museum Add. MS.53785.

—. *The Interpreters*. New York: Collier, 1970.

—. *The Jero Plays*. London: Methuen, 1973.

—. *Kongi's Harvest*. London: Oxford University Press, 1967.

—. *The Lion and the Jewel*. London: Oxford University Press, 1963.

—. *Madmen and Specialists*. London: Methuen, 1971.

—. *The Road*. London: Oxford University Press, 1965.

—. *Three Short Plays: The Swamp Dwellers, The Trials of Brother Jero and The Strong Breed*. London: Oxford University Press, 1969.

Tutuola, Amos. *The Palm-Wine Drinkard*. New York: Grove Press, 1953.

—. *My Life in the Bush of Ghosts*. New York: Grove Press, 1954.

Critical Sources

Abrahams, Roger, "The Literary Study of the Riddle." *Texas Studies in Literature and Language*, 14, No. 1 (1972), 177-97.

—. "Ritual for Fun and Profit, or the Ends and Outs of Celebration." Unpublished MS.

Achebe, Chinua. *Morning Yet on Creation Day*. London: Heinemann, 1975.

Ackley, Donald. *"The Interpreters."* Black Orpheus, 2, Nos. 5 and 6 (1972), 50-57.

Anozie, Sunday. *Christopher Okigbo*. New York: Africana, 1972.

—. "Structure and Utopia in Tutuola's *The Palm-Wine Drinkard,*" *The Conch,* 2, No. 2 (1970), 80-88.

Armah, Ayi Kwei. "African Socialism: Utopian or Scientific?" *Présence Africaine,* No. 64 (1967), pp. 6-30.

Armstrong, Robert Plant. *The Affecting Presence: An Essay in Humanistic Anthropology.* Urbana: University of Illinois Press, 1971.

Auerbach, Erich. *Mimesis: The Representation of Reality in Western Literature.* Trans. Willard Trask. 2nd ed. New York: Anchor, 1957.

Awoonor, Kofi. *The Breast of the Earth: A Survey of the History, Culture and Literature of Africa South of the Sahara.* Garden City, N.Y.: Anchor-Doubleday, 1975.

—. *Guardians of the Sacred Word: Ewe Poetry.* New York: Nok, 1974.

—. "A Study of the Influences of Oral Literature on the Contemporary Literature of Africa." Diss. State University of New York at Stony Brook, 1972.

Bascom, William. "Folklore and Literature." *The African World .* Ed. Robert A. Lystad. New York: Praeger, 1965, pp. 469-90.

—. *The Yoruba of Southwestern Nigeria.* New York: Holt, Rinehart and Winston, 1969.

Bidney, David. "Myth, Symbolism, and Truth." *Myth: A Symposium.* Ed. Thomas A. Sebeok. Bloomington: Indiana University Press, 1965, pp. 3-24.

Burke, Kenneth. *Counter-Statement.* Chicago: University of Chicago Press, 1953.

—. *A Grammar of Motives.* Berkeley: University of California Press, 1969.

—. *Language as Symbolic Action.* Berkeley: University of California Press, 1968.

—. *The Philosophy of Literary Form.* New York: Vintage, 1961.

—. *A Rhetoric of Motives.* Berkeley: University of California Press, 1969.

Busia, K.A. "The Ashanti." *African Worlds.* Ed. Daryll Forde. London: Oxford University Press, 1955, pp. 190-209.

Campbell, Joseph. *The Hero with a Thousand Faces.* 2nd ed. Princeton: Princeton University Press, 1972.

—. "The Historical Development of Mythology." *Myth and Mythmaking.* Ed. Henry A. Murray. New York: George Braziller, 1960, pp. 19-45.

Caute, David. *Frantz Fanon*. New York: Viking, 1970.

Collins, Harold R. "The Ironic Imagery of Armah's *The Beautyful Ones Are Not Yet Born*: The Putrescent Vision." *World Literature Written in English*, No. 20 (1971), pp. 37-50.

Dodson, Don. "The Role of the Publisher in Onitsha Market Literature." *Research in African Literatures*, 4 (1973), pp. 172-88.

Dorson, Richard M., ed. *African Folklore*. New York: Anchor Books, 1972.

Douglas, Mary. *Purity and Danger: An Analysis of Concepts of Pollution and Taboo*. 2nd ed. Harmondsworth: Pelican, 1970.

Duerden, Dennis and Cosmo Pieterse, eds. *African Writers Talking: A Collection of Radio Interviews*. New York: Africana, 1972.

Fanon, Frantz. *Black Skin, White Masks*. Trans. Charles Lam Markmann. New York: Grove Press, 1967.

—. *The Wretched of the Earth*. Trans. Constance Farrington. New York: Grove Press, 1968.

Finnegan, Ruth. *Oral Literature in Africa*. Oxford: The Clarendon Press, 1970.

Forster, E.M. *Aspects of the Novel*. 2nd ed. Harmondsworth: Pelican, 1962.

Fortes, Meyer. *Oedipus and Job in West African Religion*. London: Cambridge University Press, 1959.

Frye, Northrop. *Anatomy of Criticism: Four Essays*. 2nd ed. New York: Atheneum, 1967.

—. "New Directions from Old." *Myth and Mythmaking*. Henry A. Murray. New York: George Braziller, 1960, pp. 115-31.

Georges, Robert A., ed. *Studies on Mythology*. Homewood, Ill.: Dorsey Press, 1968.

— and Alan Dundes. "Toward a Structural Definition of the Riddle." *Journal of American Folklore*. 76, (1963), 111-18.

Gluckman, Max. *Custom and Conflict in Africa*. Glencoe, Ill.: Free Press, 1955.

Goldblatt, John, interviewer. "Kofi Awoonor." *Transition*, No. 41 (1972), pp. 42-44.

Goody, Jack. *The Myth of the Bagre*. London: Oxford University Press, 1972.

Griffiths, Gareth. "The Language of Disillusion in the African Novel." *Common Wealth*. Ed. Anna Rutherford. Aarhus, Denmark: Akademisk Boghandel, 1972, pp. 62-72.

—. Structure and Image in Kwei Armah's *The Beautyful Ones Are Not Yet Born.*" *Studies in Black Literature*, 2, No. 2 (1971), 1-9.

Herskovits, Melville J. and Francis. *Dahomean Narrative*. Evanston, Ill.: Northwestern University Press, 1958.

Idowu, E. Bọlaji. *Olódùmarè: God in Yoruba Belief*. London: Longmans, 1962.

Ikiddeh, Ime. "The Character of Popular Fiction in Ghana." *Perspectives on African Literature*. Ed. Christopher Heywood. New York: Africana Publishing Corp., 1971, pp. 106-16.

Jahn, Janheinz. *Muntu: An Outline of Neo-African Culture*. Trans. Marjorie Grene. New York: Grove Press, 1961.

— and Claus Dressler. *Bibliography of Creative African Writing*. Millwood, N.Y.: Kraus-Thompson, 1973.

Jakobson, Roman. "Linguistics and Poetics." *Style in Language*. Ed. Thomas A. Sebeok. Cambridge, Mass.: M.I.T. Press, 1966, pp. 350-77.

Johnson, Samuel. *The History of the Yorubas From the Earliest Times to the Beginning of the British Protectorate*. Lagos, Nigeria: C.M.S. Bookshops, 1921.

Kaplan, Irving, et al. *Area Handbook for Ghana*. Washington, D.C.: U.S. Government Printing Office, 1971.

Kluckohn, Clyde. "Recurrent Themes in Myths and Mythmaking." *Myth and Mythmaking*. Ed. Henry A. Murray. New York: George Braziller, 1960, pp. 46-60.

Laing, R.D. *The Politics of Experience*. New York: Ballantine Books, 1971.

Larson, Charles. *The Emergence of African Literature*. Bloomington, Ind.: Indiana University Press, 1972.

Laurence, Margaret. *Long Drums and Cannons*. London: Macmillan, 1968.

Leach, Edmund. "Anthropological Aspects of Language: Animal Categories and Verbal Abuse." *New Directions in the Study of Language*. Ed. Eric H. Lenneberg. Cambridge, Mass.: M.I.T. Press, 1969, pp. 23-63.

Lévi-Strauss, Claude. *Structural Anthropology*. Trans. Claire Jacobson and Brooke Grundfest Schoepf. 2nd ed. New York: Anchor, 1967.

—. *Tristes Tropiques: An Anthropological Study of Primitive Societies in Brazil*. Trans. John Russell. 2nd ed. New York: Atheneum, 1963.

Lindfors, Bernth. "Amos Tutuola: Debts and Assets." *Cahiers D'études Africaines*, 10, No. 38 (1970), 306-34.

—. *Black African Literature in English: A Guide to Information Sources*. Detroit, Mich.: Gale Research Co., 1979.

—. "The Folktale as Paradigm in Chinua Achebe's *Arrow of God*." *Studies in Black Literature*, 1, No. 1 (1970), 1-15.

—, Ian Munro, Richard Priebe, and Reinhard Sander, eds. *Palaver: Interviews with Five African Writers in Texas*. Occasional Publication No. 3, Austin, Texas: African and Afro-American Research Institute, 1972.

Linn, Michael. "Degrees of Grammaticalness in Amos Tutuola's *The Palm-Wine Drinkard*." Paper presented at the Annual Meeting of the African Studies Association, Chicago, 1974.

Lloyd, P.C. "Sacred Kingship and Government Among the Yoruba," *Africa*, 30, No. 3 (1960), 221-37.

Mbiti, John S. *African Religions and Philosophy*. New York: Anchor Books, 1970.

Moore, Gerald. *Seven African Writers*. 2nd ed. London: Oxford University Press, 1966.

—. *Twelve African Writers*. Bloomington, Indiana: Indiana University Press, 1980.

—. *Wole Soyinka*. New York: Africana, 1971.

—. "The Writer and the Cargo Cult." *Common Wealth*. Ed. Anna Rutherford. Aarhus, Denmark: Adakemisk Boghandel, 1972, pp. 73-84.

Morton-Williams, Peter. "An Outline of the Cosmology and Cult Organization of the Oyo Yoruba." *Africa*, 34, No. 1 (1964), 243-60.

—. "The Yoruba Ogboni Cult in Ọyọ." *Africa*, 30, No. 4 (1960), 362-74.

—. "Yoruba Responses to the Fear of Death." *Africa*, 30, No. 1 (1960), 34-40.

Murray, Henry A., ed. *Myth and Mythmaking*. New York: George Braziller, 1960.

Nketia, J.H. *Funeral Dirges of the Akan People*. Achimota, Ghana, 1955.

Nukunya, G.K. *Kinship and Marriage Among the Ewe*. New York: Humanities Press, 1969.

Ogunba, Oyin. "The Traditional Content of the Plays of Wole Soyinka." *African Literature Today*, No. 4 (1970), pp. 2-18 and No. 5 (1971), pp. 106-15.

Ojo, G.J. Afolabi. *Yoruba Culture*, Ife, Nigeria: University of Ife Press, 1966.

Oluwasanmi, Edwina, ed. *Publishing in Africa in the Seventies.* Ile-Ife, Nigeria: University of Ife Press, 1975.

Patten, Margaret D. *Ghanaian Imaginative Writing in English, 1950-1969.* Legon, Ghana: Department of Library Studies, 1971.

Priebe, Richard. "An Examination of the Use of Pidgin in the Works of Three Nigerian Authors." *Texas Working Papers in Sociolinguistics,* No. 11 (1972), pp. 1-24.

—. "Popular Writing in Ghana: A Sociology and Rhetoric." *Research in African Literatures,* 9, No. 3 (1978), 395-432.

—. "Tutuola, Fagunwa, and Shakespeare." *The Journal of Commonwealth Literature,* 8, No. 1 (June 1973), 110-11.

Rieff, Philip. "A Modern Mythmaker." *Myth and Mythmaking.* Ed. Henry A. Murray. New York: George Braziller, 1960, pp. 240-75.

Schorer, Mark. "The Necessity of Myth." *Myth and Mythmaking.* Ed. Henry A. Murray. New York: George Braziller, 1960, pp. 354-58.

Scott, Christopher. "Some Aspects of the Structural Unity of 'Idanre.'" *World Literature Written in English,* No. 20 (1971), pp. 11-14.

Sebeok, Thomas, ed. *Myth: A Symposium.* Bloomington: Indiana University Press, 1965.

Snyder, Emile. "New Directions in African Writings," Publication 71-92. Waltham, Mass.: African Studies Association, 1971. Reprinted in *Pan-African Journal,* 5 (1972), 253-61.

Soyinka, Wole. "Amos Tutuola on Stage." *Ibadan,* 16 (1962), 23-24.

—. "The Fourth Stage: Through the Mysteries of Ogun to the Origin of Yoruba Tragedy." *The Morality of Art.* Ed. D.W. Jefferson. London: Routledge and Kegan Paul, 1969, pp. 119-34.

—. "From a Common Back Cloth." *The American Scholar,* 32, No. 4 (1963), 387-96.

—. *The Man Died.* London: Rex Collings, 1972.

—. *Myth, Literature and the African World.* London: Cambridge University Press, 1976.

—. "Modern Negro-African Theatre: The Nigerian Stage, A Study in Tyranny and Individual Survival." *Colloquium on Negro Art.* 1st World Festival of Negro Arts, Dakar, April 1-24, 1966. Paris: *Présence Africaine,* 1968, pp. 495-504.

—. "Towards a True Theatre." *Transition,* No. 8 (1963), pp. 21-22.

—. "The Writer in a Modern African State." *The Writer in Modern Africa*. Ed. Per Wästberg. New York: Africana, 1969, pp. 14-21.

Stone, R.H. *Yoruba Lore and the Universe*. Occasional Publication No. 4, Ibadan, Nigeria: Institute of Education, University of Ibadan.

Thompson, Robert Farris. "An Aesthetic of the Cool: West African Dance." *African Forum*, 2, No. 2 (1966), 85-99.

—. *Black Gods and Kings: Yoruba Art at UCLA*. Occasional Papers of the Museum and Laboratories of Ethnic Arts and Technology, University of California, No. 2, Los Angeles, 1971.

Turner, Victor. *The Forest of Symbols: Aspects of Ndembu Ritual*. Ithaca, New York: Cornell University Press, 1967.

—. *The Ritual Process: Structure and Anti-Structure*. Chicago: Aldine, 1969.

Van Gennep, Arnold. *Rites of Passage*. Trans. Monika B. Vizedom and Gabrielle L. Caffee. Chicago: University of Chicago Press, 1960.

Walker, Bill. "Mime in *The Lion and the Jewel*." *World Literature Written in English*, 12, No. 1 (1973), 37-44.

Weinstock, Donald and Cathy Ramada. "Symbolic Structure in *Things Fall Apart*." *Critique: Studies in Modern Fiction*, 2 (1969), pp. 22-41.

Wescott, Joan. "The Sculpture and Myths of Eshu-Elegba, The Yoruba Trickster." *Africa*, 32, No. 4 (1962), 336-54.

Wiedner, Donald L. *A History of Africa South of the Sahara*. New York: Vintage, 1962.

Willet, Frank. *Ife in the History of West African Sculpture*. London: Thames and Hudson, 1967.

Williams, Denis. "The Iconology of the Yoruba Edan Ogboni." *Africa*, 34, No. 2 (1964), 139-65.

Wilson, Colin. *The Outsider*. New York: Dell, 1956.

Yankowitz, Susan. "The Plays of Wole Soyinka." *African Forum*, 1, No. 4 (1966), 132-33.

Index

Abbam, Kate, 161, 162
Abiku. See Ogbanje; Soyinka, Wole
Abruquah, Joseph, 151
Achebe, Chinua, 1, 4, 11, 21, 139,
    165, 167; *Arrow of God,* 5, 17-18,
    19, 24, 168, 169; as didactic writer,
    47, 159; and ethical consciousness,
    5, 12, 19, 47-55, 166-67, 169, 170;
    and ethical mode, xii, 7, 13; *A
    Man of the People,* 134, 180-81n;
    and myth, 15, 62, 168; *Things Fall
    Apart,* 5, 6, 13, 24, 47-55, 62, 70,
    167, 168
African literature: Africanity of, x;
    critical approaches to, x-xi
African writers: circumstances in
    which they work, ix-x; elite, x, 6,
    139; popular, xiii
African-Scandinavian Writer's
    Conference, 80, 136
Aidoo, Ama Ata, 21, 30, 151, 156
Alienation, 37, 99, 102, 105, 111,
    115, 119, 169
Aluko, T.M., 6
Amadi, Elechi, 6, 12
Ananse, 163-64
Ancestors, 68, 74, 82, 103, 104, 106,
    108, 110, 111
Anglophone literature, x, 165, 167
Anglophone writers, 127
Ansah, W.K., 159
Anti-structure. *See* Turner, Victor
Apocalyptic imagery, xii, 15, 19
Apocalyptic vision, 110, 112, 125
Aristotle, 58, 62

Armah, Ayi Kwei, 1, 11, 151, 164;
    *The Beautyful Ones Are Not Yet
    Born,* xii, 16, 18-19, 23, 24, 25-36,
    41, 143, 153, 155, 157; and ethical
    consciousness, 168; *Fragments,* 15,
    16, 22, 23, 31, 36-42; *The Healers,*
    6; and liminality, 23, 79; and
    monomyth, 22; and mythic con-
    sciousness, 5, 7, 12, 14, 15, 19, 66,
    79; novels, 21, 82; obscurity of, 47;
    and rhetoric of myth, xii, 20; sca-
    tological imagery, 6, 16, 29, 33, 47,
    156, 157 (*see also,* Demonic imag-
    ery); theme of corruption, 26, 29,
    31, 32, 34, 35, 36, 40, 157 (*see also*
    Corruption); theme of insanity, 30,
    41, 155, 169; *Two Thousand Sea-
    sons,* 6, 162; *Why Are We So
    Blest?,* 16, 19, 23, 31, 42-46, 155
Auden, W.H., 120
Audience, ix-x, 2, 14, 139-40, 158,
    159, 163, 164, 170, 172. *See also*
    Rhetoric
Auerbach, Erich, 167
Awoonor, Kofi, 1, 11, 81, 99, 151,
    164
—*This Earth, My Brother. . .,* 6-7,
    14, 15, 18, 65-78, 79, 82, 105, 114,
    153, 155, 169; as dirge, 65-78; and
    liminality, 7, 17, 77; ritual journey,
    15, 155; scatological imagery, 66,
    69, 70, 156, 157, 158; theme of cor-
    ruption, 65, 68, 74, 75, 156, 157;
    theme of death, 66-67, 69-70, 72

203

73125